QUESTIONS
ABOUT
QUESTIONS

QUESTIONS ABOUT QUESTIONS

Inquiries into the Cognitive Bases of Surveys

JUDITH M. TANUR

EDITOR

*Sponsored by the Committee on Cognition and Survey Research
of the Social Science Research Council*

Russell Sage Foundation   **New York**

THE RUSSELL SAGE FOUNDATION

The Russell Sage Foundation, one of the oldest of America's general purpose foundations, was established in 1907 by Mrs. Margaret Olivia Sage for "the improvement of social and living conditions in the United States." The Foundation seeks to fulfill this mandate by fostering the development and dissemination of knowledge about the political, social, and economic problems of America.

The Board of Trustees is responsible for oversight and the general policies of the Foundation, while administrative direction of the program and staff is vested in the President, assisted by the officers and staff. The President bears final responsibility for the decision to publish a manuscript as a Russell Sage Foundation book. In reaching a judgment on the competence, accuracy, and objectivity of each study, the President is advised by the staff and selected expert readers. The conclusions and interpretations in Russell Sage Foundation publications are those of the authors and not of the Foundation, its Trustees, or its staff. Publication by the Foundation, therefore, does not imply endorsement of the contents of the study.

Library of Congress Cataloging-in-Publication Data

Questions about questions: inquiries into the cognitive bases of
    surveys / Judith M. Tanur, editor.
        p.   cm.
    Includes bibliographical references and index.
    ISBN 13: 978-0-87154-842-9 (cloth) ISBN 13: 978-0-87154-841-2 (pbk)
    ISBN 10: 0-87154-842-9 (cloth) ISBN 10: 0-87154-841-0 (pbk)
    1. Social surveys—Psychological aspects.   2. Interviewing in
sociology.   3. Social perception.   I. Tanur, Judith M.
HN29.Q47   1991
301'.0723—dc20   91-18807
                                                                            CIP

First Paperback Edition 1994

The paper used in this publication meets the minimum requirements of American National Standard for Information Sciences—Permanence of Paper for Printed Library Materials, ANSI Z39.48-1984.

RUSSELL SAGE FOUNDATION
112 East 64th Street, New York, New York 10021

10   9   8   7   6   5   4   3

Contents

v

PART V
SOCIAL INTERACTION

PART VI
GOVERNMENT APPLICATIONS

Preface

A Brief History of the Movement to Study Cognitive Aspects of Surveys and the Social Science Research Council (SSRC) Committee[1]

In the United States the movement to study cognitive aspects of surveys had its roots in a 1980 conference organized by Albert Biderman for the Bureau of Social Science Research (BSSR) (Biderman, 1980). (There had been an earlier conference in England; see Moss and Goldstein, 1979.) Funded by the Bureau of Justice Statistics, the BSSR conference brought together statisticians, cognitive psychologists, and survey researchers to focus on the National Crime Survey. Whereas the many participants found the cross-disciplinary prospects exhilarating, no institutionalized structure resulted, and the only published piece of which I am aware that can be traced to that conference is the work of Loftus and Marburger (1983) on improving respondents' dating of events by landmarking. The idea that this kind of interaction and a mix of perspectives could aid the survey enterprise, however, did lead to a variety of activities.

In 1983 the Committee on National Statistics of the National Research Council, with funding from the National Science Foundation (NSF), organized an Advanced Research Seminar on Cognitive Aspects of Survey Methodology (and thereby coined the acronym CASM with the express notion that the purpose of the seminar was to attempt to build a bridge over deep interdisciplinary chasms). In a week-long retreat, statisticians, survey researchers, cognitive psychologists, anthropologists, and agency administrators addressed not only the problems arising in surveys and how cognitive theories and methods might be applied toward their solutions, but also how surveys might be used by those in the cognitive sciences to expand beyond the walls of their laboratories. By design the seminar included a mix of people from academia and from government agencies and focused on the National Health Interview Survey (NHIS) at its first meeting. A subsequent meeting

---

1. The history of the movement to explore cognitive aspects of surveys has been excerpted and adapted from Tanur and Fienberg (1990). The material on the history of the United States government laboratories was prepared for this volume by Cathryn Dippo and Janet Norwood.

focused on the General Social Survey (GSS). Jabine, Straf, Tanur, and Tourangeau (1984) give a report of the seminar and outline some of the research proposals that originated there.

Some very important institutional arrangements traceable to the CASM Seminar are a series of government laboratories set up to explore cognitive aspects of surveys. Largely because the NHIS was taken as the focus of the original CASM Seminar and because personnel from the National Center for Health Statistics (NCHS), especially Monroe Sirken, were enthusiastic participants in the seminar and active advocates thereafter, the first such laboratory was established at NCHS. It, too, was co-funded with NSF. The NCHS laboratory continues to sponsor collaborative research with universities and research centers (e.g., Means et al., 1989; Salovey et al., 1989; and Smith, Jobe, and Mingay, 1991) as well as to conduct research in its own Questionnaire Design Research Laboratory (Jobe and Mingay, 1991; Royston, Bercini, Sirken, and Mingay, 1986).

Inspired by NCHS, other agencies recognized the need for cognitive research in survey design. In 1987 the Bureau of Labor Statistics (BLS) sponsored a conference on the design of questionnaires used in the Consumer Expenditure Survey and the Current Population Survey (Bienias, Dippo, and Palmisano, 1987). The BLS sought advice from the conference participants on the types of questionnaire research that should be undertaken and on the priorities for its future cognitive research. The conference participants all advocated the incorporation of cognitive concepts into the BLS research program and suggested that research focus primarily on such issues as respondent rules, respondent and interviewer roles, questionnaire form and content, and statistical estimation.

A new impetus for cognitive research at the BLS occurred in 1988, when Congress appropriated funds for the BLS to establish a Collection Procedures Research Laboratory. BLS set up its laboratory with a small staff of social scientists with interdisciplinary skills and began laboratory work on the forms of communication used in BLS surveys as well as on survey collection issues. Since then the staff has practically doubled in size with the addition of positions for new initiatives, such as the post-1990 census redesign of the Current Population Survey, and contract work for other agencies, such as the Internal Revenue Service.

The Bureau of the Census, long before it had a formal cognitive laboratory, conducted much of its research from what might be considered a cognitive point of view. Examples include experiments on the design of the format of the decennial census questionnaire with special emphasis of who should be counted and how, and anthropological field observers working to match residents' conceptualizations of who actually lives in a residence with reports elicited by census forms. (See Rothwell, 1985, for a report on some of this research.) In recent years, however, the Bureau of the Census has also set up a laboratory to study questionnaire and response issues related to the decennial population census and some of its current surveys. The addition of the laboratory allowed Census to broaden its long-established research agenda to include cognitive laboratory-based methods. (For an example of current work using laboratory-like methods, see Campanelli, Martin, and Creighton, 1989.)

Thus, by 1988 cognitive research laboratories had been established at three United States government statistical agencies—NCHS, Census, and BLS—and informal collaboration at the staff level had been established. To provide a more formal framework for ensuring that each agency could benefit from the work of the others, BLS developed a Protocol of Cooperation, which was signed by the Directors of NCHS and Census and by the Commissioner of Labor Statistics.

Another institutional arrangement that had its roots in the CASM Seminar was the SSRC Committee on Cognition and Survey Research. In 1984 SSRC organized a working group to explore the need for such a committee and to set a preliminary agenda. The working group crafted a proposal to the NSF, which awarded funding for a total of three years' activities. Supplementary funding for the preparation of this volume and the convening of two additional workshops was awarded by the Russell Sage Foundation in 1988.

Many of the accomplishments of the committee were outgrowths of informal interaction at its meetings and workshops and the fruits of collaborations stimulated by such meetings. A listing of the formal activities of the committee follows this preface together with a list of the committee members, but we can note here some specific ties between committee activities and chapters or parts in this volume. For example, chapter 2 in part II: Meaning, "Asking Questions and Influencing Answers," by Clark and Schober, is a formalization of topics addressed in the committee's workshop on the Semantics of Interview Questions. Chapter 12 in part V: Social Interaction, "Validity and the Collaborative Construction of Meaning in Face-to-Face Surveys," by Suchman and Jordan, had its inspiration in the same workshop and used in its analysis the tapes of the NHIS and GSS originally prepared for the 1983 CASM Seminar. Also originally planned at that workshop was the research that led to chapter 3, "Direct Questioning About Comprehension in a Survey Setting," by Groves, Fultz, and Martin. Again, chapter 4 in part II on Memory, "Personal Recall and the Limits of Retrospective Questions in Surveys," by Pearson, Ross, and Dawes, formalizes, codifies, and greatly expands material discussed at the committee's seminar on the Effects of Theory-based Schema on Retrospective Data, and the study of "Attempts to Improve the Accuracy of Self-Reports of Voting" (chapter 7), by Abelson, Loftus, and Greenwald, grew out of research planned at that seminar. All the material in Part IV, "Expression: The Case of Attitude Measurement in Surveys," was organized at the committee's workshop on Attitude Measurement in 1989.

This history is, of course, selective. It is not meant to belittle either the earlier rich methodological research in all of the United States government agencies, earlier interdisciplinary efforts in the United States (e.g., Sinaiko and Broedling, 1976), or the parallel developments in other countries that do not have explicit roots in the original CASM Seminar. I note especially the ZUMA (Zentrum für Umfragen, Methoden und Analysen) activities, which include many research studies, two international conferences, and a newsletter on cognitive aspects of surveys (see, for example, Hippler, Schwarz, and Sudman, 1987).

References

BIDERMAN, A. (1980) *Report of a Workshop on Applying Cognitive Psychology to Recall Problems of the National Crime Survey.* Washington, DC: Bureau of Social Science Research.

BIENIAS, J., DIPPO, C., and PALMISANO, M. (1987) *Questionnaire Design: Report on the 1987 BLS Advisory Conference.* Washington, DC: U.S. Department of Labor, Bureau of Labor Statistics.

CAMPANELLI, P., MARTIN, E., and CREIGHTON, K. (1989) Respondents' understanding of labor force concepts: Insights from debriefing studies. In *Proceedings of the Fifth Annual Research Conference.* Washington, DC: U.S. Department of Commerce, Bureau of the Census, pp. 361–374.

HIPPLER, H. J., SCHWARZ, N., and SUDMAN, S. (1987) *Social Information Processing and Survey Methodology.* New York: Springer-Verlag.

JABINE, T., STRAF, M., TANUR, J. M., and TOURANGEAU, R., eds. (1984) *Cognitive Aspects of Survey Methodology: Building a Bridge Between Disciplines.* Report of the Advanced Research Seminar on Cognitive Aspects of Survey Methodology. Washington, DC: National Academy Press.

JOBE, J. B., and MINGAY, D. J. (1991) Cognition and survey measurement: History and overview. *Applied Cognitive Psychology* 5, 175–192.

LOFTUS, E. F. and MARBURGER, W. (1983) Since the eruption of Mt. St. Helens, did anyone beat you up? Improving the accuracy of retrospective reports with landmark events. *Memory and Cognition* 11, 114–120.

MEANS, B., SWAN, G., JOBE, J. B., ESPOSITIO, J., and LOFTUS, E. F. (1989) Recall strategies for estimation of smoking levels in health surveys. In *Proceedings of the Section on Survey Research Methods.* Washington, DC: American Statistical Association, pp. 421–424.

MOSS, L. and GOLDSTEIN, H., eds. (1979) *The Recall Method in Social Surveys.* London: NFER Publishing.

ROTHWELL, N. (1985) Laboratory and field research studies for the 1980 Census of Population of the United States. *Journal of Official Statistics* 1, 137–157.

ROYSTON, P., BERCINI, D., SIRKEN, M., and MINGAY, D. (1986) Questionnaire design research laboratory. In *Proceedings of the Section on Survey Research Methods*. Washington, DC: American Statistical Association, pp. 703–707.

SALOVEY, P., JOBE, J., WILLIS, G., SIEBER, W., VAN DER SLEESEN, S., TURK, D., and SMITH, A. (1989) Response errors and bias in recall of chronic pain. In *Proceedings of the Section on Survey Research Methods*. Washington, DC: American Statistical Association, pp. 413–420.

SINAIKO, H. W., and BROEDLING, L. A. (1976) *Perspectives on Attitude Assessment Surveys and Their Alternatives*. Champaign, IL: Pendleton.

SMITH, A., JOBE, J., and MINGAY, D. (1991) Retrieval from memory of dietary information. *Applied Cognitive Psychology* 5, 269–280.

TANUR, J. M., and FIENBERG, S. E. (1990) Cognitive aspects of surveys: Yesterday, today, and tomorrow. Paper presented at the International Conference on Measurement Errors in Surveys, Tucson, AZ, November 13, 1990.

Acknowledgments

As editor I must make it clear that this book is most profoundly a product of the Social Science Research Council Committee on Cognition and Survey Research. Not only did the material for most of the chapters originate in the committee's meetings and workshops, but the idea of the volume itself was generated at a committee meeting. I agreed to edit the book on the condition that the committee serve as an editorial board, and this the members did faithfully, several of them taking on oversight duties for individual parts of the volume, and all of them investing time and energy at editorial meetings and in response to telephone and mail appeals. So credit for whatever virtue this book exhibits must go primarily to the contributors (and most committee members were also contributors) but also in full measure to the editorial board of committee members.

On behalf of the committee I take this opportunity to thank the Social Science Research Council for its moral and material support during the committee's lifetime. Because he was not officially a member of the committee, it seems appropriate to extend special thanks to Robert Pearson, who served as our staff; in another sense singling out Bob for such thanks seems extremely inappropriate, for his intellectual contributions to all phases of our efforts surely made him as much a member of the committee as any of us. For financial support during the gestation and life of the committee thanks are due to the National Science Foundation, and especially to Murray Aborn. Murray's vision of the new interdiscipline of survey research and the cognitive sciences helped to guide the work of the committee, and his careful reading of the draft manuscript for this volume provided line-by-line comments that greatly improved its content. Copyediting by Daniela Guggenheim was extraordinarily complete and added greatly to the integrity of the work. For additional financial support during the editorial process we thank the Russell Sage Foundation.

I must add my personal thanks to John Seely Brown at Xerox Palo Alto Research Center who provided an intellectually stimulating haven in which I was able to finish the editorial work on this volume.

GREAT NECK, NEW YORK
February 4, 1991

Members of the Social Science Research Council Committee on Cognition and Survey Research

Robert P. Abelson   Yale University, Cochair

Judith M. Tanur   State University of New York at Stony Brook, Cochair

Roy G. D'Andrade   University of California, San Diego

Michelene T. H. Chi   University of Pittsburgh

Herbert C. Clark   Stanford University

Robyn M. Dawes   Carnegie Mellon University

Stephen E. Fienberg   Carnegie Mellon University

Robert M. Groves   University of Michigan

Elizabeth F. Loftus   University of Washington

Janet L. Norwood   U.S. Bureau of Labor Statistics

Lucy A. Suchman   Xerox Palo Alto Research Center (Palo Alto, California)

Staff: **Robert W. Pearson**

Workshop on the Semantics of Interview Questions
February 1986

Participants:
Robert P. Abelson   Yale University
Roy G. D'Andrade   University of California, San Diego
Marilynn Brewer   University of California, Los Angeles
Michelene T. H. Chi   University of Pittsburgh
Herbert C. Clark   Stanford University
James A. Davis   Harvard University
Robyn M. Dawes   Carnegie Mellon University
Stephen E. Fienberg   Carnegie Mellon University
Charles J. Fillmore   University of California, Berkeley
Robert M. Groves   University of Michigan
Per Kristian Halvorsen   Xerox Palo Alto Research Center
Elizabeth F. Loftus   University of Washington
Janet L. Norwood   U.S. Bureau of Labor Statistics
Robert W. Pearson   Social Science Research Council
Tom W. Smith   NORC (Chicago)
Judith M. Tanur   State University of New York at Stony Brook

Workshop on Theories of Questionnaire Construction
March 1986

Participants:
Robert P. Abelson   Yale University
Roy G. D'Andrade   University of California, San Diego
John Seely Brown   Xerox Palo Alto Research Center
Michelene T. H. Chi   University of Pittsburgh

William Clancey   Stanford University
Herbert C. Clark   Stanford University
Robyn M. Dawes   Carnegie Mellon University
Stephen E. Fienberg   Carnegie Mellon University
Robert M. Groves   University of Michigan
Elizabeth F. Loftus   University of Washington
Janet L. Norwood   U.S. Bureau of Labor Statistics
Robert W. Pearson   Social Science Research Council
Paul Slovic   Decision Research (Eugene, Oregon)
Lucy A. Suchman   Xerox Palo Alto Research Center
Judith M. Tanur   State University of New York at Stony Brook

Preplanning Conference
on a National Survey Program of Cognitive Skills
March 1986

Participants:
Earl B. Hunt   University of Washington, Cochair
Eleanor Singer   Columbia University, Cochair
Robert Glaser   University of Pittsburgh
Robert M. Groves   University of Michigan
Deanna Kuhn   Columbia University
Judith T. Lessler   Research Triangle Institute (Research Triangle
    Park, North Carolina)
John C. Loehlin   University of Texas
Elizabeth F. Loftus   University of Washington
Sara B. Nerlove   National Science Foundation
Robert W. Pearson   Social Science Research Council
S. James Press   University of California, Riverside
Robert J. Sternberg   Yale University
Endel Tulving   University of Toronto
William C. Ward   Educational Testing Service (Princeton, New
    Jersey)
Joseph L. Young   National Science Foundation

Seminar on the Effects of Theory-based Schemas on Retrospective Data
June 1986

Participants:
Robyn M. Dawes   Carnegie Mellon University, Chair
Roy G. D'Andrade   University of California, San Diego
Richard T. Campbell   Duke University
Linda M. Collins   University of Southern California
Stephen E. Fienberg   Carnegie Mellon University
Peter M. Lewisohn   University of Oregon
Elizabeth F. Loftus   University of Washington
Elizabeth A. Martin   U.S. Bureau of the Census
Nancy A. Mathiowetz   Westat, Inc. (Rockville, Maryland)
Colm O'Muircheartaigh   London School of Economics
Robert W. Pearson   Social Science Research Council
John P. Robinson   University of Maryland
Michael A. Ross   University of Waterloo (Waterloo, Ontario)
Wesley Schaible   U.S. Bureau of Labor Statistics
Steven J. Sherman   University of Indiana
Judith M. Tanur   State University of New York at Stony Brook
George E. Vaillant   Dartmouth Medical School
Willem A. Wagenaar   University of Leiden

Workshop on the Cognition and Measurement of Pain
April 1987

Participants:
Stephen E. Fienberg   Carnegie Mellon University, Chair
Dallas Anderson   National Institute of Health
Lawrence Bradley   Bowman Gray School of Medicine, Duke University
C. Richard Chapman   University of Washington
Kathleen Danchik   National Center for Health Statistics
Robyn M. Dawes   Carnegie Mellon University
Vicki Dorf   U.S. Social Security Administration

Thomas F. Drury   National Center for Health Statistics
Eric Eich   University of British Columbia
Jared Jobe   National Center for Health Statistics
Nancy A. Mathiowetz   National Center for Health Services
Research
Harold Mersky   London Psychiatric Hospital (London, Ontario)
David Mingay   National Center for Health Statistics
Marian Osterweis   Institute of Medicine
Robert W. Pearson   Social Science Research Council
Thomas F. Rudy   University of Pittsburgh
Judith M. Tanur   State University of New York at Stony Brook
Dennis C. Turk   University of Pittsburgh
Dewey Ziegler   University of Kansas Medical Center (Kansas City,
Kansas)

Workshop on the Role of Interviewers
in Survey Measurement
June 1987

Participants:
Robert M. Groves   University of Michigan, Chair
Paul P. Biemer   New Mexico State University
Herbert C. Clark   Stanford University
Floyd Fowler   University of Massachusetts
Nancy H. Fultz   University of Michigan
Raymond Gibbs   University of California, Santa Cruz
Sam Glucksberg   Princeton University
Robert L. Kahn   University of Michigan
Robert Krauss   Columbia University
Jon A. Krosnick   Ohio State University
Elizabeth F. Loftus   University of Washington
David Mingay   National Center for Health Statistics
Elliot B. Mishler   Harvard Medical School
Livia Polanyi   BBN Laboratories (Cambridge, Massachusetts)
Nora Cate Schaeffer   University of Wisconsin

Lucy A. Suchman   Xerox Palo Alto Research Center
Judith M. Tanur   State University of New York at Stony Brook

Workshop on Multiple Measures of Attitude Properties
July 1989

Participants:
Robert P. Abelson   Yale University, Chair
John F. Dovidio   Colgate University
Russell H. Fazio   Indiana University
Jon A. Krosnick   Ohio State University

Workshop on the Structure of the Survey Interview
March 1990

Participants:
Robert M. Groves   University of Michigan
                       and U.S. Census Bureau, Chair
Charles F. Cannell   University of Michigan
Thomas Fricke   University of Michigan
Douglas W. Maynard   University of Wisconsin
Beth Ellen Pennell   University of Michigan
Livia Polanyi   Rice University
Matt Salo   U.S. Census Bureau
Nora Cate Schaeffer   University of Wisconsin

PART

I

INTRODUCTION

1

Cognitive Aspects of Surveys and This Volume

JUDITH M. TANUR

Since sample survey technology originated in studies of London's poor in the late nineteenth century, it has undergone continual refinements. Many of these refinements have improved sampling and estimation procedures. In the 1930s the United States government agencies adopted probability sampling methods as a means of ensuring the representativeness of a sample. But probability sampling did not replace the convenience and quota sampling strategies of prior decades in many other survey organizations until these strategies were proved untrustworthy when the pre-election polls of 1948 "elected" Thomas Dewey but the voters chose Harry Truman (see Fienberg and Tanur, 1989). By now, although issues of improving the efficiency of sampling and the accuracy of estimation remain active areas of investigation, researchers have sufficiently perfected probability sampling methods for telephone, mail, and face-to-face surveys that the errors such methods introduce into the results of surveys are controllable and quantifiable.

The 1960s and 1970s saw the development of new analytical technologies, especially the hardware and software associated with high-speed electronic computers. These developments permitted more people to do more surveys more cheaply and analyze them more quickly than ever before possible. They also meant that more people became respondents to both legitimate and less legitimate surveys than ever before—gone forever were the days when Phyllis McGinley (1954), after complaining that no polltaker had yet sought her opinions, could beg:

> Before the unpolled generations trample me,
> Won't someone sample me?

Indeed, during the 1970s survey researchers found that sampled respondents were increasingly refusing to grant interviews. Such refusals raise the cost of

3

surveys because they necessitate callbacks and degrade the accuracy of results if chosen respondents cannot be persuaded to cooperate. If refusals were occurring, even in part, because of the content of survey questionnaires, it behooved researchers to improve those questionnaires to make them less onerous.

During the same period, government agencies and academic researchers initiated longitudinal surveys, and the United States government initiated large survey-based social experiments to discover the effects of such projected reforms as a negative income tax and universal health insurance. These joined such important government surveys as the Current Population Survey carried out monthly to estimate the nation's unemployment rate, the National Crime Survey collecting data on victimizations to supplement the police-report-based Uniform Crime Reports, and the National Health Interview Survey providing data on prevalence of illnesses and their effects. This proliferation of surveys has made them part of the very fabric of our lives, providing data for academic research and for crucial government policy. But questions were arising: Were respondents able to recall accurately victimizations, visits to doctors, whether they had looked for work during the previous four weeks, and other autobiographical events that survey interviewers were asking them to report? How valid were these data on which academic research and government policy were increasingly based, and what could be done to make surveys yield more valid data? A panel of the National Academy of Sciences reflected these concerns in a report on the National Crime Survey (Penick and Owens, 1976).

Although issues of rising refusal rates and costs of surveys and of the validity of data used for policy purposes made these questions especially urgent, they were not new. For many years, survey research methodologists had been concerned with such problems of questionnaire construction and administration as the effects of interviewers, wording, open versus closed questions, the existence of middle or don't-know alternatives, question ordering, and failures of recall. But by the middle of the 1970s, the social science community reacted to the urgency by increasingly turning its attention to that part of the survey enterprise that remains today an art, but one that we shall see has lately been augmented by a better understanding of the cognitive processes that underlie the process of asking and answering questions.

One response of the social science community was to hold a series of conferences. The Department of the Navy had placed a prohibition on surveys in the early 1970s, a time when tensions arising from the changing composition of naval personnel made it crucial to measure and understand attitudes of those serving in the navy. The Office of Naval Research jointly with the Navy Personnel Research and Development Center sponsored an interdisciplinary conference on Perspectives on Attitude Assessment Surveys and Their Alternatives (Sinaiko and Broedling, 1976). In 1980 Albert Biderman organized a conference for the Bureau of Social Science Research (Biderman, 1980) that brought together statisticians, cognitive psychologists, and survey researchers to focus on the National Crime Survey, and in 1983 the Committee on National Statistics of the National Research Council organized an Advanced Research Seminar on Cognitive Aspects of Survey Methodology (and thereby coined the acronym CASM with the express notion that the purpose of the seminar was to attempt to build a bridge over deep interdisciplinary chasms). Spawning many research proposals and inspiring the establishment of such institutional arrangements to nurture interdisciplinary research as cognitive laboratories in government statistical agencies and the Social Science Research Council (SSRC) Committee on Cognition and Survey Research, the CASM conference stands as a landmark in the history of the effort to bring together the cognitive sciences and survey research. (See Jabine, Straf, Tanur, and Tourangeau, 1984.) It began an effort that aims to encourage and maintain a dialogue between survey methodologists and researchers in the cognitive sciences in hopes of throwing new light on old survey problems and perhaps ultimately resolving them, opening up totally new opportunities for verifying or modifying laboratory-based cognitive theories in more naturalistic test beds, and creating a new interdiscipline with a research agenda of its own. The Preface to this volume contains a more detailed history of this movement.

This volume is an attempt by the SSRC Committee on Cognition and Survey Research to weave together some strands of research and theory that have developed out of part of the movement that aims to understand the cognitive bases of survey responding, many nurtured in the committee's meetings, workshops, and other activities. Thus, its focus is mainly on the contributions of the cognitive sciences to understanding issues in survey research rather than on the twinned aim of the movement, the expansion of the empirical bases of the cognitive sciences. This introduction will discuss the contributions of this volume and point to some fulfilled and some as yet unfulfilled promises of the movement.

Why This Volume?

As the movement to study cognitive aspects of survey methodology enters its second decade, the time seems ripe to look backward to take stock of progress and forward to get some hint of where the movement is going. There have been other such efforts. For example, Jobe and Mingay (1991) have recently carried out a fine review of many of the empirical studies conducted under the movement's banner, Aborn (1989) has prepared an evaluation of the progress of the movement, and Hippler, Schwarz, and Sudman (1987) have compiled a volume of work in the tradition. But most of the output of the movement to study cognitive aspects of surveys has appeared in reports, journal articles, and conference proceedings.

We see the special purpose of this book to be the tying together of theorizing and empirical research on the interface between the cognitive sciences and survey research. The organization of two of the parts makes that interplay especially salient, with an introductory chapter setting out theoretic themes and problems, followed by one or more empirical chapters that respond to aspects of the stated theme.

The roots of the movement to study cognitive aspects of surveys in a joint academic–government enterprise continue to influence the growth of efforts to join the cognitive sciences and survey research. Thus, much of the research has been carried out in government agencies or under contract from such agencies. Further, there is an emphasis, even in much research funded from sources other than government statistical agencies, on the kinds of "factual" questions usually asked in government surveys. This emphasis on factual questions pervades many chapters of this volume, but we have been careful to include a part on the measurement of attitudes as another important area where the importation of cognitive theories and methodologies has been informing the survey enterprise. Because few United States government surveys ask questions about attitudes or opinions, such research tends to be cross-disciplinary within academe rather than in government–academic partnership.

Following this Introduction, the volume contains five further parts, four dealing with cognitive domains implicated in the survey process and the last an overview of research carried out at the Bureau of Labor Statistics, presented as an example.

Part II is entitled "Meaning," reflecting the view that a respondent must share the meaning of a question intended by the survey researcher if he or she is to respond usefully. The part starts with a thematic overview by Herbert H. Clark and Michael F. Schober, "Asking Questions and Influencing Answers." The authors place the problem of meaning—issues that survey methodologists have studied under the rubrics of the effects of question wording, of response alternatives, of question ordering, and of context—in the perspective of the psycholinguistic concept of intentions. They point out how rules for making sense of ordinary conversations carry over to survey interviews, both providing the occasion for response effects and a systematic framework for studying and perhaps reducing them. We should note, however, that some of their vivid examples are more extreme demonstrations of ambiguous meaning and alternative interpretation than typically appear in surveys. An empirical study by Robert M. Groves, Nancy Fultz, and Elizabeth Martin, "Direct Questioning About Comprehension in a Survey Setting," explores how closely respondents' and researchers' intended meanings correspond.

These authors find that an open-ended question used as a follow-up gives useful information on the perceived meaning of a survey question.

Part III is entitled "Memory," reflecting the next step in a respondent's cognitive processing of a survey question: the retrieval of information. The thematic overview article by Robert W. Pearson, Michael Ross, and Robyn M. Dawes, "Personal Recall and the Limits of Retrospective Questions in Surveys" (chapter 4), gives a framework for understanding the processes that sometimes introduce errors into retrospective reports and some guidance on when such reports are more or less trustworthy. Then, three empirical papers explore ways in which problems caused by imperfect retrospective reports can be overcome, preceded by an introductory paper setting the experimental stage, "Improving Episodic Memory Performance of Survey Respondents" by Robert T. Croyle and Elizabeth F. Loftus (chapter 5). Chapters 6 and 7 explore the use of a two-time-frame procedure (pioneered by Crespi and Swinehart, 1982) in reducing telescoping, a tendency for respondents to move events forward in time, and thus report as occurring during a specified reference period events that actually took place earlier. In "Memory and Mismemory for Health Events," Elizabeth F. Loftus, Kyle D. Smith, Mark R. Klinger, and Judith Fiedler use the technique successfully, whereas in "Attempts to Improve the Accuracy of Self-Reports of Voting," Robert P. Abelson, Elizabeth F. Loftus, and Anthony G. Greenwald find no reduction of overreporting of voting when using a two-time-frame procedure. Loftus et al. also find that directed backward recall (reverse chronological order) is significantly better for retrieving visits to healthcare providers of the respondent's spouse, and slightly better for recalling the respondent's own visits. The remaining chapter in part III on memory, "Applying Cognitive Theory in Public Health Investigations: Enhancing Food Recall with the Cognitive Interview" (chapter 8), by Ronald P. Fisher and Kathryn L. Quigley, explores another technique that has proved useful in the laboratory for overcoming problems of retrospection and suggests ways it might be useful in field applications in surveys.

Part IV deals with the reporting of what is retrieved, opening up issues of social desirability, attitude strength, and unobtrusive measures. We have chosen to deal with these problems of expression only in the context of questions about attitudes. Robert P. Abelson presents a thematic overview on "Opportunities in Survey Measurement of Attitudes" (chapter 9), and two empirical chapters follow. The issue of the correspondence between attitudes and behavior is one of long standing (see, for example, Deutscher, 1973, and the discussion in Schuman and Presser, 1981). These two chapters treat the issue systematically from a cognitive point of view. Jon A. Krosnick and Robert P. Abelson make "The Case for Measuring Attitude Strength in Surveys" (chapter 10), presenting evidence that strong attitudes are more likely than weak ones to covary with other variables, including behavior, and thus they urge that the extra questions (and hence interview time) needed to measure attitude strength be routinely invested in surveys. John F. Dovidio and Russell H. Fazio present in chapter 11 "New Technologies for the Direct and Indirect Assessment of Attitudes." They approach the problem of the correspondence between attitudes and behavior systematically, arguing that the more likely an individual's attitude is to be activated from memory when he or she encounters an attitude object, the more likely he or she is to act in accordance with that attitude, at least when social desirability is not involved. Further, they argue that one can measure the accessibility of an attitude by the latency of its self-report; the more rapid the response, the more accessible the attitude.

Part V on "Social Interaction" is comprised of a single chapter, "Validity and the Collaborative Construction of Meaning in Face-to-Face Surveys" (chapter 12) by Lucy Suchman and Brigitte Jordan. An earlier version of this chapter appeared in the *Journal of the American Statistical Association* (from which it is reprinted with permission). Suchman and Jordan raise questions about the rigid standardization imposed on the survey interview in the pursuit of reliable data. They suggest that because such standardization violates the usual norms of conversational behavior, it may well endanger the validity of data thus collected. The *Journal of the American Statistical Association* publication included several commentaries on the Suchman and Jordan work. Although we republish neither those commentaries nor the response by Suchman and Jordan, the version of the work appearing here takes many of those commentaries into account.

Part VI, our final section, "Government Applications," presents an overview in chapter 13 by Cathryn S. Dippo and Janet L. Norwood of empirical work recently carried out in the Collection Procedures Research Laboratory at the Bureau of Labor Statistics (BLS). Three United States government statistical agencies now operate cognitive laboratories. The committee wanted to present the flavor of the research going on in those laboratories, but for reasons of space in this volume was reluctant to try to survey them all. BLS was chosen as representative for the simplest of reasons: Janet Norwood, Commissioner of Labor Statistics, was a member of our committee and was familiar with the special concerns motivating this volume.

Promises Fulfilled and Pending[1]

We believe that there is general agreement that the establishment of the cognitive laboratories in government agencies is a major contribution of the

1. Much of the evaluative material in this Introduction has been excerpted and adapted from Tanur and Fienberg (1990).

movement to bring together the cognitive sciences and survey research. The importation of tools from the cognitive sciences and the development of a new level of awareness of the implications of the ideas that emanate from the use of these tools have enriched United States government survey enterprises. These enterprises have a long history of methodological care and experimentation; but traditionally methodological survey experiments were carried out primarily in the form of full-scale field tests. The cognitive laboratories in the government agencies now use such tools as think-aloud protocols and cognitive interviewing with small numbers of subjects to do early pretesting and to secure insight into redesign options, sometimes even options favored by previous field testing (see, for example, Tucker, Miller, Vitrano, and Doddy, 1989). Of course, field tests of innovations are crucial before a change is made in an operational survey, and an experiment properly embedded in a survey is the way such a field test should be carried out (see Fienberg and Tanur, 1988, 1989), but this new approach of going back and forth between the laboratory and the field surely adds flexibility and perhaps reduces costs.

The CASM Seminar envisaged a two-way street. Not only would the insights of the cognitive sciences shed new light on problems of survey research and perhaps lead to their eventual solution, but also survey research would open a wider laboratory for testing theories of the cognitive sciences. Jobe and Mingay (1991) and Aborn (1989) point to ways in which the movement has benefited the cognitive sciences, and cognitive psychology in particular. They note, among other things, the unanticipated ability of cognitive psychologists to take theories generated in the analysis of surveys and survey-based experiments into the laboratory for testing as well as their more anticipated ability to test laboratory-generated theories in the field. So far the results seem to be more in the direction of disproof rather than confirmation. For example, Bradburn, Rips, and Shevell (1987) hypothesized that telescoping is the result of clarity of memory (arising from the vividness or salience of an event) misleading a respondent who is using an availability heuristic to gauge the recency of an event. This hypothesis was not supported in a laboratory experiment by Thompson, Skowronski, and Lee (1988), in which misdating was not related to memorableness as rated by subjects at the time of recall. This refutation points to a system of mechanisms more complicated than those previously envisaged. On the other hand, the laboratory studies of Loftus and Fathi (1985) and those reported in this volume by Loftus, Smith, Klinger, and Fiedler suggest that recall is more efficient in a backward direction (most recent event first). Additional experiments that include the alternative of free recall, however, and the work of Jobe et al. (1991) on the National Health Interview Survey/National Medical Expenditures Survey Linkage Field Test, found that free recall of doctors' visits was at least as accurate as recall in which the respondents were instructed as to order. Similarly, in this volume Loftus et al. found that the two-time-frame procedure was useful in aiding recall of healthcare visits; but Abelson, Loftus, and Greenwald had no success with the technique in curbing overreporting of voting. While these examples suggest that cognitively based research has just begun to yield cumulation by confirmation, there does seem to be more continuity in the research than before the CASM movement existed, both to provide a structure and to bring together researchers who might otherwise not have talked to one another.

We see systematization as another contribution of the CASM movement. As old problems that have plagued the field of survey research are explained to and explored by investigators with training in the cognitive sciences, the new perspectives these recruits from other disciplines bring to bear inspire new models and suggest new avenues of empirical research. For example, in this volume we have seen that Clark and Schober look at response effects in the psycholinguistic context of speakers' intentions; Pearson, Ross, and Dawes offer a framework for understanding when and why retrospective reports are likely to be valid; and Suchman and Jordan help us to understand systematically the kinds of problems that standardization may be introducing into survey data collection. The research of Dovidio and Fazio draws upon previous psychological work on the distinction between spontaneous and deliberate behaviors and uses these ideas to shape our understanding of the link between the expression of attitudes and subsequent behavior, mediated by the social desirability of the attitudes. Whereas there is a substantial survey research literature that looks at the link between attitudes and behavior, and part of it invokes the concept of social desirability, that previous literature does not give an integrated perspective rooted in the accessibility of memory. Indeed, at the joint Office of Naval Research/Navy Personnel Research and Development Center Conference in 1975, James Dabbs suggested some physiological measures of attitudes and said explicitly, "I have no rigorous derivation linking arousal to interest, affect, and stress . . ." (1976, p. 159).

Surely, this systematizing effect is not peculiar to the work presented in this volume. For example, Tanur and Fienberg (1990) cite at length the work of Huttenlocher, Hedges, and Bradburn (1990), which explores the issue of telescoping that has long concerned survey researchers. Huttenlocher et al. draw on insights from the psychological literature to construct a model for reporting errors that takes into account effects due to bounding as well as effects associated with rounding to various types of culturally prototypic values for the number of days elapsed time since an autobiographical event. The heaping-up of reported events at boundaries of reference periods as well as at selected special values is not a new observation, but the new perspective that Huttenlocher et al. bring offers an integrated interpretation of the previously observed phenomena and a framework in which further discussions about them can take place.

Thus, we believe that the movement to bring together the cognitive sciences and survey research has so far raised more questions than it has answered. Several of the empirical findings remain contradictory. But in these contradictions lie the seeds for a better understanding of cognitive processes and improved means of asking questions in surveys. Insights and tools from the cognitive sciences have established a firm role in guiding research on survey procedures. We have not yet, however, been able to use cognitive theories directly to shape survey innovations or to predict the results of using innovative variations on established procedures. We must hope that such theoretical advances lie in the future. Surely, if survey researchers expected that they would find a panacea in the cognitive sciences that would quickly solve all the problems they had been wrestling with for decades, they have been sorely disappointed in the results of the movement so far. But if their hopes were more modest, if they had considered the development of new perspectives and systematic ways of looking at measurement errors in surveys to be progress in the improvement of the survey enterprise, and if they envisage eventual but not immediate cognitive theories of surveys, then the verdict is different. In that case, we believe, the movement to explore cognitive aspects of surveys has offered, and continues to offer, promise.

References

ABORN, M. (1989) Is CASM bridging the chasm? Evaluation of an experiment in cross-disciplinary survey research. Paper presented at the American Statistical Association 1989 Winter Conference, San Diego, CA, January 4–6.

BIDERMAN, A. (1980) *Report of a Workshop on Applying Cognitive Psychology to Recall Problems of the National Crime Survey.* Washington, DC: Bureau of Social Science Research.

BRADBURN, N. M., RIPS, L. J., and SHEVELL, S. K. (1987) Answering autobiographical questions: The impact of memory and inference on surveys. *Science* 236, 157–161.

CRESPI, I., and SWINEHART, J. W. (1982) Some effects of sequenced questions using different time intervals on behavioral self-reports: A field experiment. Paper presented at the Annual Conference of the American Association for Public Opinion Research, May.

DABBS, J. M., JR. (1976) Physiological and physical measures of attitudes. In SINAIKO, H. W., and BROEDLING, L. A. (eds.). *Perspectives on Attitude Assessment Surveys and Their Alternatives.* Champaign, IL: Pendleton, pp. 159–170.

DEUTSCHER, I. (1973) *What We Say/What We Do.* Glenview, IL: Scott, Foresman.

FIENBERG, S. E., and TANUR, J. M. (1988) From the inside out and the outside in: Combining experimental and sampling structures. *Canadian Journal of Statistics* 19, 135–151.

_____ (1989) Combining cognitive and statistical approaches to survey design. *Science* 243, 1017–1022.

HIPPLER, H. J., SCHWARZ, N., and SUDMAN, S. (1987) *Social Information Processing and Survey Methodology*. New York: Springer-Verlag.

HUTTENLOCHER, J., HEDGES, L. V., and BRADBURN, N. M. (1990) Reports of elapsed time: Bounding and rounding processes in estimation. *Journal of Experimental Psychology: Learning, Memory, and Cognition* 16, 196–213.

JABINE, T., STRAF, M., TANUR, J. M., and TOURANGEAU, R., eds. (1984) *Cognitive Aspects of Survey Methodology: Building a Bridge Between Disciplines*. Washington, DC: National Academy Press.

JOBE, J. B., and MINGAY, D. J. (1991) Cognition and survey measurement: History and overview. *Applied Cognitive Psychology* 5, 175–193.

JOBE, J. B., WHITE, A. A., KELLEY, C. L., MINGAY, D. J., SANCHEZ, M. J., and LOFTUS, E. F. (1990) Recall strategies and memory for health care visits. *Millbank Memorial Fund Quarterly/Health and Society* 68, 171–189.

LOFTUS, E. F., and FATHI, D. (1985) Retrieving multiple autobiographical memories. *Social Cognition* 3, 280–295.

McGINLEY, P. (1954) "The Forgotten Woman." In *The Love Letters of Phyllis McGinley*. New York: Viking Press, pp. 87–89.

PENICK, B. K., and OWENS, M. E. B. (1976) *Surveying Crime*. Washington, DC: National Academy of Sciences.

SCHUMAN, H., and PRESSER, S. (1981) *Questions and Answers in Attitude Surveys: Experiments on Question Form, Wording, and Context*. New York: Academic Press.

SINAIKO, H. W., and BROEDLING, L. A., eds. (1976) *Perspectives on Attitude Assessment Surveys and Their Alternatives*. Champaign, IL: Pendleton.

TANUR, J. M., and FIENBERG, S. E. (1990) Cognitive aspects of surveys: Yesterday, today, and tomorrow. Paper presented at the International Conference on Measurement Errors in Surveys, Tucson, AZ, November 13.

THOMPSON, C. P., SKOWRONSKI, J. J., and LEE, D. J. (1988) Telescoping in dating naturally occurring events. *Memory and Cognition* 16, 461–468.

TUCKER, C., MILLER, L., VITRANO, F., and DODDY, J. (1989) Cognitive issues and research on the Consumer Expenditure Diary Survey. Paper presented at the annual conference of the American Association for Public Opinion Research, May.

PART
II
MEANING

2

Asking Questions and Influencing Answers

HERBERT H. CLARK
and MICHAEL F. SCHOBER

On the face of it, survey interviews are simple. An interviewer steps into the home of a randomly selected member of the public, asks a series of questions, records the answers, and departs with new facts or opinions to add to her collection. (For convenience let us think of the interviewer as female and the respondent as male.) The information she takes away is determined by the questions she asks—how they are worded and what they require of the respondent. Properly designed, they will give her the facts and opinions she wants.

But this view of survey interviews is too simple, as the history of surveys has shown again and again. How a question is worded makes a difference, but so do many other factors—how the question is introduced, what questions come before and after, what answers are allowed, and much, much more. The factors are so diverse that they may seem impossible to account for. Even wording is mystifying.

From the perspective of language use, many of these factors aren't so mysterious. At least this is what we will argue. What makes them seem that way is the common misconception that language use has primarily to do with words and what they mean. It doesn't. It has primarily to do with people and what *they* mean. It is essentially about *speakers' intentions*—what speakers intend in choosing the words they do, and what their addressees take them as intending. Once we understand the role of speakers' intentions in language use, we will find many of the problems of survey design more tractable.

Our goal is to convince you that you can't understand what happens in survey interviews without understanding the role of intentions in language use. We will begin by describing five basic principles of language use that

15

apply wherever language is found. We will then look at how they might help account for many so-called response effects in survey interviews. Along the way we will formulate a number of general propositions about how you can ask questions and influence answers.

Understanding and Responding

Language use is fundamentally a social activity. Words and sentences are merely the props people need as they engage in the social activity—whether it is gossiping, telling stories, arguing, transacting business, or courting. In each of these activities, the participants have social goals, and language is just one means they have for reaching them. Survey interviews are no exception. When an interviewer questions a respondent, the two of them take part in a social process—in the manufacture and exchange of information. What they do with language, and what they understand, depends on how they construe that process.

Speaker's Meaning

The idea is that language use, whether it is in conversations, interviews, debates, or writing, is built on what people intend by what they say and do. An essential part of these intentions is captured in this principle:

Principle of speaker's meaning:

Speakers and their addressees take it for granted that the addressees are to recognize what the speakers mean by what they say and do.

When Ann utters "Sit down" to Ben, she *means something*. She intends Ben to recognize that she wants him to sit down—and that she has this particular intention (Grice, 1957); that is, she is trying to make certain of her intentions public—open, accessible, shared, mutually known—between Ben and her, and she won't have established her meaning until she has succeeded in making them public.

What counts, then, is not the meanings of words per se, but what speakers mean by using them. The point is so obvious that we rarely give it a second thought. Take these actual newspaper headlines (Perfetti et al., 1987):

Girl, 13, Turns in Parents for Marijuana, Cocaine

Toronto Law to Protect Squirrels Hit by Mayor

Deer Kill 130,000

Although each headline has many interpretations, we assume the newspaper intended only one. The drugs were the parents' problem and not the girl's reward. The mayor criticized the law and didn't beat up squirrels. And there were 130,000 deer and not people killed. For each headline, we tacitly ask, "What could they have meant by that?" and we work out its interpretation accordingly.

All sentences have alternative interpretations or readings, though usually not as blatant or silly as these headlines. Most words have more than one conventional sense—think of *post, blue, hot, for, by*—and most sentences fit more than one construction, as in, "I watched the man with a telescope" and "They are cooking apples." Yet we rarely notice the alternatives. We infer the intended readings quickly, unconsciously, and without apparent effort. How do we do this?

Common Ground

The key to recognizing the speaker's meaning is the *common ground* between the speaker and addressees—the information they believe they share. Technically it consists of their mutual knowledge, mutual beliefs, and mutual suppositions (Clark and Marshall, 1981; Lewis, 1969; Schiffer, 1972; Stalnaker, 1978). Speakers choose their words, we suggest, according to this principle:

Principle of utterance design:

Speakers try to design each utterance so that their addressees can figure out what they mean by considering the utterance against their current common ground.

People try to say things their addressees will understand. To do that, they need to root what they say in information they believe they share with them—their common ground. That makes common ground an essential ingredient of language use.

As a simple example, take what Veronica could mean by "Two please." At a cinema ticket window on the right night, she could mean, "I'd like two adult tickets to *Animal Crackers*." How? By relying on the common ground she assumed she shared at the moment with the ticket seller. On entering an elevator, she could mean, "Please push the button for the second floor." She could assume that the common ground between her fellow passenger and her included the fact that she had just got on, that he was near the buttons, and that she was looking at them. Or with a dentist's receptionist, she could mean, "I'd like my dentist appointment to be at two o'clock on Thursday, March 20, please." She could exploit the fact that the receptionist had just asked, "Would you prefer one or two o'clock on March 20?" In every situation she would count on her addressees to use their common ground to fill in what she had left unsaid.

Common ground divides roughly into *cultural common ground* and *personal common ground*. Two people's cultural common ground draws on information that is common to the cultural groups they belong to. Their personal common ground draws on joint personal experiences as viewed against their cultural common ground.

When Veronica and John meet at a party, and as they establish the cultural groups they have in common, they can each assume an enormous body of cultural common ground. Once they realize they are both university graduates, for example, they can assume as common ground all those facts and beliefs they assume university-educated people take for granted. These range from theories of gravity, light, and biological systems to the basic facts of geography, history, and social organization. Or as two speakers of western American English, they can assume as common ground the phonology, syntax, and vocabulary of that dialect of English. As two baseball fans, they can assume as common ground the names of the major players, their statistics, and such jargon as *rbi* and *era*. Here are some common cultural communities:

Language (English, California dialect, San Francisco high school argot)

Education (grade school, high school, university)

Geography (United States, California, San Francisco, Nob Hill)

Profession (psychology, plumbing, law, pediatrics, sheep ranching)

Avocation (skiing, Giants' baseball fan, classical music, philately)

Once two people jointly establish they are both members of any of these communities, they are licensed to add vast quantities of information to their common ground.

Cultural common ground is essential in interpreting everything people say. Suppose it is 1981 and you are handed a picture of then President Ronald Reagan and his budget director David Stockman sitting side by side (Clark, Schreuder, and Buttrick, 1983). The interviewer, without pointing at either man, asks you one of two questions:

1. You know who this man is, don't you?
2. Do you have any idea at all who this man is?

Which man, Reagan or Stockman, did the interviewer mean by "this man"? When fifteen people on the Stanford University campus were asked question

1, fourteen of them said, "Sure, Reagan," or pointed at him. But when fifteen others were asked question 2, seven of them said, "Sure, Stockman," or pointed at Stockman; only two pointed at Reagan. (The remainder asked, "Which one?") Most people assumed that the reference in question 1 was to Reagan but the reference in question 2 was to Stockman—or at least not Reagan. Why?

Respondents drew on two main pieces of common ground in construing "this man." One was the interviewer's explicit presupposition about "this man." In question 1 "this man" was presupposed to be familiar, but in question 2, unfamiliar. The other was the respondents' assumption that Reagan was more recognizable to the public than Stockman, a belief about cultural common ground. Afterward all the respondents judged Reagan to be more recognizable than Stockman, even though they were able to identify both men. As utterance design predicts, they tried to figure out what the interviewer meant by considering the utterance against their current common ground.

Accumulating Common Ground

Veronica and John build up their personal common ground as they talk and experience things together. They add to it when they jointly witness a car hit a tree or hear a soprano sing an aria. They also add to it each time one asserts something to the other. Personal common ground is established from joint perceptual and linguistic experiences interpreted against cultural common ground. But how does this work?

In language use, common ground accumulates in a highly systematic way, as expressed in this principle:

Principle of accumulation:

In a conversation the participants add to their common ground each time they contribute to it successfully.

When Veronica speaks, John interprets her utterance against their initial common ground, and then they both add the content of what she says to that common ground. Then when John speaks, Veronica interprets him against their updated common ground, and the two of them update their common ground once more. And so it goes. Every successful contribution adds to the common ground of the participants. In orderly discourse, common ground is cumulative.

Each contribution adds to the common ground in a special way (Clark and Haviland, 1977; Haviland and Clark, 1974; Prince, 1981). When Veronica says, "The guy next door just bought a motorcycle," she *presupposes* there is a man John can readily identify in their common ground as "a guy next door." She treats this as *given information*. What she and John are to add to their common ground is her belief that the person so identified just bought a motorcycle. She treats this as *new information*. But listeners often have to draw *bridging inferences* to get the speaker's presuppositions to fit into their current common ground (Clark, 1977; Lewis, 1979). If John goes on, "And how bad is the noise?" he presupposes that there is a uniquely identifiable "noise" in common ground. Since there has been no explicit mention of any noise, Veronica has to draw the bridging inference that the motorcycle makes noise, and that is the noise John is referring to. This is a simple inference. Others are far more elaborate. Bridging inferences are ubiquitous in discourse.

Perspective

Perspective is an important part of what speakers establish with their presuppositions. When Veronica speaks of "the guy next door," she is viewing him as a guy next door. If she had said "that awful pest you met," she would be viewing him as an awful pest John had just met. She can refer to the same person from an infinity of different perspectives. Which perspective she chooses can be critical. By deciding to view him as awful pest, for example, Veronica can imply that the motorcycle is a nuisance.

Speakers ordinarily expect their addressees to accept their perspectives. When Veronica says "the guy next door" or "that awful pest you met," she takes it for granted that she and John will now view the man this way. That is the way presuppositions work. If John doesn't object, he implies that he accepts her perspective, at least for the moment. If he cannot accept her perspective, it is incumbent on him to say so. Suppose a friend asks you, "How many sociologists came to your party last night?" If you had no party last night, you should object, "But I had no party last night." It would be uncooperative, even deceptive, to answer "None," even though that is in one sense correct. If you don't demur, you tacitly accept her presupposition—that there *was* a party last night—which she then incorrectly believes to be common ground.

Perspectives are easy to plant in the common ground of a discourse. There are many perspectives that speakers can take on a situation, and for addressees it often matters little which one is selected. It is also polite for addressees to accept speakers' perspectives. After all, speakers choose perspectives they judge their addressees will accept, so to object is to question their judgment. It also takes special effort to object—as by saying, "But he isn't an awful pest." Perspectives usually get established automatically, without notice, as the participants in a discourse proceed with what they have to say.

The perspectives that get established should influence listeners' responses, and they do. In an experiment by Loftus and Palmer (1974) on eyewitness accounts, people were shown brief movies of car accidents and were then asked questions about them. For one movie, they were asked, "How fast were the cars going when they contacted each other?" in which the final verb was *contacted, hit, bumped, collided*, or *smashed*. The more violent the verb, the more violent the collision presupposed. If the eyewitnesses accepted the questioner's perspective, they should add that information to their common ground, and that should influence the speeds they estimated. In fact, the average estimates increased systematically from 31.8 mph for *contacted* to 40.8 mph for *smashed*. And when eyewitnesses returned a week later, they were more likely to report broken glass in the accident if they had been asked the *smashed* question than if they had been asked the *hit* question.

Perspectives are especially influential in defining vague situations. How often do you get headaches? "Well," you think, "that depends on what you call a headache—how severe it has to be, what counts as one or two headaches, and so on." In a study by Loftus (1975), people were asked one of these two questions:

1. Do you get headaches frequently, and if so, how often?
2. Do you get headaches occasionally, and if so, how often?

By presupposing that people get headaches either frequently or occasionally, the interviewer helps respondents calibrate just what it means to get a headache. For question 1, respondents replied, on average, that they got 2.2 headaches per week, but for question 2, only .7 headaches per week. The perspective helped define an otherwise vague situation.

Perspectives get established more generally by how speakers *frame* what they say. Framing an issue includes not merely choices of wording—for example, *contact* versus *smash*, or *frequently* versus *occasionally*—but other choices as well. Consider the following two ways of describing what amounts to the same situation:

1. A company is making a small profit. It is located in a community experiencing a recession with substantial unemployment but no inflation. The company decides to decrease wages and salaries 7% this year.
2. A company is making a small profit. It is located in a community experiencing a recession with substantial unemployment and inflation of 12%. The company decides to increase salaries only 5% this year.

In a telephone interview, respondents given scenario 1 judged it as "unfair" or "very unfair" 62% of the time. This proportion was only 22% for scenario 2

(Kahneman, Knetsch, and Thaler, 1986; see also Tversky and Kahneman, 1981, 1986). The "nominal increase" perspective was less unpleasant than the "real loss" perspective, even though they both imply the same financial loss. Perspective is influential everywhere.

Common Purpose

Whenever we take part in a discourse, we do so purposefully. Some of our goals are private, even embarrassing if they were to come out. But others become public, a shared, mutually recognized part of the discourse. When you plan a party with a friend, your primary goal is to arrive at a plan, and it must be mutually recognized as such if you and your friend are to progress. As Grice (1975, p. 45) said:

> Our talk exchanges do not normally consist of a succession of disconnected remarks, and would not be rational if they did. They are characteristically, to some degree at least, cooperative efforts; and each participant recognizes in them, to some extent, a common purpose or set of purposes, or at least a mutually accepted direction.

The participants take these common purposes, or the mutually accepted direction, to be part of their common ground, and they design their utterances accordingly. According to Grice, they do so by observing this principle:

Cooperative principle:

Make your conversational contribution such as is required, at the stage at which it occurs, by the accepted purpose or direction of the talk exchange in which you are engaged (p. 45).

If people observe this principle, the mutually accepted purpose should be essential in figuring out the speaker's meaning, and all evidence suggests that it is.

Suppose you run a restaurant, and one day a woman with a pleasant voice telephones, says "Hello," and asks one of three questions:

1. Do you accept American Express cards?
2. Do you accept credit cards?
3. Do you accept any kinds of credit cards?

With each question she asks whether you accept something, but what that something is varies from "American Express cards" to "credit cards" to "any kinds of credit cards." As it happens, you can answer yes to each one, so if you take her literally, you should respond simply, "Yes, we do." But would you?

No, you wouldn't. The percentages of responses actually elicited from fifty restaurateurs per question in the San Francisco area go as follows (Clark, 1979):

Response Examples	Question		
	1	2	3
Yes, we do	100	44	10
Yes, we do. We accept American Express and Visa	0	38	56
We accept American Express and Visa	0	16	34
Other	0	2	0
Total	100	100	100

For "Do you accept American Express cards?" restaurateurs took the caller as asking merely whether they accepted American Express cards. But for "Do you accept credit cards?" many took her as asking, in addition, for a list of the credit cards they accepted. And when she explicitly spoke of "any kinds of credit cards," even more took her as asking for the list of acceptable cards.

Restaurateurs interpreted the caller by inferring her purpose. They supposed that she wanted to patronize their restaurant and pay with a credit card, so she wanted to know if they accepted a card she owned. She signaled the cards she was interested in by her question. She specified an American Express card in question 1 but credit cards in general in questions 2 and 3. By mentioning "any kinds" of cards in question 3, she showed an interest in the *particular* cards they accepted, and most restaurateurs told her about them. So restaurateurs looked for the caller's mutually recognizable purpose, and their responses were attempts to satisfy it.

This example brings out an important point: Questions can themselves serve many different purposes. We usually think of questions as *information questions*, as asking for information the questioner doesn't or couldn't possibly know. In our example, "Do you accept American Express cards?" is taken as an information question. But there are also *exam questions*, which ask for information the questioner already could or does know. These are common in the classroom, as when a teacher demands, "What is the capital of South Dakota?" or "What is the longest river in Scotland?"

Still other questions serve as *presequences*. With these, questioners check on a precondition for the next action they want to take (Levinson, 1983; Schegloff, 1980). Take this exchange at a food counter (Merritt, 1976):

Customer:	Do you have hot chocolate?
Server:	Mmhmm
Customer:	Can I have hot chocolate with whipped cream?
Server:	Sure (leaves to get)

The first question serves as a *prerequest* because it opens the way for a request of hot chocolate. Prerequests are often interpreted as requests proper as well, as illustrated by the customer's, "Can I have hot chocolate with whipped cream?" The server not only answers this question but also treats it as a request for hot chocolate with whipped cream. Prerequests are common, as in "Do you have a watch?" and "Can you pass the butter?" So are preinvitations ("What are you doing tonight?"), preannouncements ("Do you know what happened to me yesterday?"), and prequestions ("Do you know anything about New Guinea?"). In the restaurant example, "Do you accept any kinds of credit cards?" is a prequestion. In most presequences, speakers are less interested in the question itself than in the request, invitation, announcement, or question that it prefigures. Often, the question isn't expected to be taken seriously at all, and it is treated as merely pro forma (Clark, 1979).

People interpret a speaker's purpose against the accumulating common ground. Suppose Veronica asks John two questions in a row, "How is your wife?" and then "How is your family?" In answering the first, John updates their common ground with news about his wife's health. So when Veronica asks the second, he construes her goal as finding out about the rest of the family—she already knows about his wife—and interprets "your family" as referring to family members *other than* his wife. Interpreting the speaker's purpose is complicated simply because the current common ground changes moment by moment.

Grounding

Fundamental to everyday language use is a process called *grounding* (Clark and Brennan, 1991; Clark and Schaefer, 1987, 1989; Clark and Wilkes-Gibbs, 1986; Isaacs and Clark, 1987; Schober and Clark, 1989). When Veronica and John talk to each other, they work to formulate utterances that express what they mean. But by the principle of accumulation, they must make sure what they say becomes part of their common ground; that is, they must also *ground* what gets said, as expressed in this principle:

Principle of grounding:

For each contribution to discourse, the participants try to reach the mutual belief that the addressees have understood what the speaker meant to a criterion sufficient for current purposes.

Grounding is ordinarily achieved through collaboration, through joint actions. When Veronica speaks, she looks for evidence from John that he has understood her. John, in turn, tries to provide that evidence by saying "uh huh," nodding his head, or taking the relevant next turn. If he hasn't understood her, he will ask her to repeat, confirm, or paraphrase what she said (Clark and Schaefer, 1989; Jefferson, 1972; Schegloff, Jefferson, and Sacks, 1977; Schegloff, 1972, 1982).

What Veronica and John accomplish in this process is a shared construal of what Veronica meant. Consider this example from spontaneous conversation (Svartvik and Quirk, 1980):

A   well wo uh what shall we do about uh *this* boy then

B   Duveen?

A   m

B   well I propose to *write*, uh saying (continues)

In his first turn A tries to ask B a question, but his reference to the boy isn't explicit enough for B. B therefore asks for confirmation before he is willing—or even able—to answer the question. It takes the two of them to establish the reference to the boy. In general it takes speaker and addressee working together to establish intended word meanings, intended interpretations of full utterances, implications of utterances, mutually recognized purposes, and many other such things. Grounding and the collaboration it requires are essential to everyday language use.

So far, then, we have argued for five principles of language use. Speakers mean things by what they say, and their addressees are expected to recognize that meaning (principle of speaker's meaning). Speakers design what they say so that their meaning can be worked out by appealing to the common ground they currently share with their addressees (principle of utterance design). In orderly discourse this common ground accumulates (principle of accumulation) as the participants collaborate in establishing a shared understanding of what the speaker meant (principle of grounding). And when people engage in a discourse, they have mutually recognizable purposes. These are salient parts of their current common ground and are essential in determining what speakers are understood to have meant (cooperative principle).

Responses to Survey Interviews

Over the years survey researchers have puzzled over a number of unexpected problems with surveys. Reword a question and the answers often change. Move a question from one survey to another and the answers often change.

Switch the order of two questions and the answers often change. Alter the response alternatives for a question and the answers often change. "Response effects" like these have been the bane of survey researchers (Cannell, 1985b; Converse and Presser, 1986; Hippler and Schwarz, 1987; Schuman and Presser, 1981; Sudman and Bradburn, 1974, 1982). Where do they come from?

Many of these effects, we will argue, have ultimately to do with speaker intent. Survey interviews are in many ways like any other discourse: They are a collective activity in which people—here, the interviewer and respondent—use language to accomplish some purpose. But they are unlike most types of discourse in at least three features. They are built around a single type of exchange: questions and answers. Their course is predetermined by a written schedule. And the person who is really asking the questions, the writer of the questions, isn't present. Some response effects arise because respondents treat the survey interview like any other type of discourse, and others arise as respondents try to deal with these special features (see Suchman and Jordan, chapter 12 in this volume). Let us consider some of these consequences.

Interviewers as Intermediaries

The questions in survey interviews are special in several ways. When Veronica asks John, "How's your wife?" in conversation, the two of them take several features for granted. First, she is asking the question because she herself wants to know the answer. She is speaking on her own behalf and not on behalf of anyone else. Second, she is formulating the utterance extemporaneously. And third, she will make use of John's answer—say, "She's fine, and so is the baby"—in deciding what to say next. Everyday conversation is unmediated, extemporaneous, and interactive. But survey interviews are mostly mediated, predetermined, and noninteractive, features that have a range of influences on interpreting and responding to questions.

In survey interviews, who is really asking the questions? Who really wants to know the answers? Certainly not the interviewer. She is merely acting on behalf of the survey researcher, the person who has written the survey, as his intermediary. For convenience, we will call this person the *surveyer*, and we will consider him male. It is his intentions, his meaning, that are at issue. The interviewer and the respondent take all this for granted. They both recognize that the interviewer has little or no authority. Ordinarily she cannot change the questions. Sometimes she cannot even interpret them. This encourages respondents to assume that what the surveyer means should be self-evident, and they interpret him that way.

Also unlike everyday conversation, survey interviews follow a route planned in advance. Ordinary talk is controlled by the participants working together. But in survey interviews the respondent has no say in the direction of the talk, except in special branching questions. It is the written survey schedule that controls the topics raised, the questions asked, and the answers recorded. The course of the discourse is determined by the surveyer working unilaterally through his intermediary. All respondents surely recognize this too. After all, the questions are couched in such nonconversational language and are read out in such a manner that they would never be mistaken for extemporaneous ones.

Indeed, survey interviews preclude most of the usual techniques for grounding. The interviewer doesn't check for understanding, at least not to the degree people do in everyday conversation. Nor can the respondent do much when he doesn't understand. He might get the interviewer to repeat a question. But if he asks, say, "What do you mean by 'military spending'?" she is sometimes required to reply, "Whatever it means to *you*." This reply would be nonsense in ordinary conversation. It is the speaker who is the final arbiter of what she means, not the addressee. If the interviewer does offer a definition of "military spending," she reads it from a script, and it isn't open to further clarification. If the interviewer is a mere intermediary, and if she doesn't command complete authority about what the surveyer means, then the ordinary course of establishing what the speaker means is blocked.

The Presumption of Interpretability

Respondents, therefore, make the *interpretability presumption*: "Each question means what it is obvious to me here now that it means." They assume the surveyer chose his wording so they can understand what he meant—and can do so quickly. After all, he prepared and edited the question carefully, and since he knows they have no way of getting clarification, he must think a question won't need clarification. If a word seems vague, ambiguous, or strange, it isn't really vague, ambiguous, or strange, because the surveyer is confident respondents can figure out what it means. The interpretability presumption has several surprising consequences.

1. RESPONDENTS ANSWER VAGUELY WORDED QUESTIONS IN IDIOSYNCRATIC WAYS. Whenever a surveyer chooses a vague word, as just noted, respondents can presume that he means something specific by it, namely, the interpretation most obvious to them at that moment. These interpretations will often be idiosyncratic just because vague words allow such latitude of interpretation.

Idiosyncratic interpretations turn up surprisingly often. In one survey interview (Belson, 1981) respondents were asked a series of questions about television, and they seemed quite certain about the meanings of such general terms as *usually, children, few,* and *have*. Yet, when the respondents were

questioned after the interviews, they revealed strikingly different interpretations of almost every question. In one question *few* (in "over the last few
years") was interpreted as "no more than two years" by seven of the fifty-nine
respondents interviewed, as "seven years or more" by nineteen of them, and
as "ten years or more" by eleven of them. In a survey about politics (Fee,
1979), the term *energy crisis* was interpreted in *nine* distinct ways. Respondents think, "If the surveyer thinks this word has an obvious meaning, then it
must be the meaning that is obvious to me at the moment." Surveys differ, of
course, and respondents can show considerable agreement with the surveyer
in their interpretations (e.g., Smith, 1989).

2. RESPONDENTS FAIL TO SEE WHEN THE SURVEYER IS USING WORDS DIFFERENTLY FROM
THE WAY THEY USE THEM.   Respondents can generally assume that the surveyer
is using each word in the way it is conventionally used in their culture or
subculture. One survey went awry in a European country because the
researchers didn't realize that in that country the word translating English
washing machine referred to a hand-turned agitator that fits over the top of a
washtub (Payne, 1951, p. 28). The point of this example may be obvious, yet
in subtler form the problem has plagued a good many surveys. Words vary in
unexpected ways not only in translation from one language to the next, but in
unchanged form from one culture and subculture to the next. In a study
carried out in Mexico,[1] villagers in the Yucatán were asked in Spanish, "How
many children do you have?" (*"Cuántos niños tienen Ustedes?"*). The count
would have been wrong if it hadn't been discovered that these villagers
interpreted the word *niños* to include not only living children but also
unsuccessful pregnancies and children who had died. And in one set of
studies (Belson, 1981), respondents were found to give terms in an interview
interpretations not intended by the surveyer more than 70% of the time. And,
again, the respondents felt entirely comfortable with their interpretations.

3. RESPONDENTS SEEM TO HAVE STABLE OPINIONS ON ISSUES THEY KNOW NOTHING ABOUT.
This is another consequence of the interpretability presumption. Respondents tacitly reason, "When the surveyer asks me a question, he assumes it is
one I can answer, one I have valid opinions about. So it must be about an issue
I *do* have an opinion on. (Also, if he assumed this, I would lose face if I
admitted I couldn't answer the question, so I must.)" In one study (Hartley,
1946) college students were asked for their opinions about three nationalities
that didn't exist—Danireans, Pireneans, and Wallonians—and they gave
their opinions willingly. If they were supposed to know about these nationalities, they must. In another study (Schuman and Presser, 1981) respondents

---

1. Brigitte Jordan, personal communication.

were asked about a proposed law they knew nothing about (the law was fictitious). About 30% of them were willing to provide an opinion; 10% were willing even after they were told they could say they didn't know about the law.

The first three response effects, then, come about from the interpretability presumption. In ordinary language use, when people ask us questions, they choose their words with us in mind. They ask them confident we can make the intended interpretation. And if we run into problems, we can ask for clarification: "What do you mean by 'a few'?" In survey interviews respondents can make an even stronger presumption of interpretability. After all, the questions are prepared ahead of time, are worded very carefully, and often cannot be clarified. The trouble with the interpretability presumption lies not with respondents but with surveyers. Surveyers cannot possibly write perfect questions, self-evident to each respondent, that never need clarification. And because they cannot, the answers will often be surprising.

Perspective

Every question, as we noted, implies a perspective. Suppose you are one of those eyewitnesses to the car crash and you are asked, "How fast were the cars going when they smashed into each other?" The questioner presupposes that the cars are to be viewed as smashing, not contacting, hitting, bumping, or colliding, and this way she establishes a particular perspective on the collision. Now, unless you demur, it becomes common ground that you accept her perspective. Ordinarily, it is more than just polite to take a questioner's perspective—although there is that pressure, too. You must express your answer from some perspective, and unless you create a new one, the questioner will interpret your answer, by default, from the perspective she has established. Worse yet, in the eyewitness report you have no opportunity to demur. You are almost forced to accept her perspective. So it isn't surprising that answering questions is influenced by the questioner's perspective.

4. LOADED TERMS HELP SET THE PERSPECTIVE FROM WHICH QUESTIONS ARE TO BE ANSWERED.   Many terms are politically loaded. There is *pro-choice* versus *proabortion*, and *pro-life* versus *antiabortion*. There is *freedom fighters* versus *antigovernment guerrillas*, and *peacekeeping forces* versus *occupation army*, and *war* versus *armed conflict*, and *neutron bomb* versus *enhanced radiation device*, and *MX missile* versus *Peacekeeper*. There is the *Department of War* (the United States department until 1947) versus the *Department of Defense*. There is *taxes* versus *revenues*. Suppose respondents are asked one of these two questions:

1. Do you favor increasing government revenues to pay for new roads?
2. Do you favor increasing taxes to pay for new roads?

They will assume that the term chosen—*revenues* versus *taxes*—reflects the perspective from which they are to answer the question. They will interpret the two terms differently (no two terms are exactly synonymous), so they might suppose, for example, that revenues are fees paid for services rendered whereas taxes are just, well, taxes. If so, they might say yes to question 1 but no to question 2. Or suppose respondents are asked a question whose perspective they cannot accept, such as, "Are you in favor of aborting babies on demand?" Since they cannot object—"Do you mean, am I pro-choice?" to which they might answer yes—they have to answer from the surveyer's perspective and say no.

No one would be surprised that loaded questions—questions with loaded terms—influence responses by the perspectives they establish. But it is often difficult to recognize loaded questions for what they are. Compare these two questions (Mueller, 1973; Schuman and Presser, 1981):

1. If a situation like Vietnam were to develop in another part of the world, do you think the United States *should* or *should not* send troops to stop a communist takeover?
2. If a situation like Vietnam were to develop in another part of the world, do you think the United States *should* or *should not* send troops?

In a 1974 SSRC survey the first question was agreed to 33% of the time and the second only 18%. During the Cold War, whenever a survey question referred to communist activities, Americans tended to assume it was being asked from the perspective of defending American interests from foreign aggressors, and they were more likely to support American military operations (Mueller, 1973; Payne, 1951). Examples like this are common.

It is futile to search for truly neutral questions. They don't exist. Every question carries presuppositions, so every question establishes a perspective. So for each question we must ask: Is the perspective taken really the one from which we want the respondent to answer? If the answer is yes—if we can justify the perspective—then we can also justify the question.

5. THE RESPONSE ALTERNATIVES TO A QUESTION HELP DETERMINE THE DOMAIN OF INQUIRY IN WHICH IT IS TO BE ANSWERED.   When a friend asks, "What type of wine do you like, red or white?" the *domain of inquiry* is red and white wines only. If she had said "red, white, or rosé," it would have included rosé wines as well. The two questions specify distinct perspectives on what is of current interest, and you will also go about answering them very differently. So it goes in survey

interviews. Respondents confronted with "Which do you believe, A or B?" assume a different domain of inquiry from those confronted with "Which do you believe, A, B, or C?" As Schuman and Kalton (1985, p. 648) put it, "the rules of the game call for working within the categories offered." The game isn't special to surveys. It is played wherever language is used. The categories help specify the questioner's perspective.

One famous example is the *forbid-allow* discrepancy. Compare these two questions (Rugg, 1941):

1. Do you think the United States should forbid public speeches against democracy?
2. Do you think the United States should allow public speeches against democracy?

Both questions are answered yes or no, but these are really different alternatives. In question 1 yes and no mean "forbid" and "not forbid," but in question 2 they mean "allow" and "not allow." Of course, to forbid a speech is to not allow it, and vice versa, so saying yes to question 1 is logically equivalent to saying no to question 2. Still, 54% of the respondents to question 1 said yes, public speeches against democracy should be forbidden, whereas fully 75% of the respondents to question 2 said no, such speeches should not be allowed. Questions 1 and 2 elicited discrepant answers—a difference of 21%. The same discrepancy has been noted in many other domains (Schuman and Presser, 1981).

How are questions 1 and 2 different? They present different perspectives on public speeches precisely because of the response alternatives offered. To agree to question 1 (to "forbid" speeches) implies a real act of opposition. But to disagree with question 2 (to "not allow" those same speeches) means merely to abstain from support. Respondents without strong opinions on the matter should be willing to say no to both questions: "I don't oppose such speeches, but I also don't support them." Indeed, according to Hippler and Schwarz (1986), this is exactly where the discrepancy arises.

There is another striking change when the alternatives to a question include "don't know." In one survey (NORC–1974, reported in Schuman and Presser, 1981, p. 120) respondents were asked, "In general, do you think the courts in this area deal too harshly or not harshly enough with criminals?" They responded as follows:

Too harshly	5.6%
Not harshly enough	77.8%
About right (volunteered)	9.7%
Don't know (volunteered)	6.8%

Their responses changed dramatically when "or don't you have enough information about the courts to say?" was included at the end of the question:

Too harshly	4.6%
Not harshly enough	60.3%
About right (volunteered)	6.1%
Not enough information to say	29.0%

As in other questions of this sort, some 22% more people answered "don't know" for the second question. Why is this? When "don't know" isn't an explicit alternative, the implication is that they are to give their general impression. They are to answer from what they know. When the alternatives do include "don't know," the implication is that respondents are to give only informed judgments. They are to answer only if they *do* know. As expected from the presumption of interpretability, almost no one refused to answer substantively when "don't know" wasn't an alternative.

6. QUESTIONS WITH AND WITHOUT RESPONSE ALTERNATIVES IMPLY DIFFERENT PERSPEC-TIVES. Imagine being asked, "What type of fruit do you like best?" The inferred domain of inquiry is the full gamut of fruit, though you might give more attention to common than to uncommon ones. Now imagine being asked, "What type of fruit do you like best—apples, oranges, grapes, or watermelons?" in which the fruits are the ones most often thought of by other respondents. By specifying the four fruits, the questioner restricts the domain of inquiry to them alone and, indeed, invites you to consider each one about equally. These two types of questions are called *open* and *closed* questions. Their domains of inquiry differ in both range and distribution.

Survey questions, too, can be open or closed, and the difference may be dramatic. One example comes from a 1977 telephone survey (Schuman and Presser, 1981) in which people were asked about the most important problem currently facing the United States. The question they were asked took one of two forms:

1. What do you think is the most important problem facing this country at present?
2. Which of these is the most important problem facing this country at present? Unemployment, crime, inflation, quality of leaders, breakdown of morals and religion.

For question 1 fully 22% responded that fuel and energy shortages were the most important problem, making it the second most frequent response. This isn't surprising, since the survey was taken during the coldest winter in recent history. But for question 2 only one of 592 respondents even mentioned the energy crisis. Of the respondents to question 2, fully 99% answered with one of the five options they were given.

Which are better in surveys—open or closed questions? There has been a long debate about this. Open questions are time-consuming to administer and their answers hard to analyze. Closed questions are quicker and easier. For years survey researchers assumed that open and closed formats would elicit similar responses as long as the closed questions had the right response alternatives. But they don't and the differences are large enough to matter (see Hippler and Schwarz, 1987; Schuman and Presser, 1981). When respondents in one survey were asked what is the most important thing for children to learn to prepare them for life, 62% picked "to think for themselves" from a list of five options, but only 5% spontaneously came up with that answer in an open format (Schuman and Presser, 1981).

Why are the differences so large? In open questions respondents have to judge whether the first answer they think of lies within the surveyer's domain of inquiry. If the answer seems self-evident, they won't give it; after all, it is already part of their common ground with the surveyer. But if it is an explicit alternative, they infer that it is part of the domain of inquiry—a legitimate answer—and they are happy to give it. They assume the surveyer put it among the alternatives for a reason, so it must be relevant to his intent. An explicit list of alternatives may remind them of things they might not otherwise have thought of (Hippler and Schwarz, 1987). But more than that, respondents infer they were intended to consider the rare alternatives on the same footing as the common ones. They are then as free to choose a rare alternative as a common one.

7. RESPONSE ALTERNATIVES ARE OFTEN CONSTRUED AS WHAT IS TYPICAL OR NORMAL IN THE POPULATION. In a study by Schwarz, Hippler, Deutsch, and Strack (1985), Germans were asked, "How many hours a day do you spend watching TV?" Half were given the response alternatives in set 1, and the other half those in set 2.

Set 1	Set 2
up to ½ hour	up to 2½ hours
½ to 1 hour	2½ to 3 hours
1 to 1½ hours	3 to 3½ hours
1½ to 2 hours	3½ to 4 hours
2 to 2½ hours	4 to 4½ hours
more than 2½ hours	more than 4½ hours

Estimates of TV watching differed dramatically between the two groups of respondents. Of those given set 1, the number who watched more than 2½ hours of TV each day was 16%, but of those given set 2, it was 38%. Indeed, respondents used the response alternatives they were given to infer what is normal for German TV viewing. Later, when asked in an open format, "What is the average TV consumption of German citizens?" Set 1 respondents estimated 2.7 hours and set 2 respondents, consistent with the higher alternatives, estimated the higher average of 3.2 hours. Conversely, when asked later, "How important a role does TV play in your life?" set 1 respondents gave an average rating of 4.6 (on a 1 to 10 scale), and set 2 respondents, the reliably lower average of 3.8—that is, set 1 respondents judged TV to be more important than did set 2 respondents, even though set 1 respondents estimated that they watched less TV.

Why should response alternatives be taken as typical or normal? These are part of what the surveyer presupposes, or takes for granted, in asking the question. Respondents can therefore assume that he chose them because they specify a perspective that is appropriate, hence normative, for the people he is surveying. The alternatives given specify the norm they are to compare themselves to. Respondents have no choice but to accept the perspective anyway: they have no easy way to object to it. They are forcefully invited to think of the alternatives as more than an arbitrary set of categories.

Pressure to Respond

Questions and answers form a unit of language use called *adjacency pairs* (Schegloff and Sacks, 1973). Other adjacency pairs include request and compliance, offer and acceptance, invitation and acceptance, apology and acceptance, thanks and acceptance, compliment and agreement, greeting and greeting, and farewell and farewell. Each pair has a first and a second part spoken by two different people. The crucial property is conditional relevance. Once Veronica has asked John a question, it is relevant and expectable that he provide the answer in the very next turn, and the same goes for other adjacency pairs.

In this way questions and answers are subject to the conventions governing turn taking in conversation (Sacks, Schegloff, and Jefferson, 1974). Veronica, in asking John a question, designates him as the next speaker. He in turn is obligated to begin his turn the moment she completes hers. Ordinarily, he will start in on his answer without a pause. But if he cannot, he must show Veronica that he realizes that it *is* his turn at that moment. He is under pressure to say something—for example, "um"—within about one second (Jefferson, 1989).

The pressure to answer immediately has its effects. John cannot take much time thinking about his answer, so he will usually give the type of answer he could be expected to formulate in the time he has. If Veronica asks, "How many meals did you eat out last week?" he doesn't have time to recall each one. He is forced to estimate, "Oh, about three." Indeed, John will interpret Veronica as requesting only an estimate, since she couldn't have expected anything more in so short a time. Veronica, of course, can take the pressure off ("Take one minute to recall and count the meals you ate out last week and tell me the number"), but ordinarily she won't. So time pressure affects both the interpretation of the question and the precision of the answer. Here are two consequences for surveys.

8. RESPONDENTS ESTIMATE FACTUAL ANSWERS THAT WOULD TAKE TOO LONG TO FIGURE OUT PRECISELY. Respondents tacitly reason, "The surveyer is asking me a question I should be able to answer immediately. So even though he seems to be asking for a precise answer, he couldn't be, because he couldn't possibly expect me to compute it in the time available. So I will make a best guess." This way precise questions get less precise answers than surveyers expect.

One manifestation of this is what is called *telescoping*. People often include more events in a time interval than they should. In a police study (Garofalo and Hindenlang, 1977), about 20% of the crimes reported by victims to have happened in a particular period of time actually happened before the beginning of that period, as determined by comparing their reports with actual police records. In a study of purchases of housewares and small appliances (Sudman and Ferber, 1970), people reported buying 43% more in the last three months than the department store records indicated they had. For other questions people include too few events in the reported time interval. Telescoping of both types has turned up in questions about voting, doctor visits, illnesses, accidents, grocery shopping, leisure activities, and many other types of events (Cannell, 1985a; Sudman and Bradburn, 1973, 1982).

People telescope, we suggest, largely because they assume the questioner wants to know only about the events they can think of quickly, so they estimate rather than compute their answers. Telescoping itself can often be traced to people's uncertainty about when or how often past events occurred (Bradburn, Rips, and Shevell, 1987; Brown, Rips, and Shevell, 1985; Loftus and Marburger, 1983; Wagenaar, 1986). Precisely what form it takes depends on people's methods of estimating. Sometimes it leads to overestimation, and other times to underestimation. The point is that telescoping can be reduced by forcing respondents to take their time, recall each event, and count the events (Cannell, Oksenberg, and Converse, 1977; Neter and Waksberg, 1964; Sudman and Bradburn, 1973, 1982). The more people calculate rather than estimate, generally, the more accurate they are. So, although memory accounts for the fallibility of estimating, it is the pressure to answer quickly that leads them to estimate in the first place.

9. RESPONSES TO SURVEY QUESTIONS CHANGE WITH THE MODE OF ADMINISTRATION— FACE-TO-FACE, TELEPHONE, OR SELF-ADMINISTERED QUESTIONNAIRE. Many aspects of language use change with mode of administration, and these may change communication in a variety of ways (see Clark and Brennan, 1991). One way these modes differ is in how they deal with unwanted pauses. In face-to-face interviews, respondents have the full range of verbal and nonverbal signals at their disposal. They can use not only "ums" and "wells" but also gestures and eye gaze to signal that they are still thinking about a question. On the telephone they are more limited in their signals, so pauses are more disruptive (Hippler and Schwarz, 1987). In self-administered questionnaires pauses don't even count. Hence, time pressure is strongest in telephone interviews and weakest in questionnaires (Bishop, Hippler, Schwarz, and Strack, 1988, p. 323).

Time pressure counts. Telephone interviews go more quickly than face-to-face interviews (Groves and Kahn, 1979; Williams, 1977; Wilson and Williams, 1977). On the telephone people give shorter answers to open-ended questions, and they pause less (Williams, 1978), as if they were under more pressure to answer questions quickly. By our logic they should also estimate more and calculate less when asked factual questions. On the telephone they should assume they were intended to answer more quickly and so estimate more often. And, indeed, many of these response effects are stronger over the telephone than in self-administered questionnaires (Bishop et al., 1988). Mode of administration has other effects, too (Bishop and Hippler, 1986; Schuman and Presser, 1981).

Structure in Survey Interviews

Survey interviews, like any discourse, have both a global and a local structure. Overall, an interview might begin with a general orientation, move to questions on health, switch to questions on employment, and end with questions about the respondent's age and occupation. The section on health would have its own local structure, consisting perhaps of an orientation followed by questions ordered by topic. In conversation we interpret each assertion, question, offer, and other speech act relative to such a structure as it accumulates in our common ground. Respondents to survey interviews do the same, and that has its consequences.

The Pressure for Consistency

In any discourse the participants are under pressure to be consistent. When Veronica speaks to John, as we noted, what she says now is to be interpreted against what she and John have said before. It is directly dependent on what they have made public so far—on their accumulating common ground. If she says one thing now and something contradictory later, John will take her as confused or, worse, deceitful. Survey interviews are no different. There, too, the participants push for consistency, and this has its consequences.

10. SO-CALLED KNOWLEDGE FILTERS CAN SUPPRESS OPINIONS IN LATER QUESTIONS. Many surveys contain what are called *knowledge filters*, such as these two questions:

1. Do you have an opinion about gasoline taxes?
2. Have you thought enough about gasoline taxes to have an opinion?

When respondents answer no to a knowledge filter, they should be less willing to offer an answer to the next substantive question, and they are. They are discouraged from doing so apparently because they think they need to know a lot in order to answer the questions. To be consistent, they should refuse to answer them. That, indeed, is the purpose of knowledge filters.

But are knowledge filters always what they claim to be—knowledge filters? Note that they really function as what we have called prequestions. They are asked merely to check on preconditions for the interviewer's next question. As we noted earlier, presequences are not always intended to be taken seriously. When you are asked, "Can you tell me the time?" you usually don't say yes before giving the time. You take the question of ability as pro forma, as a mere gesture of politeness. The same goes for many knowledge filters. It is natural to view question 1 as pro forma, but not question 2. For question 1 respondents could respond immediately with their opinion ("I think they are too low"), but for question 2 they couldn't easily do that. That makes them likely to treat question 2 as a true knowledge filter, but to interpret question 1 as a mere gesture of politeness. That would make question 2 a stronger filter than question 1. Indeed, the more strongly a filter is worded, the more it discourages answers to the later questions (Hippler and Schwarz, 1987).

11. PEOPLE USE THEIR EARLIER ANSWERS AS EVIDENCE FOR THEIR LATER JUDGMENTS. We have already noted an example of this proposition in the study on TV watching. People whose earlier answer led them to believe they watched TV

more than average judged that TV played a *more* important role in their lives. The difference was induced entirely by the response alternatives they were offered with the first question, set 1 or set 2. Likewise, in a study of images of foods (Noelle-Neumann, 1970), 30% of the respondents rated potatoes as "particularly German." This figure rose to 48% after they had just rated rice. Earlier questions help set the structure of the interview by indicating what the later question is relative to.

Although most questions in survey interviews are what we have called information questions, others are interpreted as exam questions—with all the implications that exam questions usually carry. The structure they add to the interview can therefore be especially influential. In a study by Bishop (1987), Ohio residents were asked, among other things, one of two exam questions:

1. Do you happen to remember anything special that your United States representative has done for your district or for the people in your district while he has been in Congress? (Yes 12%; no 88%)

1′. Do you happen to know the name of the governor of Ohio? (Yes 69%; no 31%)

Then they were asked, either immediately or later in the interview:

2. Would you say you follow what's going on in government and public affairs most of the time, some of the time, only now and then, or hardly at all?

Respondents who said no to either question 1 or 1′ were, in effect, giving the interviewer evidence that they were not really following public affairs. Indeed, once they had said no to either question 1 or 1′, they were less likely to say they followed public affairs "most of the time" for question 2. But since question 1 prompted more no answers than question 1′, it should also keep people from saying "most of the time" more than question 1′ would. It did, by a reliable margin of 32% to 26%. Respondents, trying to be consistent, brought their later answers into line with their earlier ones.

The influence of one question on the next in circumstances like this has at least two possible explanations. One is priming. "Specific features" of the current question have been automatically "activated" or "primed" in memory by the previous question, and that directly affects people's answers to the current question (Strack and Martin, 1987). A second explanation is that respondents pursue consistency—either publicly, privately, or both. So as they build up common ground with the interviewer, they may try to appear to have a consistent set of beliefs as part of their public self-presentation. Or, privately, they may see themselves as competent people with a coherent set of beliefs, and to maintain that image, they try to be consistent in what they do.

The pressure for consistency seems to be the major, if not sole, explanation for these effects. Memory, of course, is required for participants to keep track of their common ground—to check that an answer now is consistent with earlier answers. If priming were necessary, the influence of one question on another should disappear if enough irrelevant questions are asked in between. But it doesn't disappear. In Bishop's study, questions 1 and 1' influenced the responses to question 2, whether they came immediately before or five questions before. Such an influence may last as long as the interview and even longer (Schwarz and Strack, 1981). Evidence like this suggests that priming per se is not very important in these effects; consistency is.

The pressure for consistency can be very influential indeed. In a well-known study by Hyman and Sheatsley (1950), people were asked two questions:

1. Do you think the United States should let communist newspaper reporters from other countries come in here and send back to their papers the news as they see it?
2. Do you think a communist country like Russia should let American newspaper reporters come in and send back to America the news as they see it?

When the respondents were asked question 1 first, 36% of them said yes. But when they were asked question 2 first, the number saying yes to question 1 jumped to 73%. Likewise, 90% of the respondents said yes to question 2 when it was asked first, but the number dropped to 66% when it was asked after question 1. Why? Apparently, the respondents were again trying to be consistent. People who would never allow a communist reporter into the United States will do it just to follow rules of fair play—that is, when they have just let a United States reporter into a communist country. Consistency effects like this are common in surveys (Link, 1946; Rugg and Cantril, 1944; Schuman and Presser, 1981; Turner and Krauss, 1978).

The Quest for Structure

In conversation, speakers are not always explicit about how their current utterance is to be related to the previous ones, so we are expected to infer the relation. Suppose a friend tells you:

1. John féll. He stood up again.
2. John fell. He broke his arm.
3. John fell. He tripped on a rock.
4. John fell. He wanted to scare Mary.

Your friend has used no explicit connectives. If she had, they would have been "and then" in item 1, "and therefore" in item 2, and "because" in items 3 and 4. Still, she intends you to infer the connections, and you do, without giving it a thought. Indeed, we build these connections as a part of the bridging inferences we draw as we relate each utterance to the current common ground. These connections can take dozens of shapes (Clark, 1977; Mann and Thompson, 1986). We have illustrated the relations of sequel in item 1, consequence in item 2, physical cause in item 3, and reason in item 4, but there are many more.

People should infer these connections in survey interviews as readily as they do in conversation, news stories, or novels. And they do. They sometimes even infer relations that surveyers didn't intend. None of this should be surprising. If people search for the structure they think the surveyer intended, they will infer the obvious relations, unless they are told not to. Here are several consequences.

12. PEOPLE INTERPRET SUCCESSIVE QUESTIONS AS RELATED IN TOPIC—UNLESS THEY ARE TOLD OTHERWISE.   Ordinarily, survey questions either continue the current topic of conversation or introduce a new topic. When a question is heard as continuing the current topic, it should be interpreted as related to the previous questions, and it is. In one study (Hippler and Schwarz, 1987) respondents were asked, "What are the major problems facing the country today?" Those who had just been asked, "Is the president doing enough about the drug problem?" were more likely to mention drugs in answer to the second question. It is as if they inferred the bridging connective "and so." In another survey (Sears and Lau, 1983) respondents were asked to evaluate the president's overall performance. Those who had just answered a question about their personal income were more likely to rate the president's performance on the basis of his economic success. The relations that respondents infer, however, are not merely vague connections. They usually take quite definite shapes.

13. WHEN A GENERAL QUESTION FOLLOWS A SPECIFIC QUESTION ON THE SAME TOPIC, IT MAY GET AN EXCLUSIVE OR AN INCLUSIVE INTERPRETATION, DEPENDING ON THE CIRCUMSTANCES.   We have argued throughout that people expect common ground to accumulate in discourse. Recall what happens when Veronica asks

John, "How is your wife?" and then, "How is your family?" He reasons, "Veronica has already asked me about my wife. That is already part of our common ground. So by 'your family' she must be referring to family members other than my wife." Let us call this the *exclusive* interpretation of "your family." But when Veronica asks only, "How is your family?" John interprets "your family" as including his wife—the *inclusive* interpretation. So whether John takes "How is your family?" to have an inclusive or an exclusive interpretation depends on the circumstances—here, on its connection with a previous question.

Exclusive and inclusive interpretations often arise in a general question that follows a specific one. In one study respondents were asked two questions:

1. Do you think it should be possible for a pregnant woman to obtain a legal abortion if she is married and does not want any more children?

2. Do you think it should be possible for a pregnant woman to obtain a legal abortion if there is a strong chance of serious defect in the baby?

Of these two questions, 1 is general and 2 is specific, much as "How is your family?" is general and "How is your wife?" is specific. When question 1 came first, 61% of the respondents answered yes, but when it followed question 2, only 48% did; that is, once people had been asked about birth defects—and 84% of them said yes to question 2—they appeared to interpret question 1 exclusively and not inclusively. They excluded birth defects from consideration in question 1 and were less likely to approve of abortions in cases other than birth defects. Respondents assumed that they were not to repeat an opinion they had already rendered (Schuman and Presser, 1981; Strack and Martin, 1987).

General questions following specific ones may also get inclusive interpretations. In a study by Strack, Martin, and Schwarz (1988), respondents were asked these two questions, among others:

1. How happy are you with life in general?

2. How often do you normally go out on a date? about ____times a month

Here, question 1 is general and question 2 is specific. When question 1 came after question 2, respondents heard it as a summary question that *included* the information they had just provided in question 2. It is as if they read it: "Now, considering what you have just told me about dating, how happy are you with life in general?" Indeed, the two answers were highly correlated (.66). But when question 1 came *before* question 2, the two questions pertained to very different topics, and indeed the two answers were almost uncorrelated ($-.12$).

What is the difference in the two situations? A general question can bear many relations to the specific question it follows. Just as with successive assertions, the bridging connective inferred might be "and also," "and therefore," "for example," or "and in summary." Precisely what relation is inferred depends on the information asked for, the wording, and many other factors. For the general abortion question 1, the content leads to "and also," forcing an exclusive interpretation. For the general happiness question, the phrase "in general" suggests "and therefore" or "and in summary," which forces an inclusive interpretation. We suggest that it is futile to look for only one or several factors that distinguish the two circumstances. These factors, like the connections themselves, are probably open-ended.

14. EXPLICITLY STATED CONNECTIONS ORDINARILY TAKE PRECEDENCE IN RESPONDENTS' QUEST FOR STRUCTURE.   Suppose your friend says the following:

John fell. He got a speck of dirt in his eye.

Depending on the circumstances you could infer the connection to be "and then," "and therefore," "because," or many others. Whatever bridging inference you drew would be preempted if she had said "and then," "and therefore," or "because." This is common sense. You assume that your friend chose the connectives so that you could infer her intent.

Explicit structure like this can be powerful. Let us return to the study of happiness (Strack, Martin, and Schwarz, 1988) when general question 1 was asked *after* question 2. Recall that question 1 was taken as a summary question that included people's response to question 2, and the two answers were highly correlated (.66). Another group of respondents heard this preface before being asked question 2 and then question 1:

Now we would like to learn about two areas of life that may be important for people's overall well-being: (a) happiness with dating, (b) happiness with life in general.

This preface was designed to get people to treat the two questions as independent, and it did. With the preface the answers to the two questions were almost uncorrelated (.15). Once again, priming offers no explanation. High satisfaction with dating didn't automatically "prime" a judgment of great happiness with life in general. Respondents were trying to infer the surveyer's intent, and the explicit structure in the preface helped them do that.

Summary

When people are interviewed in a survey, they don't leave behind the principles they would ordinarily apply in using language. They proceed much as they would in ordinary conversation, though with limitations. They look for the speaker's intent. They look for common ground to accumulate. They deal with the speaker's perspective. But interviews also have their limitations. People realize that the interviewer is only an intermediary for the surveyer and that she has little authority. Also, since the form of the interview is writ in stone, it isn't easy to ask for clarification or qualify answers. So, for example, they make an even stronger presumption of interpretability than they ordinarily would.

The principles of language use that people bring with them to survey interviews have a range of consequences. We have documented only some of them, but our point should be clear. To understand surveys and the data they produce, we must see survey interviews as a type of discourse, as a specialized arena of language use. Only then will we resolve many of the puzzles of survey design.

We thank the members of the SSRC Committee on Cognition and Survey Research for their valuable counsel on this paper. The preparation of the paper was supported in part by Grant BNS 83-20284 from the National Science Foundation.

References

BELSON, W. A. (1981) *The Design and Understanding of Survey Questions*. Aldershot, England: Gower.

BISHOP, G. F. (1987) Context effects on self-perception of interest in government and public affairs. In HIPPLER, H. J., SCHWARZ, N., AND SUDMAN, S. (eds.). *Social Information Processing and Survey Methodology*. New York: Springer-Verlag, pp. 179–199.

BISHOP, G. F., and HIPPLER, H. J. (1986) Response effects in self-administered and telephone surveys: An experiment in Germany and the United States. Paper presented at the Annual Conference of the American Association for Public Opinion Research (AAPOR), St. Petersburg, FL.

BISHOP, G. F., HIPPLER, H. J., SCHWARZ, N., and STRACK, F. (1988) A comparison of response effects in self-administered and telephone surveys. In GROVES, R. M.,

BIEMER, P. B., LYBERG, L. E., MASSEY, J. T., NICHOLLS II, W. L., and WAKSBERG, J. (eds.). *Telephone Survey Methodology.* New York: Wiley, pp. 321–340.

BRADBURN, N. M., RIPS, L. J., and SHEVELL, S. K. (1987) Answering autobiographical questions: The impact of memory and inference on surveys. *Science* 236, 157–161.

BROWN, N. R., RIPS, L. J., and SHEVELL, S. K. (1985) The subjective dates of natural events in very-long-term memory. *Cognitive Psychology* 17(2), 139–177.

CANNELL, C. F. (1985a) Experiments in the improvement of response accuracy. In BEED, T. W., and STIMSON, R. J. (eds.). *Survey Interviewing: Theory and Techniques.* Winchester, MA: Allen & Unwin, pp. 24–62.

⸺ (1985b) Overview: Response bias and interviewer variability in surveys. In BEED, T. W., and STIMSON, R. J. (eds.). *Survey Interviewing: Theory and Techniques.* Winchester, MA: Allen & Unwin, pp. 1–23.

CANNELL, C. F., OKSENBERG, L., and CONVERSE, J. M. (1977) Striving for response accuracy: Experiments in new interviewing techniques. *Journal of Marketing Research* 14(3), 306–315.

CLARK, H. H. (1977) Inferences in comprehension. In LA BERGE, D., and SAMUELS, S. J. (eds.). *Basic Processes in Reading: Perception and Comprehension.* Hillsdale, NJ: Erlbaum, pp. 243–263.

⸺ (1979) Responding to indirect speech acts. *Cognitive Psychology* 11, 430–477.

CLARK, H. H., and BRENNAN, S. E. (1991) Grounding in communication. In RESNICK, L. B., LEVINE, J., and TEASLEY, S. D. (eds.). *Perspectives on Socially Shared Cognition.* Washington, DC: American Psychological Association, pp. 127–149.

CLARK, H. H., and HAVILAND, S. E. (1977) Comprehension and the given-new contract. In FREEDLE, R. O. (ed.). *Discourse Production and Comprehension.* Hillsdale, NJ: Erlbaum, pp. 1–40.

CLARK, H. H., and MARSHALL, C. R. (1981) Definite reference and mutual knowledge. In JOSHI, A. K., WEBBER, B., and SAG, I. A. (eds.). *Elements of Discourse Understanding.* Cambridge, England: Cambridge University Press, pp. 10–63.

CLARK, H. H., and SCHAEFER, E. F. (1987) Collaborating on contributions to conversation. *Language and Cognitive Processes* 2, 19–41.

⸺ (1989) Contributing to discourse. *Cognitive Science* 13, 259–294.

CLARK, H. H., SCHREUDER, R., and BUTTRICK, S. (1983) Common ground and the understanding of demonstrative reference. *Journal of Verbal Learning and Verbal Behavior* 22, 245–258.

CLARK, H. H., and WILKES-GIBBS, D. (1986) Referring as a collaborative process. *Cognition* 22, 1–39.

CONVERSE, J. M., and PRESSER, S. (1986) *Survey Questions: Handcrafting the Standardized Questionnaire.* Beverly Hills, CA: Sage.

FEE, J. (1979) Symbols and attitudes: How people think about politics. Ph.D. dissertation. Chicago, IL: University of Chicago.

GAROFALO, J., and HINDENLANG, M. J. (1977) *An Introduction to the National Crime Survey.* Washington, DC: U.S. Department of Justice.

GRICE, H. P. (1957) Meaning. *Philosophical Review* 66, 377–388.

———— (1975) Logic and conversation. In COLE, P., and MORGAN, J. L. (eds.). *Syntax and Semantics, vol. 3: Speech Acts.* New York: Academic Press, pp. 41–58.

GROVES, R. M., and KAHN, R. L. (1979) *Surveys by Telephone: A National Comparison with Personal Interviews.* New York: Academic Press.

HARTLEY, E. (1946) *Problems in Prejudice.* New York: Kings Crown Press.

HAVILAND, S. E., and CLARK, H. H. (1974) What's new? Acquiring new information as a process in comprehension. *Journal of Verbal Learning and Verbal Behavior* 13, 512–521.

HIPPLER, H. J., and SCHWARZ, N. (1986) Not forbidding isn't allowing: The cognitive basis of the forbid-allow asymmetry. *Public Opinion Quarterly* 50, 87–96.

———— (1987) Response effects in surveys. In HIPPLER, H. J., SCHWARZ, N., and SUDMAN, S. (eds.). *Social Information Processing and Survey Methodology.* New York: Springer-Verlag, pp. 102–122.

HYMAN, H. H., and SHEATSLEY, P. B. (1950) The current status of American public opinion. In PAYNE, J. C. (ed.). *The Teaching of Contemporary Affairs: Twenty-first Yearbook of the National Council of Social Studies.* Washington, DC: National Council for the Social Studies, pp. 11–34.

ISAACS, E. A., and CLARK, H. H. (1987) References in conversation between experts and novices. *Journal of Experimental Psychology: General* 116(1), 26–37.

JEFFERSON, G. (1972) Side sequences. In SUDNOW, D. (ed.). *Studies in Social Interaction.* New York: Free Press, pp. 294–338.

———— (1989) Preliminary notes on a possible metric which provides for a "standard maximum" silence of approximately one second in conversation. In ROGER, D., and BULL, P. (eds.). *Conversation: An Interdisciplinary Perspective.* Philadelphia: Multilingual Matters, pp. 166–196.

KAHNEMAN, D., KNETSCH, J. L., and THALER, R. (1986) Fairness as a constraint on profit seeking. *American Economic Review* 76(4), 728–741.

LEVINSON, S. C. (1983) *Pragmatics.* Cambridge, England: Cambridge University Press.

LEWIS, D. K. (1969) *Convention: A Philosophical Study.* Cambridge, MA: Harvard University Press.

———— (1979) Scorekeeping in a language game. *Journal of Philosophical Logic* 8, 339–359.

LINK, H. C. (1946) The Psychological Corporation's index of public opinion. *Journal of Applied Psychology* 30, 297–309.

LOFTUS, E. F. (1975) Leading questions and the eyewitness report. *Cognitive Psychology* 7, 560–572.

LOFTUS, E. F., and MARBURGER, W. (1983) Since the eruption of Mt. St. Helens, has anyone beaten you up? Improving the accuracy of retrospective reports with landmark events. *Memory and Cognition* 11(2), 114–120.

LOFTUS, E. F., and PALMER, J. C. (1974) Reconstruction of automobile destruction: An example of the interaction between language and memory. *Journal of Verbal Learning and Verbal Behavior* 13, 585–589.

MANN, W. C., and THOMPSON, S. A. (1986) Relational propositions in discourse. *Discourse Processes* 9, 57–90.

MERRITT, M. (1976) On questions following questions in service encounters. *Language in Society* 5(3), 315–357.

MUELLER, J. E. (1973) *War, Presidents and Public Opinion.* New York: Wiley.

NETER, J., and WAKSBERG, J. (1964) A study of response errors in the expenditures data from household interviews. *Journal of the American Statistical Association* 59, 18–55.

NOELLE-NEUMANN, E. (1970) Wanted: Rules for wording structured questionnaires. *Public Opinion Quarterly* 34, 191–201.

PAYNE, S. L. (1951) *The Art of Asking Questions.* Princeton, NJ: Princeton University Press.

PERFETTI, C. A., BEVERLY, S., BELL, L., RODGERS, K., and FAUX, R. (1987). Comprehending newspaper headlines. *Journal of Memory and Language* 26(6), 692–713.

PRINCE, E. F. (1981) Towards a taxonomy of given-new information. In COLE, P. (ed.). *Radical Pragmatics.* New York: Academic Press, pp. 223–256.

RUGG, D. (1941) Experiments in wording questions: II. *Public Opinion Quarterly* 5, 91–92.

RUGG, D., and CANTRIL, H. (1944) The wording of questions. In CANTRIL, H. (ed.). *Gauging Public Opinion.* Princeton NJ: Princeton University Press, pp. 23–50.

SACKS, H., SCHEGLOFF, E., and JEFFERSON, G. (1974) A simplest systematics for the organization of turn-taking for conversation. *Language* 50, 696–735.

SCHEGLOFF, E. A. (1972) Notes on a conversational practice: Formulating place. In SUDNOW, D. (ed.). *Studies in Social Interaction.* New York: Free Press, pp. 75–119.

_____ (1980) Preliminaries to preliminaries: "Can I ask you a question?" *Sociological Inquiry* 50, 104–152.

_____ (1982) Discourse as an interactional achievement: Some uses of "uh huh" and other things that come between sentences. In TANNEN, D. (ed.). *Analyzing Discourse: Test and Talk. Georgetown University Roundtable on Languages and Linguistics 1981.* Washington, DC: Georgetown University Press, pp. 71–93.

SCHEGLOFF, E., JEFFERSON, G., and SACKS, H. (1977) The preference for self-correction in the organization of repair in conversation. *Language* 53, 361–382.

SCHEGLOFF, E., and SACKS, H. (1973) Opening up closings. *Semiotica* 8, 289–327.

SCHIFFER, S. (1972) *Meaning.* Oxford, England: Clarendon Press.

SCHOBER, M. F., and CLARK, H. H. (1989) Understanding by addressees and overhearers. *Cognitive Psychology* 21(2), 211–232.

SCHUMAN, H., and KALTON, G. (1985) Survey methods. In LINDZEY, G., and ARONSON, E.

(eds.). *Handbook of Social Psychology*, vol. 1, 3rd ed. New York: Random House, pp. 635–697.

SCHUMAN, H., and PRESSER, S. (1981) *Questions and Answers in Attitude Surveys: Experiments on Question Form, Wording, and Context.* New York: Academic Press.

SCHWARZ, N., HIPPLER, H. J., DEUTSCH, B., and STRACK, F. (1985) Response categories: Effects on behavioral reports and comparative judgments. *Public Opinion Quarterly* 49, 388–395.

SCHWARZ, N., and STRACK, F. (1981) Manipulating salience: Causal assessment in natural settings. *Personality and Social Psychology Bulletin* 6, 554–558.

SEARS, D. O., and LAU, R. R. (1983) Inducing apparently self-interested political preferences. *American Journal of Political Science* 27, 223–252.

SMITH, T. W. (1989) Random probes of GSS questions. *International Journal of Public Opinion Research* 1, 305–325.

STALNAKER, R. C. (1978) Assertion. In COLE, P. (ed.). *Syntax and Semantics, Vol. 9: Pragmatics.* New York: Academic Press, pp. 315–332.

STRACK, F., and MARTIN, L. L. (1987) Thinking, judging, and communicating: A process account of context effects in attitude surveys. In HIPPLER, H. J., SCHWARZ, N., and SUDMAN, S. (eds.). *Social Information Processing and Survey Methodology.* New York: Springer-Verlag, pp. 102–122.

STRACK, F., MARTIN, L. L., and SCHWARZ, N. (1988) The social determinants of information use in judgments of life-satisfaction. *European Journal of Social Psychology* 18, 429–442.

SUDMAN, S., and BRADBURN, N. M. (1973) Effects of time and memory factors on response in surveys. *Journal of the American Statistical Association* 68, 805–815.

_____ (1974) *Response Effects in Surveys: A Review and Synthesis.* Chicago: Aldine.

_____ (1982) *Asking Questions: A Practical Guide to Questionnaire Design.* San Francisco: Jossey-Bass.

SUDMAN, S., and FERBER, R. (1970) *Experiments in Obtaining Consumer Expenditures in Durable Goods by Recall Procedures.* Urbana, IL: Survey Research Laboratory, University of Illinois.

SVARTVIK, J., and QUIRK, R. (1980) *A Corpus of English Conversation.* Lund, Sweden: Gleerup.

TURNER, C. F., and KRAUSS, E. (1978) Fallible indicators of the subjective state of the nation. *American Psychologist* 33, 456–470.

TVERSKY, A., and KAHNEMAN, D. (1981) The framing of decisions and the psychology of choice. *Science* 211, 453–458.

_____ (1986) Rational choices and the framing of decisions. *Journal of Business* 59(4), 251–278.

WAGENAAR, W. A. (1986) My memory: A study of autobiographical memory over six years. *Cognitive Psychology* 18(2), 225–252.

WILLIAMS, E. (1977) Experimental comparisons of face-to-face and mediated communications: A review. *Psychological Bulletin* 84(5), 963–976.

―――― (1978) Visual interaction and speech patterns: An extension of previous results. *British Journal of Social and Clinical Psychology,* 101–102.

WILSON, C., and WILLIAMS, E. (1977) Watergate words: A naturalistic study of media and communications. *Communication Research* 4(2), 169–178.

3

Direct Questioning About Comprehension in a Survey Setting

ROBERT M. GROVES, NANCY H. FULTZ,
and ELIZABETH MARTIN

Background

Survey questionnaires are useful measurement instruments to the extent that questions convey to the respondent the desired intent of the researcher. For much of survey research this has been assumed to be an unproblematic part of the measurement process. Yet throughout the history of survey research, there has been a stream of methodological research, now grown large with the application of concepts from cognitive psychology to surveys, which has challenged that assumption.

One of the initial cognitive acts by a survey respondent upon hearing a question is the attribution of meaning to the oral presentation by the interviewer. This step of comprehension involves the retrieval from semantic memory of relevant facts concerning meaning of words and phrases. It also involves recognition of the implied meanings of combinations of words. These retrievals are made in the context of the survey interview, in which relevant stimuli may include the topics discussed prior to this particular question, the respondent's perception of interviewer beliefs, and speech behaviors of the interviewer during delivery of the question.

Following this logic, one possible source of variation in responses to a single survey question is differences in perceived intent or meaning of the question. Whereas there has been much attention paid to the impact of question wording in the survey methodology literature, there have been only a few attempts to examine perceived meaning directly as a cause of sensitivity

49

to question wording. One of the earliest was Cantril's (1944) study of the question:

> After the war is over, do you think people will have to work harder, about the same, or not so hard as before?

> 1. Harder
> 2. About the same
> 3. Not so hard
> 4. Don't know

On a special subsample Cantril followed up the question with:

> When you said that people would have to work (harder, about the same, not so hard), were you thinking of people everywhere and in all walks of life—laborers, white collar workers, farmers and businessmen—or did you have in mind one class or group of people in particular?

Depending on the answer to this question, Cantril used other questions to attempt to understand the perceived meaning of different words or phrases in the question. (He found that one-third of the respondents believed "people" meant a certain class, and only a little more than one-half thought it meant everyone.)

Later Nuckols (1953) asked respondents to use their own words to describe what a question was asking. He also concluded that standardization of words does not automatically imply standardization of meaning. Belson (1981) did further work along this line by asking people in reinterviews what specific phrases meant in the context of survey questions. Ferber (1956) did the same thing for all respondents on an attitudinal question and found people readily expressing opinions about issues which they could not define. This fact later became a cornerstone of Converse's notion of "nonattitudes" (1970), which hypothesized that some attitudinal questions failed to measure well-defined affective states for some respondents. The result was low reliability of answers over replications of the measurement.

Many of the studies above used small samples and failed to address the question of a methodology suitable for ongoing surveys. Schuman's idea of the "random probe" (1966) comes closer to such a method. He argues that a notion of the quality of answers can be obtained by following a closed question, on random subsamples, with the probe, "Could you tell me a little more about that?" or "Could you explain a little about that?" This probe differs from the ones mentioned above by not measuring meaning directly, but instead asking for an elaboration of an answer. (It is not known whether this probe indeed does produce different answers than the meaning probes, but on the surface it appears to seek different information.)

The final alert to problems of shared meaning comes from the new critics of standardized survey interviewing (e.g., Mishler, 1986; Briggs, 1986; and Suchman and Jordan, chapter 12 in this volume). These researchers note that analysis of the interaction between respondents and interviewers uncovers repeated failures of the respondent to comprehend the question as desired by the researcher. Most of this work notes that the standardized interview (which heavily restricts both parties of the interaction to a small number of behaviors) is poorly suited to repair the misconceptions that arise. Further, they note that the responses in such circumstances typically will pass normal edit checks during data processing. They are "invisible" to normal survey quality control procedures.

Some of the procedures used in past work to measure perceived meaning of terms in questions rely on direct questioning of respondents. The criticisms of these approaches come from two perspectives. One, from the Nisbett and Wilson (1977) logic, would state that respondents could only reconstruct likely perceived meaning after the question was answered. They would not be privy to the actual cognitions experienced at the moment of comprehension and would be giving freshly obtained perceptions. In that sense the questions on meaning would themselves be subject to large measurement errors. The second perspective notes that open questions seeking meaning of a prior (target) question might entail different burdens for respondents with limited verbal skills than for those who are very articulate. Thus, groups with potentially different perceptions about the intent of the question may vary in response errors to the open question. For either reason, the follow-up question would be plagued with its own response-error problems.

The criticism relating to burdens on verbal articulation of thoughts might be addressed directly with a test using both open and closed questions following a target question. The Nisbett and Wilson argument is more difficult to address. It appears to require a theory relating answers on the target question to perceived intent of the question.

This paper presents the results of a small study examining the use of follow-up questions probing the perceived intent of a question about self-perceived health status. The data collection involved the use of several follow-up questions that asked respondents to describe the meaning they attributed to words in the question and the method of constructing their answers to the question.

Design

The data were collected as part of a pretest for the 1986 General Social Survey. Approximately one hundred pretest interviews were collected by NORC field interviewers, using quota-sampling schemes to represent major demographic groups. At the end of an interview lasting about 1.5 hours, a series of questions about self-perceived health status were asked.

Respondents were first asked to rate their own health status:

Would you say your own health, in general, is excellent, good, fair, or poor?

This question was followed by a series of questions, both open and closed, asking the respondents what they had thought about when they answered the health-status question. The series started with an open question:

When you answered the last question about your health, what did you think of?

Then there was a series of closed questions, asking the respondents to report whether, in answering the question, they compared their health to that of others, whether they compared it to their own at an earlier time, and whether they were thinking of the last few years or more recent times. They were also asked, in open questions, what was bad or good about their health. Finally, they were asked whether, in answering the question, they considered how "happy or sad" they had been feeling.

Data Analysis Strategy

Past literature (e.g., Waldron, 1983) has shown that women tend to give lower self-perceived health-status ratings than do men. These differences remain after controls are applied for differential health conditions. It has been hypothesized that some of the difference might be attributable to women's inclusion of more psychological health criteria than men's. In short, the meaning of the phrase "health status" might tend to differ between the sexes.

The responses to the health-status question appear in table 1 separately by sex of respondent. As with past studies, males in the pretest tended to report "excellent" health compared to females (43 percent of the males; 28 percent of the females, approximate standard error of 15-point difference is about 9.5).

The most important purpose of the pretest was the examination of responses to questions about meaning. Related to this was the question of whether open and closed questions would provide similar information about what respondents had perceived as the intent of the health-status question.

Table 1   Reported Health Status by Gender.

Health Status	Gender		Total
	Male	Female	
Excellent	43%	28%	35%
Good	39	58	49
Fair	16	8	12
Poor	2	6	4
Total	100%	100%	100%
n	49	50	99

Further, it was hypothesized that, to the extent that respondents were inferring different meanings from the question, different responses to the health question could be expected. Finally, it was hoped that any differences found in the ways respondents perceived and thus answered the health status question would help to explain the finding that men tend to rate their health status higher than do women. It was acknowledged, however, that tests of this hypothesis would be distorted by lack of analytic controls on true health conditions, which might differ between males and females in the pretest.

From the data analyzed here, there is reason to believe that respondents did perceive the intent of the health-status question in differing ways, and that open and closed questions provided different kinds of information about their comprehension of the question. Results pertaining to the gender differential were less clear. Most of these conclusions are severely limited by the small number of cases in the pretest ($n = 100$).

Analysis of the data was divided into three stages. In the first stage, coding of the open-question responses was completed. In the second, comparisons were made between several closed questions and the open question. Finally, in the third stage, analysis of the possible explanations of the gender differential in health-status ratings was implemented.

Coding of Open-Question Responses

Respondent reports of what they had thought about when they answered the health-status question were coded into ten categories. These categories include:

1. Health behaviors ($n = 14$)
2. Affect ($n = 3$)

3. Health-service usage ($n = 6$)
4. Outcome of physical examination ($n = 5$)
5. Physical performance or ability ($n = 7$)
6. Absence or presence of illness ($n = 31$)
7. Feelings ($n = 10$)
8. Health, not specified ($n = 7$)
9. Other ($n = 14$)
10. Don't know or not asked ($n = 3$)

Whereas some of these category labels may seem clear, others are less clearly defined. Health behaviors include those which affect health either positively or negatively (for example, exercising or smoking). Affect responses include responses such as "I'm happy" or "I feel sad." Respondents who cited the frequency with which they utilized health services were grouped into the third category. These respondents were considered separate from those who specifically mentioned the outcome of a physical examination, and these respondents were coded into the fourth category. Respondents who mentioned that they were either able or unable to perform any physical task (for example, walking up stairs) were coded into the performance or ability category. Respondents who said they had thought about either the absence or presence of illness in their lives were coded into the illness category. The feelings category included those respondents who specifically mentioned that "they felt good" or "they felt bad." Finally, the respondents coded into the "Health, not specified" category differ from those in the "Other" category in that, when asked what they had thought about, they stated merely that they had thought about their health. These responses offered little additional information to the original health-status rating. Whereas up to three responses were coded for each person, analysis was only undertaken for first-mentioned responses.

The first test of the open question was whether respondents could supply anything more than merely a repeating of the question. About 90 percent of respondents gave some response that was more than just a restating of the question. Hence, the test offers some hope for the methodology.

The second question is whether the answer provides some insight into differences in response-formation processes. Given the coding scheme, respondents' answers tended to fall within two clusters. The first may be considered an *external* cluster, the result of some labeling of the respondent by another or by some experience that made the health status a salient characteristic of the respondent. The contrasting sets are named *internal* meanings. The term *external* refers to the idea that these respondents have concrete, external cues to help them in rating their health status. Respondents from the third, fourth, and sixth categories were combined to create the external group ($n = 42$). For example, respondents who have had a physical examination within the last few weeks are able to use the results of that examination as a concrete indicator of their health status. Their knowledge of their health status comes from an outside source, specifically their doctor. Respondents who are visitors to health facilities have objective (i.e., separate from their own evaluation) indicators of their health status that they may use in answering the health question. For these respondents the question of determining their health status may be one of recalling a particular event, or set of events, and then from that recall deciding the proper response.

The response task is somewhat different for those respondents who fall into the second category, the *internal* cluster. For these people it appears that no external source is relevant to help them rate their health status. The answers they give are not based on specific events that they have recalled, but rather are based on some other, less concrete, source. For example, some of the respondents in this category reported that they thought about feelings or emotions when they answered the health-status question.

These two clusters seem somewhat different from the contrast of the psychological and physiological meanings that has been suggested to distinguish male and female assessments of health. Rather, they are two sets of meanings that are heavily dependent on life experiences and contact with others.

Comparisons
of Open and Closed Questions

Given this distinction between the two types of responses found with the open question, it seems relevant to compare these findings with the responses to the closed questions. Closed questions were used because of the fear that respondents with low verbal skills could not provide useful responses to the open question. If similar information were obtained by both, then the economical form of a single open question might be preferable. Thus, studying the relationship between the two types of questions takes on increasing importance in the attempt to obtain the most accurate data possible.

Three questions from the General Social Survey (GSS) pretest were of particular interest in studying the relationship between the open and closed questions. The first of these asked the respondents whether they had compared their health to the health of others when they had answered the health-status question. It was hypothesized that those people who had been labeled as *internal* would be more likely to answer this question affirmatively than would those respondents labeled *external*. The reasoning behind this hypothesis stemmed from the idea that without the aid of external cues people would be more likely to compare their health to others' in an attempt to reach a decision about their own health status. Data from the GSS pretest appear to support this hypothesis (see table 2).

Of those respondents classified as *external*, only 12% reported comparing their own health to the health of others, compared to 31% of the respondents classified as *internal*. (Standard error of the difference of 19 percentage points is about 8.0).

A second question included in the pretest asked respondents whether they had compared their health at the present time to their health at an earlier age when they answered the health-status question. Similar to the hypothesis above, it was thought that respondents classified as *internal* would be more likely than the *external* respondents to make comparisons to an earlier age in an attempt to rate their health status. Again, this would be due to the lack of more recent, concrete indicators available to them in making this judgment. The data in table 3 provide only limited support for this hypothesis. These results do not show any significant differences between the two groups. However, the findings are in the expected direction, with slightly more of the *external* respondents reporting that they did not compare their health now to their health at an earlier age in an attempt to rate their health status.

One final question that was used from the pretest asked respondents:

When you said your health was (excellent/good/fair/poor), were you thinking about your health over the last few years, recent months, the last few weeks, or now?

Table 2 Percentage Comparing Health to Others by External Versus Internal Responses to Health-Status Question.

Did R Compare Health to Others?	Type of Meaning Attributed to Health-Status Question			
	External	Internal	DK/NA	Total
Yes	12%	31%	0%	22%
No	88	69	67	77
DK/NA	0	0	33	1
Total	100%	100%	100%	100%
n	42	55	3	100

Table 3   Percentage Comparing Health to That at an Earlier Age by Type of Response to Health-Status Question.

Did R Compare Health to Earlier Age?	Type of Meaning Attributed to Health-Status Question			
	External	Internal	DK/NA	Total
Yes	40%	47%	0%	43%
No	60	53	67	56
DK/NA	0	0	33	1
Total	100%	100%	100%	100%
n	42	55	3	100

For the purpose of this analysis, these categories were dichotomized so that "the last few years" was considered "the past" and the other three categories were defined as "recent times." (In retrospect the response categories seem to overemphasize distinctions among recent times.) Those respondents relying on external labeling of their health status were expected to refer to the date of the event (a date uncontrolled in the data collection). It was expected that those relying on self-evaluation would use current feelings and conditions as information relevant to judgments about their health status. Data in table 4 show that those using *internal* assessments tended to reference recent times more often than those using *external* information.

One conclusion that can be reached from the data discussed above is that the open question and the three closed questions generate different information from respondents. This finding suggests the importance of

Table 4   Percentage Thinking of the "Last Few Years" Versus More Recent Times in Answering Health-Status Question by Perceived Meaning of Question.

Time Reference	Type of Meaning Attributed to Health-Status Question			
	External	Internal	DK/NA	Total
Last Few Years	50%	36%	33%	42%
Recent Times	50	64	33	57
DK/NA	0	0	34	1
Total	100%	100%	100%	100%
n	42	55	3	100

including both types of questions in future surveys. Had the responses for the two types of questions been more similar, an argument could have been made for eliminating the three closed questions in favor of the one open question. Despite the increased costs of coding an open question, the overall expenditure would probably be less than the cost of including three questions. For each target question to be investigated, however, a different set of closed questions would be required, motivated by relevant theories of alternative meanings of the target question.

Gender Differentials
in Health-Status Ratings

A second area of interest for these data is the question of gender differences in health-status reporting. Past researchers have found that men tend to report that they are in better health than do women. One explanation for this finding is that women have more frequent medical examinations than men, and thus have more objective views of their health. The GSS pretest is poorly suited to investigate the underlying causes of these differences because many confounding variables (e.g., actual health conditions, health-service usage) are not measured. Despite these weaknesses, it is useful to examine whether the meaning probes help to explain the gender differences. First, there is some tendency for males to report higher health status than females in the GSS pretest. As Table 1 showed, about 43% of the men rated their health as excellent compared to only 28% of the women (standard error on the difference of 15 percentage points is about 9.5).

The question of primary interest, however, is whether the gender differences merely reflect the use of different meanings for the health-status question. It was hypothesized that controlling for the inferred meaning of the question would decrease the gender difference in health-status ratings. Thus, it might be possible that women report lower health statuses than men because they are more likely to use objective indicators in judging their health. In order to test this, we compare health status by gender controlling first for the external-internal indicator and then for each of the three closed questions. Results from the open question are discussed first. Data are presented in table 5.

Table 5 shows that controlling for the perceived meaning of the question does not eliminate the gender differences. Among both the *externals* and the *internals*, a 15-point difference exists in the percentage rating their health excellent.

Similar analyses were conducted for the three closed questions. The first two yielded no statistically significant results. When controlling for whether

Table 5 Reported Health Status by Gender
by Perceived Meaning of Question.

| | Gender | | |
	Men	Women	Total
External Labels			
Excellent	37%	22%	28%
Good	37	56	48
Fair	26	9	17
Poor	0	13	7
Total	100%	100%	100%
n	19	23	42
Internal Labels			
Excellent	47%	32%	40%
Good	40	60	49
Fair	10	8	9
Poor	3	0	2
Total	100%	100%	100%
n	30	25	55

the respondents had compared their health to the health of others, the percentage difference between men and women was 32 for those who did compare, and 11 for those who did not. Similarly, the percentage difference when controlling for whether or not the respondents had compared their health to an earlier age was 26 for those who had made the comparison, and 14 for those who had not. The only significant results were found for the question that asked respondents what period of time they had been thinking about when they rated their health. These results are summarized in table 6. Among those considering the past few years, there are no significant gender differences on health status. For those thinking of more recent times, however, men tend to rate their health excellent much more than do women (32 percentage point difference, approximate standard error, 11 points).

Conclusions

Most respondents appear to be able to give useful information in a follow-up open question on meaning. Further, their responses on meaning are related to their health-status ratings. There are several alternatives that could be used for this question (e.g., "In your own words, what did you think the question

**Table 6 Reported Health Status
by Time Reference Used for Health-Status Response.**

	Gender		
	Men	Women	Total
Considered Health over Last Few Years			
Excellent	41%	44%	43%
Good	41	44	43
Fair	12	8	9
Poor	6	4	5
Total	100%	100%	100%
n	17	25	42
Considered Health in More Recent Times			
Excellent	44%	12%	30%
Good	37	72	53
Fair	19	8	14
Poor	0	8	3
Total	100%	100%	100%
n	32	25	57

meant?" "What information do you think the question was seeking from you?"). In addition, the random-probe wording might be used (e.g., "Tell me more about that."). It is not clear whether very different information would be obtained from the different questions.

The closed questions did not capture the same dimensions of meaning that were revealed by the open question. In the open question no one mentioned explicit comparisons to others or to themselves at an earlier age (although some answers involving use of physical activities had implied temporal references). In retrospect it seems clear that some of the closed questions were seeking reports on cognitive strategies for judging an appropriate answer—that is, they might have gone beyond an attempt merely to measure meaning of the question. As a result, they may have been more difficult to answer accurately than a question about meaning alone.

The pretest was inconclusive (as it was likely to be, given the small sample size) in explaining the gender difference on the health-status question. We were hampered, however, by the lack of control variables on health conditions. The basic hypothesis still stands—indeed, the finding that the difference between men and women disappears among respondents who consider the distant past suggests further lines of research and perhaps changes in survey practice. If an over-time evaluation is what the researcher is looking for, perhaps the question wording should include explicit reference periods.

References

BELSON, W. A. (1981) *The Design and Understanding of Survey Questions*. Aldershot, England: Gower.

BRIGGS, C. L. (1986) *Learning How to Ask: A Sociolinguistic Appraisal of the Role of the Interview in Social Science Research*. Cambridge, England: Cambridge University Press.

CANTRIL, H. (1944) *Gauging Public Opinion*. Princeton, NJ: Princeton University Press.

CONVERSE, P. (1970) Attitudes and nonattitudes: Continuation of a dialogue. In Tufte, E. R. (ed.) *The Quantitative Analysis of Social Problems*. Reading, MA: Addison-Wesley, pp. 168–189.

FERBER, R. (1956) The effect of respondent ignorance on survey results. *Journal of the American Statistical Association* 51, 576–586.

MISHLER, E. (1986) *Research Interviewing*. Cambridge, MA: Harvard University Press.

NISBETT, R. E., and WILSON, T. D. (1977) Telling more than we can know: Verbal reports on mental processes. *Psychological Review* 84(3), 231–259.

NUCKOLS, R. (1953) A note on pre-testing public opinion questions, *Journal of Applied Psychology* 37(2), 119–120.

SCHUMAN, H. (1966) The random probe—A technique for evaluating the validity of closed questions, *American Sociological Review* 31(2), 218–222.

SUCHMAN, L., and JORDAN B. Validity and the collaborative construction of meaning in face-to-face surveys, chapter 12 in this volume.

WALDRON, I. (1983) Sex differences in illness incidence, prognosis, and mortality: Issues and evidence. *Social Science and Medicine* 17(16), 1107–1123.

PART

III

MEMORY

4

Personal Recall
and the Limits
of Retrospective Questions
in Surveys[1]

ROBERT W. PEARSON, MICHAEL ROSS,
and ROBYN M. DAWES

Memory belongs to the imagination. Human memory is not like a computer which records things; it is part of the imaginative process, on the same terms as invention.

—Alain Robbe-Grillet,
author, scriptwriter, *Last Year at Marienbad*

Herein lies a difficulty in any autobiographical sketch which purports to deal with one's mental development. It is a story of oneself in the past, read in the light of one's present self. There is much supplementary inference—often erroneous inference—wherein "must of been" masquerades as "was so."

—Lloyd Morgan
1930/1961, p. 237.

Introduction

Retrospective, or memory-based, responses to interview questions provide an indispensable window onto our past. Often, retrospective questions are

1. Portions of this chapter are based on Ross (1988).

the only means available to monitor individual or social states, or their change. The responses to such questions are used, for example, to:

- Estimate the nation's monthly unemployment rate. (Respondents who are not employed are asked to report whether they looked for work within the last four weeks, to differentiate between the unemployed and those not in the labor force.)

- Estimate the lifetime prevalence rate of depression. (Respondents are asked whether they ever had a continuous period of two weeks or more during which they felt so depressed that it interfered with their daily activities.)

- Assess the effect of parental behavior on a person's current mental state. (Clinically depressed subjects are asked to report on the nature of their relationship with their parents when the subjects were growing up.)

- Assess the likelihood of a child abuser having been abused by his or her own parents. (Child abusers are asked to recall whether they were abused as children to determine whether others who have been abused as children may be prone to abuse their own children.)

- Provide estimates of the prevalence rates of various crimes. (Respondents in a national sample of households are asked whether they were robbed within the last six months.)

- Evaluate the effectiveness of participating in programs designed to improve academic performance. (Students are asked to evaluate the effectiveness of skills-improvement programs by comparing their present skills to those they recalled having prior to participation in the program.)

Much research in the social sciences depends upon personal recall. Some researchers have also been misled by it. Not long ago, for example, psychologists formulated theories of development on the basis of parents' retrospective descriptions of their child-rearing practices. Research suggests that such descriptions are often invalid evidence. For example, after Dr. Spock's book on child rearing became popular, mothers recalled that their parenting of just a few years earlier had been much more permissive than the concurrent evidence indicated (Robbins, 1963). Researchers now seek more direct—often prospective—evidence for studies of development across the life span (Yarrow, Campbell, and Burton, 1970).

Researchers and practitioners, however, continue to make considerable use of retrospective self-reports. In addition to those uses noted above, they include reports of voting, medical care, purchases, and finances. On the basis of such self-reports, social scientists evaluate theories of human behavior and offer advice on public policy. It is important, therefore, to know how personal memories are formed and how accurate they may be.

Peoples' responses to retrospective questions are affected by such factors as the amount of time permitted for the response, the order of events being recalled, the presence or absence of anchors or comparisons, and so on (see Schuman and Kalton, 1986; Sudman and Bradburn, 1982). What we wish to emphasize in this chapter is that responses to questions of retrospective nature are also greatly influenced by the current psychological and environmental state of the respondents, and by the explicit or implicit theories which consist of schemata, narratives, or scripts they hold about themselves and society.

A Theory of Personal Recall

Memory is often a construction in which images of the past and present are combined with inferences drawn from implicit theories about self and society (Bartlett, 1932; Mead, 1934). In the current chapter we focus on the memory of personal attributes such as prior beliefs, traits, and behaviors.

The recall of personal attributes often involves a two-step process (Ross and Conway, 1986). First, the individual begins by noting his or her present status on the attribute in question. The present serves as a benchmark because it is generally more salient and available than a person's earlier standing on an attribute. As a result, construction of the past consists, in large part, of characterizing the past as different from or the same as the present. To determine their attitude toward capital punishment five years ago, for example, individuals may first ask themselves: Is there any reason to believe that I felt differently then than I do now?

Second, people often invoke an implicit theory of stability or change to guide their construction of past attributes. These implicit theories include specific beliefs regarding the inherent stability of an attribute as well as a set of general principles concerning the conditions likely to promote personal change or stability. The theories are implicit in that they encompass rarely discussed but strongly held beliefs about oneself or society.

An implicit theory can affect the kind of information retrieved from memory as well as the individual's understanding of it. Memories consistent with peoples' beliefs are often more accessible than memories that are inconsistent with beliefs. Ambiguous information retrieved from memory may also be interpreted as supportive of the belief (Anderson and Pichert, 1978; Bartlett, 1932; Cantor and Mischel, 1977; Hamilton, 1981; Hastie, 1981; Loftus, Miller, and Burns, 1978; Markus, 1977; Mischel, Ebbesen, and

Zeiss, 1976; Rothbart, 1981; Rothbart, Evans, and Fulero, 1979; Schank and Abelson, 1977; Snyder and Uranowitz, 1978; Spence, 1982; Taylor and Crocker, 1981). An implicit theory may thus serve to organize memories into a coherent pattern of information that is consonant with the theory. In addition, when theory-relevant information cannot be recalled, an individual may guess about the past by using the implicit theory and present status as guides (Bellezza and Bower, 1981).[2]

Implicit Theories of Stability and Change

What is the nature of theories that are hypothesized to guide recall? There are a host of implicit theories that are potentially relevant, including theories about the course of various personal traits across the life span, theories about the impact of life events (e.g., motherhood) on behavior and personality, and theories about the characteristics of various social groups (e.g., males and females). At a more generic level, however, it is possible to identify two overarching theories: (1) a theory of personal stability and (2) a theory of personal change.

People often perceive their attributes as stable over time. In general I say that I am the same today as I was yesterday (Epstein, 1973; Erikson, 1968; James, 1980). When the consistency principle is invoked, people tend to view their current standing on an attribute as an accurate reflection of their past status. Consequently, if individuals adopt a theory of consistency in the face of actual change, they exaggerate the similarity of the past to the present.

Although people frequently assume consistency, at other times they see alterations in themselves. Individuals can maintain a sense of personal identity in the face of change by explaining how their current self emerged from an earlier version. In constructing their past, people impose coherence by connecting what is unconnected (Mead, 1964). Hence, I may believe I am a better teacher than I used to be because of experience, or that I am physically weaker because of age. These examples suggest that people possess implicit theories of change and ideas about the conditions that are likely to foster alterations in themselves and others. In such instances people's theories may lead them to overestimate the amount of change that has occurred.

Evidence for these general beliefs about the stability or constancy of

2. Although we focus on personal recall in the present chapter, the processes we describe seem to be as applicable in accounting for responses that attribute a characteristic to someone else. They may also be used in constructing collective memories, as suggested, for example, by recent research in the history and anthropology concerning collective personal testimony (see Crapanzano, Ergas, and Modell, 1986; Bodnar, 1989).

different personal attributes is found, for example, in Ross's (1987) study of how university and high school students expect personality traits, abilities, and opinions to change or remain constant throughout the life course. Participants in this study were instructed to start at age five and draw a plot, indicating the degree of each attribute the target would evince at every age. Four dominant prototypes were most prevalent in each of the attribute categories, although the ordering of their frequency of use differed. Two of the dominant prototypes emphasized stability over all or most of the life span, whereas the remaining two indicated change. For abilities, an inverted U-shaped prototype was most common (accounting for 29% of the plots), significantly exceeding use of the other prototypes. The inverted U prototype indicates that an ability was seen to improve, remain steady for a period, and then worsen across the life span. For opinions, the predominant prototype (accounting for 30% of the plots) indicated stability across the life span. Thus, the stability prototype was used to code 53% of the plots of attitudes toward Canadian Indians over the life span, 65% of the plots of attitudes toward Jews, and 67% of the plots of attitudes toward Catholics. Apparently, attitudes toward groups acquired early in the socialization process are thought to be maintained through the life span. The prototype coding of an attribute was typically unaffected by the target being rated (e.g., self, best friend, or average college student) and the gender of the subject.

While the most general set of implicit theories concern personal beliefs about change and stability, other types of theories may operate to fill in details; for example, to specify the nature of a change or the impact of various environmental factors on behavior and personality. These theories, illustrated in the next section, are especially important because they may mirror the theories that we wish to test through our questioning. For example, if we ask questions of current alcoholics about their relationship with their parents while the respondents were young, we may actually tap cultural theories, broadly shared in society, concerning the relationship between child rearing and psychological development, which the research itself is intended to test.

The Evidentiary Basis
of a Theory of Personal Recall

This chapter now turns to several examples of how the construction of the past can as a result be largely independent of experience. We cover both memories for specific events (e.g., an illness) and generalizations about past events (e.g., one's state of health for the past five years), some of which may be quite judgmental (e.g., the degree of caring by one's parents). In a concluding section, we consider implications of the findings for survey practices.

Most of the research reviewed below shares several properties. An investigator asks a subject to describe a current personal attribute; for example, the amount of pain he or she is experiencing. Later, these same individuals are asked to recall their initial report as well as describe the attribute again in the present. At the time of the first rating, individuals do not know that they will subsequently be asked to remember their prior response.

This procedure provides a clear criterion for the accuracy of personal recollections. In contrast, much of the cognitive psychology and life-span development research on autobiographical memory employs methods that do not permit such assessment (Barclay, 1986). For example, subjects are presented with activities (e.g., going to a library) or feelings (e.g., unhappy) and asked to describe relevant memories invoked by these cues (see Crovitz and Schiffman, 1974; Fitzgerald, 1980; Reiser, Black, and Kalamarides, 1986). It is not possible to determine the accuracy of the memories reported in such research.

There are also several disadvantages to the procedures employed in the studies that we review. The responses being recalled are often unfamiliar activities, such as an evaluation of the severity of one's pain on a ten-point scale. As a result, what appears to be errors in recall may actually reflect random fluctuations in scale usage. For example, an individual may assign the same degree of pain to slightly different scale ratings at two points in time. Unreliability per se, however, would not pose significant interpretational problems. We focus on systematic biases in this chapter.

A more serious limitation of these studies is that the researchers have established the focus, content, and time frame (which is usually based on convenience or other arbitrary criteria) for recall. They examine what people remember when prompted, rather than what they remember spontaneously (Linton, 1986). Recalling with prompts, however, is exactly the task of survey research, or any research requiring subjects to answer questions about their past state. Moreover, attempts to study behavior without prompts—or with minimal prompts, such as those used in projective tests—have produced little success (Dawes, 1988, chapter 11).

Despite the limitations of the studies, there is much that can be learned from a careful analysis of this research. Our aim is to interpret and integrate what may appear to be an unrelated and diverse set of research findings and survey practices. We do not claim, however, that the current analysis yields the only plausible interpretation of any particular research results. Major alternative explanations of the research findings are evaluated following the next section.

Let us begin, then, by considering a series of studies that yield results consonant with the hypothesis that people should exaggerate the similarity between the present and the past when they adopt a theory of consistency in the face of actual change.

Exaggerating the Consistency Between the Present and Past

LABORATORY INDUCED ATTITUDE CHANGE.   A number of researchers have examined people's recall of their earlier opinions after they have experienced an experimentally induced shift in attitudes. The typical finding is that people exaggerate the consistency between their present (new) attitudes and their past opinions. They presume that they always felt the way they do now. The first experiment along these lines was conducted by Bem and McConnell (1970). Their results have been replicated a number of times (e.g., Goethals and Reckman, 1973; Ross and Shulman, 1973; Wixon and Laird, 1976).

The Goethals and Reckman study is perhaps the most intriguing in that it involved a controversial attitude topic and massive attitude change. At the initial experimental session, Massachusetts high school students completed an opinion questionnaire, indicating their attitudes on various political and social topics. They returned four to fourteen days later for a group discussion on one of the attitude issues—the busing of students to achieve racial balance in United States schools. Students were told that the discussion was being conducted to assess high school students' thoughts on various topical issues. Groups were composed of students who were either all pro- or all anti-busing on the initial questionnaire, and a confederate of the experimenter. The confederate, a respected high school senior, attempted to change the attitudes of the group members. He was armed with persuasive arguments and dominated the conversation.

After group discussion the students were asked to indicate, in private, their current attitudes toward busing. Their responses revealed large shifts in opinion. Subjects were also asked to recall as accurately as possible the attitudes that they had reported at the first session. Despite a dramatic shift in attitudes, the students recalled their initial opinions as being very similar to their post-discussion attitudes toward busing.[3]

---

3. In many of the studies described here, respondents were required to report their present state before they were asked to recall their past status. Does the consistency effect in recall only occur when the present state is rendered highly salient in this fashion? No. Several studies of laboratory-induced attitude change assessed recall of past attitudes and behaviors without first asking subjects to state their current opinions (Bem and McConnell, 1970; Ross, 1985; Ross, McFarland, Conway, and Zanna, 1983; Ross, McFarland, and Fletcher, 1981). In the Bem and McConnell experiment, subjects wrote a counterattitudinal essay arguing for decreased student control over courses. They were then asked to recall their earlier attitude responses on this topic. Subjects recalled being less favorable to student control of courses than they had been. In a second condition, subjects were not asked to recall their earlier attitude reports, but instead were asked to indicate their current attitudes after writing the counterattitudinal essay. These subjects evidenced strong shifts in attitudes. As Bem and McConnell observed, the attitude-recall means paralleled the attitude-change means: "The figures are so similar . . . that it would appear that we had asked [attitude-recall] subjects for their current attitudes rather than their initial attitudes" (p. 28). In sum, it would appear that the consistency bias in recall does not depend on experimental procedures that highlight present attitudes.

In this and other experimental studies of attitude recall, the researchers were sensitive to the possibility that subjects might choose to present themselves as consistent over time by deliberately misreporting their earlier attitude responses. The researchers introduced strong demands for accuracy to reduce the likelihood that self-presentational concerns would affect recall. Subjects were asked to complete the attitude scales exactly as they had in the initial experimental session. More important, they were explicitly informed that the experimenter would evaluate the accuracy of their recall by comparing the two sets of responses.

When asked to recall their attitudes, subjects may have used the best information available, their current views, and, adopting a theory of stability, assumed that their past attitudes were similar. We have observed that people expect attitudes to be stable over long periods of time (Ross, 1987).

Ross (1985) provided more direct evidence of the processes mediating attitude recall in the attitude-change context. In this research the attitude-consistency effect in recall was replicated successfully with a different topic and attitude-change manipulation. Subjects were presented with a tape-recorded persuasive message by a noted medical authority, who argued that vigorous physical exercise, such as jogging, tends to have more harmful than beneficial effects. Pretesting indicated that subjects exposed to this message subsequently expressed more negative attitudes toward exercise than control subjects who had not heard the message.

In the experiment proper, subjects were not asked to report their current attitudes after exposure to the message, but instead were asked to recall the attitudes toward vigorous exercise that they had reported on an attitude questionnaire completed three to four weeks earlier in their introductory psychology class. Subjects exposed to the persuasive message recalled reporting significantly more negative attitudes toward exercise than subjects who had not heard the message. More important, the experiment included an additional dependent measure introduced to assess the biases of subjects' recall. Immediately after they recalled their earlier attitude response, subjects were asked how they remembered it. They were to write down the thoughts that went through their heads as they attempted to recall their initial attitude report.

Four categories accounted for 97% of the recall strategies reported by these subjects. Fifty-one percent of the responses reflected the use of a temporal consistency principle (e.g., "I answered the question now and figured that my opinion probably hasn't changed much in a month or so."). Twenty-two percent of the responses indicated use of a temporal consistency principle together with the person's current standing on a facet of the self relevant to the attitude response (e.g., "I do not remember what number I wrote in class, but being someone who exercises fairly regularly, and not too vigorously, I would say 9."). An additional 22% of the responses reflected strategies to promote recall. For example, subjects reported efforts to put themselves in the same frame of mind as when the original episode occurred (e.g., "First I tried to recall the psychology class that I was in, who I was sitting with, and, most importantly, how I was feeling that day."). Finally, 2% of the subjects reported actual memory of their initial response (e.g., "I seem to recall marking 12 in class."). The same four response categories were found to account for 95% of the recall strategies reported in a subsequent study, and the pattern of responding was virtually identical (Buehler, 1987). Moreover, in both studies, subjects who had received the attitude-change manipulation reported using recall strategies similar to those reported by control subjects who had not received the message, but who were asked to recall their initial attitude responses.

The strategies coded in the first two categories reflect use of present status and a principle of temporal consistency to construct a previous response. Interestingly, subjects did not always focus directly on the attribute in question. They sometimes drew inferences about the target attribute from related traits or behaviors. Thus, subjects' responses imply implicit theories about both temporal consistency and the relationships among various attributes. The other major category of responses seems to involve a quite different set of implicit theories. Subjects employed their understanding of the memory process itself to devise strategies to facilitate recall.

The responses reported most frequently in these studies are consonant with the recall process we are positing. It is not clear, however, that one should take such self-reports of mental processes at face value (Ericsson and Simon, 1980; Nisbett and Wilson, 1977). It seems reasonable to consider the reports of recall strategies as offering some, but not definitive, support for the present interpretation of the attitude-consistency finding.

People's implicit theories of attitudes go beyond temporal consistency. People also seem to believe that their own attitudes and behavior are, or should be, compatible.[4] Suppose, then, people are asked to recall attitude-relevant behaviors after they have changed their opinions. The research on attitude recall suggests that individuals assume that they have held their new attitudes for some time. If individuals assume a correspondence between these attitudes and their earlier behavior, they can infer that they have already engaged in actions consistent with their new attitudes.

In one study along these lines, university students listened to a persuasive communication on the negative consequences of frequently brushing one's

4. Indeed, many attitude theorists also assume attitude-behavior consistency. Consequently, social psychologists believe that it is important to explain the lack of attitude-behavior correspondence observed in some research (e.g., Fazio and Zanna, 1981).

teeth (Ross, McFarland, and Fletcher, 1981). Subjects were dismissed after making some judgments about the communication. In a different context they were subsequently asked to recall how often they had brushed their teeth during the previous two weeks. Students whose attitudes toward toothbrushing had shifted in a negative direction recalled brushing less often than control subjects whose attitudes had not been altered. Similar findings have been reported by Olson and Cal (1984).

It can be argued that the consistency effect in memory described to this point depends on experimental deception. In all cases the researchers hid the fact that they were attempting to change subjects' attitudes. By masking the purposes of the studies, the researchers may have contributed to subjects' perceptions that their attitudes had not shifted. Next, we review studies that demonstrate a consistency effect in recall when people's beliefs develop and change in natural settings.

NATURALLY OCCURRING ATTITUDE AND BEHAVIOR CHANGE.   McFarland and Ross (1987) assessed university students' evaluations of their dating partners at two points a few months apart. Some students became more favorable toward their partners over the time period, and others became less favorable. More interesting, the participants underestimated the amount of change that had occurred. In general, they recalled their earlier impressions as being more consistent with their current opinions than was the case. This consistency effect in recall had been anticipated because the evaluations were obtained primarily on traits that control subjects rated as stable over time (e.g., honesty and reliability). The consistency effect was not obtained on happiness, the one trait included in the study that was perceived to be unstable by control subjects. There is an obvious analogy between such results and the rewriting of history that occurs in regimes to make past events seem more compatible with current views (Berger, 1963; Greenwald, 1980).

Markus (1986) reported an analysis of data from a panel study of parents ($n = 898$) and their children ($n = 1,135$) that permits an examination of long-term recall of attitudes. In 1973 and 1982 respondents indicated their positions on welfare spending, affirmative action toward minorities, marijuana penalties, government job guarantees, equality of women, and political ideology (liberal versus conservative). In 1982 they were also asked to recall their 1973 positions. The children were about 25 years old in 1973 and 34 in 1982, and the parents were 54 and 63 years old, respectively.

The views that respondents reported were moderately stable over time, with the mean correlation between 1973 and 1982 opinions being .42 in parents and .44 in children. There was also a moderate relation between the stated positions in 1973 and those positions as recalled in 1982. The mean correlations were .39 for parents and .44 for children. There was a considerably stronger correlation between the positions stated in 1982 and 1982 recollection of 1973 positions. The mean correlations were .79 for parents and .56 for children. In summary, current attitudes predicted recall better than initial attitudes did.

Why is the relation between present and recalled opinions significantly higher for the parents than for the children? Respondents may be invoking the implicit theory that older people's opinions are more stable than those of younger people. Markus obtained some support for this hypothesis. Subjects were asked to respond to the question, "Thinking back over the last 10 years or so, would you say that your basic political ideas have changed a great deal, somewhat, or hardly at all?" Sixty-one percent of the parents and only 36% of the offspring chose "hardly at all," although the actual degree of stability in attitudes was about the same in the two generations. Apparently, the younger generation believed that they had passed through a stage in life in which there is a shift in political opinions. As a result, the parents were more likely than the children to recall their past attitudes as being similar to their current ones.

Research on the recall of political partisanship also supports the hypothesis that people may exaggerate their consistency over time. In a United States panel study, reports of partisanship were obtained in 1972 and 1976 (Niemi, Katz, and Newman, 1980). In 1976 respondents were asked to recall their party identification in 1972 (Democrat, Independent, or Republican). Approximately 78% of the 1,284 respondents reported the same party identification in 1972 and 1976. Among those who did not change party identification, 96% correctly reported no change. Of those who did change, 91% incorrectly reported not changing. The evidence suggests that most participants theorized that their political identification is stable over a four-year period. For 78% of the sample, partisanship was indeed stable; an implicit theory of stability would engender accurate recall in these respondents.

The consistency finding in recall has been obtained in domains other than attitudes and political affiliation. The effect is ubiquitous, as illustrated in the four following studies that yield analogous results in quite disparate contexts.

PAIN RECALL.   Eich and his associates asked patients with chronic headaches to keep diaries in which they made hourly ratings of pain intensity on ten-point scales (Eich, Reeves, Jaeger, and Graff-Radford, 1985). At the end of the week, they visited a clinic for a treatment session. Patients were asked to rate the intensity of pain they were experiencing at that moment, and to recall the maximum, minimum, and usual levels of pain they had experienced in the past week. The patients were suffering from chronic pain; as a result, there was no reason for them to assume much change in pain intensity during this brief period of time. Indeed, subjects with high levels of present pain overestimated their prior pain levels. Similarly, those experiencing low levels of present pain underestimated their earlier pain levels.

RECALL OF SUBSTANCE USE.   Collins and her associates examined the relation between reported use and recalled use of tobacco, marijuana, and alcohol among high school students over a two-and-a-half-year period (Collins, Graham, Hansen, and Johnson, 1985). The data were presented as a series of hierarchical regressions in which past and current use predicted recalled use. Past use was always entered into the model before current use. This procedure allowed all of past use, including that shared with current use, to account for the variance in recalled use.

The impact of current use on recalled use was significant, accounting for between 9% and 14% of the variance in recall at one year and for between 15% and 19% of the variance at two and a half years. The effect of current use on recalled use was greater when analyses were conducted only on students whose use changed from wave to wave. For these respondents, 19% to 25% of the variance in remembered substance use was attributable to current use when the recall period was one year, and 23% to 28% of the variance was attributable to current use when the recall period was two and a half years.

The data suggest that even subjects who change assume consistency in behavior. Further, as the recall period increases, respondents appear to be more dependent on theory-based construction in which present use serves as a benchmark.

RECALL OF PAST INCOME.   Withey (1954) reported the results of a panel study on income for a random sample of the United States urban population. In January 1948 and January 1949 respondents reported their income for the previous year. Income changed to an unusual degree over this period; only about one in three respondents had an income in the second year that was within 10% of their income in the previous year.

In January 1949 respondents were also asked to recall their income in 1947. Not surprisingly, their reports were quite accurate. The difference between recall and the initial response was only 4% and the correlation between the two was .84. The recall errors that did occur, however, were not random. People exaggerated the consistency between their current and past income; they recalled earning more than they had reported initially if their income had increased and less if their income had decreased.

RECALL OF DEPRESSION.   Aneshensel, Estrada, Hansell, and Clark (1987) interviewed a representative sample of Los Angeles County adults four times at roughly equal intervals between 1979 and 1980, and a fifth time in 1983.

The first and fourth interviews were conducted in person, whereas the others were conducted by telephone. Among many questions, respondents were asked whether they had ever been depressed—with depression defined as a continuous two-week period of time during which they had felt so "depressed that it interfered with their daily activities, and had lost interest in everything and everybody." The question clearly involved a retrospective account involving the respondent's entire life span ("ever had"). In addition, the CES-D Scale (Radloff, 1977) was included in the fifth interview to determine whether the respondents were suffering from depressive symptomatology at the time of that interview.

Strikingly, only 46% of the respondents who had reported in one of the previous interviews that they had been depressed at some point in their lives acknowledged such depression in the fifth interview. Most important for the argument of this chapter, recall of previous depression was significantly related to whether the subjects were currently depressed at the time of the fifth interview as assessed by a dichotomization of the CES-D responses (chi-square = 28.13). Those currently experiencing depressive symptoms were more likely to report a previous episode than were those not currently experiencing such symptoms. While the relationship between reporting depression in the fifth interview and reporting it previously is also significant (chi-square = 127.70), the large proportion of subjects who had previously reported depression but failed to report it in this fifth interview implies a very low level of accuracy for such retrospective reporting. Note that this inference can be made in the absence of whether subjects were "really" depressed in the past; a high proportion of responses in a fifth interview or in the previous ones (or in both) had to be inaccurate in order for such inconsistency to result. The inconsistency likely arises from people assuming that their prior moods were much like their current ones.

Exaggerating the Difference Between the Past and the Present

In contrast to research that suggests that people tend to bias their memories of previously held attributes in ways that deny changes that have actually taken place, the research reported below examines the coin's other side to assess whether people overestimate change when they hold a theory of change in a context of actual stability.

THE STUDY-SKILLS EXPERIMENT.   Self-improvement programs provide a setting in everyday life where an overestimation of change might be expected to occur. Many different programs flourish in North America. For example, every year new diet and exercise books head the bestseller lists. Some of these programs have apparently satisfied many people, although most are judged by informed professionals to be ineffective or even harmful (e.g., Polivy and Herman, 1983).

There are several explanations for the contrast between the skepticism of the program evaluators and the enthusiasm of the participants, including the possibility that the two groups are evaluating the program on the basis of different criteria. Let us assume, however, that a program appears to be valid, but promises more than it can deliver. The participants may believe the promises and inadvertently manufacture evidence that supports the false claims. There are two ways in which such fabrication of evidence can emerge: People can (1) distort their post-program standing or (2) revise their impressions of how they were before the program began.

Although both processes undoubtedly occur, it may sometimes be more feasible for people to alter their impressions of their past status than to enhance their present standing. For example, obese people may not be able to persuade themselves or a scale that they are thin following a diet. In contrast, they may more readily convince themselves that they were far heavier before the diet.

Conway and Ross (1984) examined the hypothesis that participants in a study-skills program overestimate their improvement because they exaggerate how poorly off they were before the program began. Conway and Ross instituted a study-skills course of the sort commonly offered in universities and colleges. Several well-conducted evaluations of such courses had indicated that participation does not improve grades, even though the courses are judged beneficial by students who take them (e.g., Chibnall, 1979; Gibbs, 1981; Main, 1980).

In the Conway and Ross research, students wishing to participate in a skills program evaluated their study skills at a first meeting and then were assigned randomly to either the skills program or a waiting list control group. After program participants had attended three weekly skills sessions, they and the waiting-list subjects returned for a final meeting. Subjects were asked to evaluate their current study skills, recall their initial evaluations of their skills, and predict their grades at the end of the semester. In addition, the researchers obtained students' actual final grades.

Program participants recalled their original evaluations of their study skills as being worse than they had reported originally; waiting-list subjects exhibited no systematic bias in recall. In short, program participants belittled their prior study skills, whereas waiting-list subjects did not. Although program participants expected to achieve much higher grades than control subjects, academic grades were not affected by the program. Interestingly, this did not prevent program participants from subsequently recalling their performance as superior. When contacted six months later, program participants remembered better grades in their major than they had actually obtained. In contrast, waiting-list subjects did not exhibit a systematic bias in recall of their grades.

In sum, program participants appeared to exaggerate their improvement in a direction consistent with their theories of what ought to be—taking a course should enhance their skills. They did so, at least in part, by retrospectively derogating their initial status. They constructed a past that enabled them to perceive improvement in a context in which the objective evidence indicated that their performance had not been affected by the course. Then, when enough time had passed, they also "doctored" the objective evidence in the appropriate direction.

A STUDY OF A PAIN-TREATMENT PROGRAM.   Linton and Melin (1982) reported results analogous to those obtained in the study-skills experiment. Participants were asked to make pain ratings before they entered a program to treat chronic pain in their back or joints. After the program they were asked to recall their baseline pain estimates. Patients remembered having experienced significantly more pain than they had actually indicated during the baseline period. Such biased recall would support the belief that the program was effective in reducing pain.

Thus, whereas Eich, Reeves, Jaeger, and Graff-Radford (1985) found an exaggeration of the consistency between present and recalled pain, Linton and Melin obtained an exaggeration of change. Both findings make sense from the standpoint of subjects' implicit theories. The recall period was relatively brief in the Eich et al. experiment; there was little reason for subjects to presume that their chronic pain levels had changed. The interval was much longer in Linton and Melin's research, and subjects could assume a change in pain level as a result of having participated in the treatment program.

Molding Recall to Be Consistent with Sociocultural Theories of Self and Society

Exaggerations of consistency or change are in part a class of more general processes in which people rely on the combination of a theory (in this case, of change or stability) and an assessment of current conditions. But such theories, schemata, or scripts need not be limited to these examples, as suggested by the following research in which the theories being used concerned men's and women's different approaches to daily stress and the personal histories of alcoholics.

STRESSFUL DAILY EVENTS.   In one of two pilot studies conducted in classroom settings, Hamilton (reported in Hamilton and Fagot, 1988) asked 126 male and 236 female undergraduates at the University of Oregon to list the daily events that they found stressful, to rate how stressful these events were, and to describe how they attempted to cope with them in general. The second study, with subjects drawn from the same population as the first, was used to check the events most frequently cited in the first study. On the basis of her survey, Hamilton compiled twenty-eight events that constituted "the most common stressful situations reported" (p. 14).

The events can be categorized into two sets: (1) those common to both males and females and (2) those specific to females. The "interpersonal" nature of those specific to females was found to be consistent with previous research. Men were more concerned with "instrumentality"; women with "relationships." For example, "destructive criticism" and "peer pressure" were reported to be more stressful for women than for men. Moreover, women reported using "internal coping strategies" more than did men, who attempted to change their environment. These reports were consistent with our cultural stereotypes or implicit theories of gender-related stress. They were, however, unrelated to what male and female freshmen actually experience, as observed in a second study by Hamilton.

Again using first-year students as subjects at the University of Oregon, Hamilton surveyed 56 females and 42 males over an eight-week period concerning stresses encountered the previous day. The two samples were comparable with respect to standard sociodemographic makeup, although those in the eight-week sample were volunteers who participated for a payment of fifty dollars. She asked respondents about each of the specific twenty-eight events that the pilot study revealed: had the event occurred the previous day, how stressful was the event that occurred, and how they coped with it. Interviews were conducted three times a week during an eight-week period.

The results of the second study differed strikingly from those of the pilot study and those reported in much previous research. Male and female freshmen did not experience events differently, they did not evaluate the stressfulness of specific recent events differently, and they did not differ in using external rather than internal coping strategies. There was no evidence of an interaction between gender and the type of event or stress rating.

Our hypothesized explanation for this finding is that college men and women are in very much the same social setting. They have the same problems associated both with the delay of "personhood" in our culture and with the demands of academic performance. Thus, the stresses to which they are exposed tend to be identical. In contrast, they have cultural theories about what stresses males and females in our society (these theories may be valid when males and females tend to be in different social contexts). Hence, in past research (most of which was retrospective) and in the pilot studies that

Hamilton conducted, men and women reported the culturally accepted theories that women have greater concern with interpersonal relationships. Moreover, since (as the data indicated) everyone may have a tendency to deal with such interpersonal stresses by internal strategies (i.e., the data revealed a high proportion of "working on feelings" as opposed to "problem-solving behaviors"), the underreporting of these events by men (or their overreporting by women) yields the conclusion that women have a greater tendency to adopt internal strategies—a misreporting that may reflect, in part, theories about men and women in society.

PERSONALITY OF ALCOHOLICS.   As can be determined by a casual reading of textbooks in psychiatry, medicine, and clinical psychology in the 1970s, the personality of people who become alcoholics was believed to differ fundamentally from that of nonalcoholic individuals. Categorizations of alcoholics ranged from "character disorder" to "psychopathic deviant." Whatever the particular theoretical orientation, there was general agreement in the literature that alcoholics were more "infantile" and less socially integrated prior to the time they became addicted than were other people (e.g., Kolb, 1977; Schilder, 1974).

More recent research suggests the contrary. One text, for example, concludes, "If there are consistent common personality features among alcohol abusers which reliably predict the development of alcohol problems, they have eluded the determined efforts of several generations of psychiatrists, psychologists, and other social scientists" (Mendelson and Mello, 1985, p. 235).

Notwithstanding this more recent research, many researchers and therapists who administer depression-treatment programs exclude alcoholics from their treatment groups on the ground that the condition is too severe and intractable to be subject to change; instead, control through Alcoholics Anonymous (AA) or Antabuse is recommended. AA strongly contends that alcoholics are fundamentally different from nonalcoholics even prior to the time they become addicted to alcohol. Equally important, many alcoholics themselves subscribe to such beliefs. For example, one alcoholic summarized her experience in the Alcoholics Anonymous handbook as follows:

> The mental twist that led up to my drinking began many years before I ever took a drink, for I am one of those whose history proves conclusively that my drinking was a "symptom of deeper trouble."
>
> Through my efforts to get down to "causes and conditions," I stand convinced that my emotional illness has been present from my earliest recollection. I never did react normally to any emotional situation.

I am an only child, and when I was seven years old my parents separated very abruptly (p. 553).

Prospective—as compared to retrospective—studies of alcoholism have led to a different assessment of the effects of these distant personal events, and in so doing have provided support for one more general inference we seek to draw here.

In particular Vaillant and Milofsky (1982) conducted a prospective study of alcoholism in "456 nondelinquent controls from the Gluecks' delinquency study" (p. 494). The subjects in this study were adolescents from a relatively poor area near Boston with a high juvenile delinquency rate. They were assessed as part of a comparison group in the Gluecks' study of juvenile delinquents; hence, they had not experienced significant legal trouble. Vaillant and Milofsky were able to interview 87% of these subjects when they were age 47, which was thirty-three years after they were assessed as part of the original study. Of the 456 subjects interviewed, 110 could be classified as "alcoholic" on the basis of the standard definition that alcohol use had been significantly involved with health, marital, employment, or legal problems.

Vaillant and Milofsky asked whether the existence of later alcoholism could be predicted from conditions assessed in adolescence over and above that which could be attributed to genetic factors. (Adoptive studies have demonstrated a much greater correlation between alcoholism in adopted children and their biological parents than between the children and their adoptive parents, which is consistent with other genetic studies of familial alcoholism.) They found none.

> When ethnicity and heredity were [statistically] controlled, childhood emotional problems and multiproblem family membership explained no additional variance in the development of alcoholism. Thus, the etiological hypotheses that view alcoholism as primarily a symptom of psychological instability may be illusions based on retrospective study[5] (p. 494).

5. Zucker and Gomberg (1986) have questioned these conclusions. They argue that it is intrinsically impossible to separate the social psychological effects of being raised by an alcoholic parent and the effect of sharing that parent's genes. Consequently, they questioned the logic by which Vaillant and Milofsky assessed the importance of these variables only in terms of their incremental predictability once the alcoholism of a parent has been entered into the prediction equation. Clearly, confounded variables have high correlations. Consequently, determination of the size and significance of their incremental effect by multiple regression techniques is related to the order in which they are considered. Zucker and Gomberg argue that variables should be entered in order of predictability ("hierarchically"), whereas Vaillant and Milofsky made a theoretically based decision to enter genetic variables first, due to findings from adoptive studies.

Summary

The research reported above is consistent with an analysis of personal recall in which responses to retrospective questions are a function of an interplay between the past, the present, and implicit theories of change, stability, and relationships among attributes. If respondents assume that their state has not changed in a significant way, they can construct their past from their current state (and will be inclined, unless otherwise motivated, to do so). If respondents assume that they have changed, their construction of their earlier state is likely to be guided by implicit theories about change. Thus, recall is likely to be biased when attributes (1) have changed, and respondents are unaware of the change; (2) have changed, and respondents uniformly miscalculate the degree or nature of the change; and (3) are stable, and respondents assume that the attributes have changed in a particular fashion.

Consistent with this analysis, the research findings indicate the existence of two forms of systematic bias in personal memories. In some studies people exaggerate their consistency over time and inappropriately infer that a prior response followed from their current state. In other studies people overestimate the extent to which their present state differs from an earlier state; they infer a prior response that was too much at variance with their current status. Further, evidence links both biases to implicit theories of stability and change for the attribute in question.

Alternative Theoretical Explanations

We now consider alternative theoretical interpretations of the research reviewed above. The interpretations fall within two categories: (1) a shift in standards and (2) impression management. We then contrast these alternatives to the present formulation.

Thus, for example, "premorbid parental criminality" (diagnosed before alcoholism), which Zucker and Gomberg believe is "also implicated in the process" (p. 790), is assessed in the Vaillant and Milofsky analysis only for its incremental predictability over and above the parental alcoholism that later "surfaces." There is no correct answer concerning which of these variables should be entered first. Entering variables according to their predictability is dependent on many factors, such as the precision of measurement. Standard statistical analyses are better suited to a priori choices of variables. Thus, even in cases where variables such as "premorbid parental criminality" are temporally prior to others, entering them simply because they predict well is a dubious procedure. Zucker and Gomberg also criticize Vaillant and Milofsky on the grounds that the subjects were not children at the original assessment, but adolescents. The implicit model behind this criticism is that greater predictability of adult behavior may be obtained from childhood than from adolescence, a dubious model even from a Freudian perspective.

Standards of Comparison

An alternative account of the consistency bias in recall can be derived from Tversky and Kahneman (1974), who noted that people often fail to make adjustments to initial standards. For example, Tversky and Kahneman asked subjects to adjust an arbitrary initial estimate of the percentage of African countries in the United Nations. Some subjects were provided with a high starting point (65%) and others with a low one (10%). The starting points had a dramatic effect on subjects' final adjusted estimates, even though they were determined by spinning a (rigged) wheel and thus had no information value for answering the later question. Those beginning at 65% produced a final estimate of 45%. Those starting at 10% produced a final estimate of 25%.

In the studies reviewed in the first half of this chapter, participants overestimated the consistency between the present and the past. In line with the Tversky and Kahneman findings, people may employ their current state as a standard and simply fail to adjust sufficiently in computing their past status. The Tversky and Kahneman explanation is similar to the present formulation, but it is more parsimonious in that it does not involve a consideration of theory-guided recall.

There are several findings, however, that seem to be better explained by a conception incorporating implicit theories. First, there is evidence in the attitude studies that many subjects see their own attitudes as consistent over time and that this theory of temporal consistency mediates their recall (Buehler, 1987; Ross, 1985). Second, there is less of a correspondence between the present and the remembered past when the attribute in question is seen as unstable (Markus, 1986; McFarland and Ross, 1987). Thus, subjects' recall appears to reflect an inference about the relation of the present to the past, rather than an "automatic" process, such as failing to adjust a standard. Finally, an inability to adjust initial standards does not seem to account for research in which people exaggerate the difference between the past and the present (e.g., Conway and Ross, 1984).

It is possible, however, to explain an overestimation of the difference between the past and the present in terms of a contrast effect resulting from a change in standards. For example, participants in the study-skills experiment may adopt more stringent standards concerning what constitutes "ideal" study behavior (Conway and Ross, 1984). They may, therefore, unwittingly lower their assessment of their initial skills, even when asked to reproduce their original responses as accurately as possible. Similarly, if the pain-treatment programs evaluated by Linton and Melin (1982) were somewhat effective, or if the subjects experienced spontaneous recovery, the initial pain levels may have seemed especially high to subjects in comparison to their posttreatment state. In these studies, then, an exaggeration of change may occur because individuals contrast their previous state to a new standard.

A contrast explanation does not seem to account for all of the data, however. In particular, it does not explain the consistency effect in recall obtained in studies reported in the first half of this chapter.

Impression Management

Subjects may wish to present themselves in the most favorable manner possible to the researcher. They may attempt to accomplish this goal by deliberately fabricating their memory of the past. Research indicates that it is socially undesirable to change one's opinions (Allgeier, Byrne, Brooks, and Revnes, 1979; Cialdini, Braver, and Lewis, 1974; Cialdini, Levy, Herman, and Evenbeck, 1973; McFarland, Ross, and Conway, 1985; Staw and Ross, 1980). Subjects in attitude-change experiments, therefore, may assume a facade of consistency by reporting past attitudes that are similar both to their present opinions and to the views expressed in experimental communications designed to alter their attitudes. Similarly, participants in improvement programs may believe that the appearance of improvement would make them look good and please the program leader. They may derogate their initial study skills or exaggerate their prior pain levels to generate an impression of improvement.

Several features of the research seem incompatible with a self-presentational interpretation of the data. In the experimental studies subjects' responses were anonymous and confidential. More important, investigators demanded accurate responses from research subjects. Finally, there are instances in which recall is not flattering, for example, the AA member.

Summary

Despite the relevance of standards of comparison and concerns for impression management to biases in recall, neither formulation provides an account of all of the research reported above. At the present time, an explanation emphasizing the impact of implicit theories and present status on recall seems to provide a better overall explanation of the findings.

The Degree of Bias in Recall

The practical implications of the research reviewed above may be considerable. The biased retrospections obtained in survey research may lead, among other things, to inaccurate conceptions of human behavior. The biases found in health settings may contribute to invalid diagnoses. The biased retrospections of participants in improvement programs may cause them to remain in worthless programs and not to search for more effective treatments. Indeed, when self-reports are a primary indicant of improvement—a source of evidence often used in decisions to renew existing programs in the absence of more rigorous evaluation designs—a conspiracy of ignorance may emerge in which both the helper and the helped erroneously believe in the achievement of their common goal.

It is important not to overestimate the extent of the bias, however. Biases are emphasized in the current chapter primarily because they contribute to an understanding of the processes by which people construct their personal histories. If we focused our review on accuracy, we would conclude that much of the research demonstrates relatively accurate recall. Whereas in some studies the degree of bias is large (e.g., Goethals and Reckman, 1973), it is small in others (e.g., Withey, 1954). There is often a substantial correlation between the past response and the recalled response (e.g., Collins, Graham, Hansen, and Johnson, 1985; McFarland, Ross, and De Courville, 1989; Withey, 1954).

At issue here is not just the discrepancy between recall and the prospective or simultaneous study of the same phenomenon. It can be argued that recall—and the global judgments based on it—are as "real" as ongoing behavior, and may in some instances be more important to an individual. Instead, the question is how this discrepancy interacts with the investigator's hypothesis and whether retrospective data lead the researcher to reach the wrong conclusion. We are not arguing that all retrospective data are useless. The magnitude of biases and error variances associated with recall varies considerably, as do the uses to which such data are put. A better understanding of the problems associated with retrospective data follows from an understanding of the conditions under which theory-based construction occurs, and from an understanding of the technique for measuring and/or reducing the magnitude of the problem.

The relatively low degree of error and bias exhibited by respondents in at least some of the studies raises the following question (Alba and Hasher, 1983; Neisser, 1986): How can an implicit theory approach to memory account for accuracy? One answer is that recall is accurate to the extent that the theory is valid (Nisbett and Wilson, 1977). A study described earlier on recall of political partisanship is illustrative (Niemi, Katz, and Newman, 1980). The vast majority of participants in this study appeared to view their partisanship as stable over the four years in question. For 78% of the sample, partisanship was stable, and an implicit theory of stability would engender accurate recall in these respondents.

Any theory of human behavior with that kind of predictive validity deserves to be taken seriously. More generally, a theory stressing the temporal consistency of personal attributes may be accurate much of the time. People sometimes exaggerate their consistency over time; but it is also evident that people's personal attributes are often stable. Studies of long-term development, for example, suggest the personality traits are quite stable over many years (e.g., Block, 1971; Woodruff and Birren, 1972).

The use of valid theories does not provide a full explanation of accurate memory, however. Sometimes, people may not use their implicit theories to guide recall. There is evidence from two quite divergent experiments that people can abandon an implicit theory or schema and engage in a less biased memory search. In a study of prose recall, Hasher and Griffin (1978) found that subjects who were provided with a theme for an ambiguous passage subsequently showed a constructive pattern of recall, as indicated by thematically related intrusions and forgetting of specific ideas. A second group of subjects was informed at the time of retrieval that the theme provided during their initial reading of the passage was invalid. These subjects showed better memory for specific details of the passage than the former group as well as fewer thematically related intrusions. Hasher and Griffin concluded that subjects who were forced to relinquish use of the theme as a retrieval guide exerted greater effort to retrieve less accessible material.

Similarly, Aderman and Brehm (1976) asked university students to recall their earlier attitude responses following an attitude-change manipulation. In one condition subjects were promised two dollars if they were able to recall exactly their initial attitude response. Aderman and Brehm found that the offer of an incentive reduced the magnitude of the consistency bias in recall.

These studies suggest that people can choose to engage in relatively effortless, theory-guided recall or a more strenuous and extensive memory search (Alba and Hasher 1983). Conceivably, several factors influence people's selection of a recall strategy. Individuals may invoke an implicit theory if it is salient and credible at the time of retrieval. An implicit theory may be less likely to be employed when relevant memories are easily accessed, or when the person believes that it is particularly important to recall specific details. In sum, people often rely on implicit theories for their reports of long-term, personal memories; however, there are circumstances in which dependence on theories may be reduced.

Implications for Survey Measurement

Our memories present an important implication for research that must rely on retrospection. People carry with them theories about the very attributes and social relationships we wish to examine, and they may use these theories in answering our questions, especially when we ask for information about a personal or social past. The theories may be more or less correct. Their validity simply cannot be tested through questions that prompt respondents' reliance on those theories to organize their responses.

At present, there are no highly reliable rules for distinguishing the role of social or personal schema, or implicit theories from that of actual events in recall. The work of Schooler, Gerhard, and Loftus (1986) on the "sensory" quality of correct recall provides one of the few cues to accuracy from retrospective memory itself, but even this work is limited to events from the recent past that the subject may reasonably be expected to "picture." A researcher simply could not know in advance how to "correct" for recall bias. The investigator can only guess about the role of implicit theories in yielding these reports.

Treatises on survey methods, such as those by Sudman and Bradburn (1982, pp. 43–51) and Schuman and Kalton (in Lindzey and Aronson, 1986, pp. 643–647), for example, devote attention to measures of recall. These and related texts suggest that memory is a function of time and of the saliency of the event or behavior being measured. In general, the more distant the event, the more likely it is to be forgotten (omission) or incorrectly moved forward in time (forward telescoping). Salient events are more likely to be recalled than nonsalient ones, where saliency is a function of the unusualness of an event, its economic and social costs and benefits, and its continuing consequences. But how such considerations interact with the effect of theory-based recall is not known at present. It would be a fruitful area for subsequent investigation.

Several "lessons" for survey practices, however, emerge from the research reviewed here. Interestingly, several of these lessons are quite consistent with current best practices, although the rationale for such practices may lie more in the survey practitioners' trial-and-error experiences than in any theory of personal recall. (It is nonetheless supportive of the theory that many practices are consistent with it.)

Surveys now employ a variety of techniques for reducing the errors and biases associated with such problems as telescoping and memory decay. These techniques and procedures appear to steer the respondent away from relying heavily on constructing the past by using implicit theories about change or stability. They often try to make access to the event or attribute being recalled more direct by (1) emphasizing to respondents through instruction and reinforcement the importance and need for accurate and precise answers; (2) reinstating the context of the event or attribute being recalled; (3) using "aided recall" methods in which respondents are provided with lists related to the event being recalled and then asked to recognize events or objects, as compared to the more difficult task of recalling them; (4) keeping the reference period short (e.g., less than six months); (5) using landmark events as memory anchors (e.g., an earthquake, the Shuttle disaster, Christmas); (6) in panel studies "bounding" the recall period by explicit reference to periods and information provided in previous interviews; and (7) asking respondents to date events—if such dating is required—only after other questions about the events have provided contextual information to assist recall.

In general, the research reviewed above suggests that retrospective questions should be asked in ways that reduce the use of implicit theories. As is suggested in chapter 7 by Abelson, Loftus, and Greenwald in this volume, care should be taken, for example, that implicit theories of stability and change about the phenomena of concern are not supplied in the sequence of questions prior to the retrospective questions. Similarly, asking questions about events or attributes that respondents cannot be expected to know well (e.g., the past behavior of friends or fellow students) invites respondents to supply culturally influenced theories of these phenomena in combination with readily observable aspects of that behavior. In addition, it may be worthwhile to emphasize to survey respondents the importance of accuracy; to encourage respondents to take their time (and to provide incentives for interviewers to establish and maintain a pace that encourages this); to offer aids for recall by providing respondents with cues, anchors, or context-reinstating descriptions of the times or events being recalled; and to suggest procedures for the recall process (e.g., starting recently and moving back in time).

Another solution is to avoid using retrospectively based methods altogether. Prospective studies would appear especially appropriate in those areas where the "cultural wisdom" about the phenomenon under study is strong but erroneous, or where the period under study is long. Prospective studies are also preferable in studies of phenomena or subjects that are known to change a great deal, but where people may believe that stability is the norm (and vice versa). Again, such folk wisdom may be correct. The problem arises when retrospective memory is used to validate it.

One cannot, however, avoid the conclusion that the resources allocated toward the measurement and understanding of the bias-and-error variance of retrospectively collected data have been deficient. Here we agree with Reiss (1981), who stressed that

> . . . theories about human behavior—such as how we cognize, store, and recall information or how organizations select, store, and process information—are more critical kinds of theory for the development of our disciplines than are theories about how nations develop their economies or how people vote. It is far more critical in this sense to develop theories about personal and social deception that will underlie methods of inquiry than to develop theories that rely upon those methods for their test (p. 15).

References

ADERMAN, D., and BREHM, S. S. (1976) On the recall of initial attitudes following counterattitudinal advocacy: An experimental reexamination. *Personality and Social Psychology Bulletin* 19, 59–62.

ALBA, J. W., and HASHER, L. (1983) Is memory schematic? *Psychological Bulletin* 93, 203–231.

ALLGEIER, A. R., BYRNE, D., BROOKS, B., and REVNES, D. (1979) The waffle phenomenon: Negative evaluations of those who shift attitudinally. *Journal of Applied Social Psychology* 9, 170–182.

ANDERSON, R. C., and PICHERT, J. W. (1978) Recall of previously unrecallable information following a shift in perspective. *Journal of Verbal Learning and Verbal Behavior* 17, 1–12.

ANESHENSEL, C. S., ESTRADA, A. L., HANSELL, M. J., and CLARK, V. A. (1987) Social psychological aspects of reporting behavior: Lifetime depressive episode reports. *Journal of Health and Social Behavior* 28, 232–246.

BARCLAY, C. R. (1986) Schematization of autobiographical memory. In RUBIN, D. C. (ed.). *Autobiographical Memory*. Cambridge, England: Cambridge University Press, pp. 82–99.

BARTLETT, F. C. (1932) *Remembering—A Study in Experimental and Social Psychology*. Cambridge, England: Cambridge University Press.

BELLEZZA, F. S., and BOWER, G. H. (1981) Person stereotypes and memory for people. *Journal of Personality and Social Psychology* 41, 856–865.

BEM, D. J. (1966) Inducing belief in false confessions. *Journal of Personality and Social Psychology* 3, 707–710.

BEM, D. J., and McCONNELL, H. K. (1970) Testing the self-perception explanation of dissonance phenomena: On the salience of premanipulation attitudes. *Journal of Personality and Social Psychology* 14, 23–31.

BERGER, P. L. (1963) *Invitation to Sociology: A Humanistic Perspective*. Garden City, NY: Doubleday.

BLOCK, J. (1971) *Lives Through Time*. Berkeley, CA: Bancroft.

BODNAR, J. (1989) Power and memory in oral history: Workers and managers at Studebaker. *Journal of American History*, March 75, 1201–1221.

BUEHLER, R. (1987) Constructing the past: A new look at the consistency bias in recall of previously held attitudes. Honours thesis, University of Waterloo, Waterloo, Ontario.

CANTOR, N., and MISCHEL, W. (1977) Traits as prototypes: Effects on recognition memory. *Journal of Personality and Social Psychology* 30, 631–637.

CHIBNALL, B. (1979) The Sussex experience. In MILLS, P. J. (ed.). *Study Courses and Counselling: Problems and Possibilities*. Surrey, England: Society for Research into Higher Education, Guilford, pp. 37–46.

CIALDINI, R. B., BRAVER, S. L., and LEWIS, S. K. (1974) Attributional bias and the easily persuaded other. *Journal of Personality and Social Psychology* 35, 38–48.

CIALDINI, R. B., LEVY, A., HERMAN, C. P., and EVENBECK, S. (1973) Attitudinal politics: The strategy of moderation. *Journal of Personality and Social Psychology* 25, 100–108.

COLLINS, L. M., GRAHAM, J. W., HANSEN, W. B., and JOHNSON, C. A. (1985) Agreement between retrospective accounts of substance use and earlier reported substance use. *Applied Psychological Measurement* 9, 301–309.

CONWAY, M., and ROSS, M. (1984) Getting what you want by revising what you had. *Journal of Personality and Social Psychology* 47, 738–748.

CRAPANZANO, V., ERGAS, Y., and MODELL, J. (1986) Personal testimony: Narratives of the self in the social sciences and the humanities. *Items* 40, 25–30.

CROVITZ, H. F., and SCHIFFMAN, H. (1974) Frequency of episodic memories as a function of their age. *Bulletin of the Psychonomic Society* 4, 517–518.

DAWES, R. M. (1988) *Rational Choice in an Uncertain World*. San Diego, CA: Harcourt Brace Jovanovich.

EICH, E., REEVES, J. L., JAEGER, B., and GRAFF-RADFORD, S. B. (1985) Memory for pain: Relation between past and present pain intensity. *Pain* 23, 375–380.

EPSTEIN, S. (1973) The self-concept revisited, or a theory of a theory. *American Psychologist* 28, 404–416.

ERICSSON, K. A., and SIMON, H. A. (1980) Verbal reports as data. *Psychological Review* 87, 215–251.

ERIKSON, E. H. (1968) *Identity: Youth and Crisis*. New York: Norton.

FAZIO, R. H., and ZANNA, M. P. (1981) Direct experience and attitude consistency. In BERKOWITZ, L. (ed.). *Advances in Experimental Social Psychology*, vol. 14. New York: Academic Press, pp. 162–202.

FITZGERALD, J. M. (1980) Sampling autobiographical memory reports in adolescents. *Developmental Psychology* 16, 675–676.

GIBBS, G. (1981) *Teaching Students to Learn*. Milton Keynes, England: Open University Press.

GOETHALS, G. R., and RECKMAN, R. F. (1973) The perception of consistency in attitudes. *Journal of Experimental Social Psychology* 9, 491–501.

GREENWALD, A. G. (1980) The totalitarian ego: Fabrication and revision of personal history. *American Psychologist* 35, 603–618.

HAMILTON, D. L. (1981) Illusory correlation as a basis for stereotyping. In HAMILTON, D. L., (ed.). *Cognitive processes in stereotyping and intergroup behavior*. Hillsdale, NJ: Erlbaum, pp. 115–144.

HAMILTON, S., and FAGOT, B. (1988) Chronic stress and coping skills: A comparison of male and female undergraduates. *Journal of Personality and Social Psychology* 55, 819–823.

HASHER, L., and GRIFFIN, M. (1978) Reconstructive and reproductive processes in memory. *Journal of Experimental Psychology: Human Learning and Memory* 4, 318–330.

HASTIE, R. (1981) Schematic principles in human memory. In HIGGINS, E. T., HERMAN,

C. P., and ZANNA, M. P. (eds.). *Social Cognition: The Ontario Symposium*, vol. 1. Hillsdale, NJ: Erlbaum, pp. 39–88.

JAMES, W. (1980) *The Principles of Psychology*, vol. 1. New York: Holt, Rinehart and Winston.

KOLB, L. C. (1977) *Modern Clinical Psychiatry*. Philadelphia: Saunders.

LINTON, M. (1986) Ways of searching and the content of memory. In RUBIN, D. C. (ed.). *Autobiographical Memory*. Cambridge, England: Cambridge University Press, pp. 50–67.

LINTON, S. J., and MELIN, L. (1982) The accuracy of remembering chronic pain. *Pain* 13, 281–285.

LLOYD MORGAN, C. (1930/1961). C. Lloyd Morgan. In MURCHISON, C. (ed.). *History of Psychology in Autobiography*, vol. 2. New York: Russell and Russell, pp. 237–264.

LOFTUS, E. F., MILLER, D. G., and BURNS, H. J. (1978). Semantic integration of verbal information into a visual memory. *Journal of Experimental Psychology: Human Learning and Memory* 4, 19–31.

MCFARLAND, C., and ROSS, M. (1987). The relation between current impressions and memories of self and dating partners. *Personality and Social Psychology Bulletin* 13, 228–238.

MCFARLAND, C., ROSS, M., and CONWAY, M. (1985) Self-persuasion and self-presentation as mediators of anticipatory attitude change. *Journal of Personality and Social Psychology* 46, 529–540.

MCFARLAND, C., ROSS, M., and DE COURVILLE, N. (1989) Women's theories of menstruation and biases in recall of menstrual symptoms. *Journal of Personality and Social Psychology* 57, 522–531.

MAIN, A. (1980) *Encouraging Effective Learning*. Edinburgh: Scottish Academic Press.

MARKUS, G. B. (1986) Stability and change in political attitudes: Observed, recalled and explained. *Political Behavior* 8, 21–44.

MARKUS, H. (1977) Self-schemata and processing information about the self. *Journal of Personality and Social Psychology* 25, 63–78.

MEAD, G. H. (1934) *Mind, Self and Society*. Chicago: University of Chicago Press.

——— (1964) *Selected Writings*. RECK, A. J. (ed.). Chicago: University of Chicago Press.

MENDELSON, J. H., and MELLO, N. K. (1985) *Alcohol Use and Abuse in America*. Boston: Little, Brown.

MISCHEL, W., EBBESEN, E. B., and ZEISS, A. M. (1976) Determinants of selective memory about the self. *Journal of Consulting and Clinical Psychology* 1, 92–103.

NEISSER, U. (1986) Nested structure in autobiographical memory. In RUBIN, D. C., (ed.). *Autobiographical Memory*. Cambridge, England: Cambridge University Press, pp. 71–81.

NIEMI, G., KATZ, R. S., and NEWMAN, D. (1980) Reconstructing past partisanship: The failure of party identification recall questions. *American Journal of Political Science* 24, 633–651.

NISBETT, R. E., and WILSON, T. D. (1977) Telling more than we can know: Verbal reports on mental processes. *Psychological Review* 84, 231–259.

OLSON, J. M., and CAL, A. V. (1984) Source credibility, attitude, and the recall of past behaviors. *European Journal of Social Psychology* 14, 203–210.

POLIVY, J., and HERMAN, C. P. (1983) *Breaking the Diet Habit*. New York: Basic Books.

RADLOFF, L. S. (1977) The CES-D Scale: A self-report depression scale for research in the general population. *Applied Psychological Measurement* 1, 385–401.

REISER, B. J., BLACK, J. B., and KALAMARIDES, P. (1986) Strategic memory search processes. In RUBIN, D. C. (ed.). *Autobiographical Memory*. Cambridge, England: Cambridge University Press, pp. 100–121.

REISS, A. J., JR. (1981) Exploring the central paradox in methods of scientific inquiry. Paper presented at the annual meeting of the American Sociological Association.

ROBBINS, L. C. (1963) The accuracy of parental recall of aspects of child development and of child rearing practices. *Journal of Personality and Social Psychology* 66, 261–270.

ROSS, M. (1985, unpublished data)

———— (1987, unpublished data)

———— (1988). The relation of implicit theories to the construction of personal histories. *Psychological Review* 96, 341–357.

ROSS, M., and CONWAY, M. (1986) Remembering one's own past: The construction of personal histories. In SORRENTINO, R. M., and HIGGINS, E. T. (eds.). *Handbook of Motivation and Cognition*. New York: Guilford Press, pp. 122–144.

ROSS, M., MCFARLAND, C., CONWAY, M., and ZANNA, M. P. (1983) Reciprocal relation between attitudes and behavior recall: Committing people to newly formed attitudes. *Journal of Personality and Social Psychology* 45, 257–267.

ROSS, M., MCFARLAND, C., and FLETCHER, G. J. O. (1981) The effect of attitude on the recall of personal histories. *Journal of Personality and Social Psychology* 10, 627–634.

ROSS, M., and SHULMAN, R. F. (1973) Increasing the salience of initial attitudes: Dissonance vs. self-perception theory. *Journal of Personality and Social Psychology* 28, 138–144.

ROTHBART, M. (1981) Memory processes and social beliefs. In HAMILTON, D. L. (ed.). *Cognitive Processes in Stereotyping and Intergroup Behavior*. Hillsdale, NJ: Erlbaum, pp. 145–181.

ROTHBART, M., EVANS, M., and FULERO, S. (1979) Recall for confirming events: Memory processes and the maintenance of social stereotypes. *Journal of Experimental Social Psychology* 15, 343–355.

SCHANK, R. C., and ABELSON, R. P. (1977) *Scripts, Plans, Goals and Understanding*. Hillsdale, NJ: Erlbaum.

SCHILDER, P. (1974) The psychogenesis of alcoholism. *Quarterly Journal of the Study of Alcoholism* 2, 277–292.

SCHOOLER, J. W., GERHARD, D., and LOFTUS, E. F. (1986) Qualities of the unreal.

Journal of Experimental Psychology: Learning, Memory and Cognition 12, 171–181.

SCHUMAN, H., and KALTON, G. (1986) Survey methods. In LINDZEY, G., and ARONSON, E. (eds.). *The Handbook of Social Psychology*, 3rd ed. Reading, MA: Addison-Wesley, pp. 635–697.

SNYDER, M., and URANOWITZ, S. M. (1978) Reconstructing the past: Some cognitive consequences of person perception. *Journal of Personality and Social Psychology* 36, 941–950.

SPENCE, D. P. (1982) *Narrative Truth and Historical Truth: Meaning and Interpretation in Psychoanalysis*. New York: Norton.

STAW, B. M., and ROSS, J. (1980) Commitment in an experimenting society: A study of the attribution of leadership from administrative scenarios. *Journal of Applied Psychology* 65, 249–260.

SUDMAN, S., and BRADBURN, N. M. (1982) *Asking Questions*. San Francisco: Jossey-Bass.

TAYLOR, S. E., and CROCKER J. (1981) Schematic bases of information processing. In HIGGINS, E. T., HERMAN, C. P., and ZANNA, M. P. (eds.). *Social Cognition: The Ontario Symposium*, vol. 1. Hillsdale, NJ: Erlbaum, pp. 89–134.

TVERSKY, A., and KAHNEMAN, D. (1974) Judgment under uncertainty: Heuristics and biases. *Science* 185, 1123–1131.

VAILLANT, G. E., and MILOFSKY, E. S. (1982) The etiology of alcoholism. A prospective viewpoint. *American Psychologist* 37, 494–503.

WITHEY, S. B. (1954) Reliability of recall of income. *Public Opinion Quarterly* 18, 197–204.

WIXON, D. R., and LAIRD, J. D. (1976) Awareness and attitude change in the forced compliance paradigm: The importance of when. *Journal of Personality and Social Psychology* 34, 376–384.

WOODRUFF, D. S., and BIRREN, J. E. (1972) Age changes and cohort differences in personality. *Developmental Psychology* 6, 252–259.

YARROW, M. R., CAMPBELL, J. D., and BURTON, R. V. (1970) Recollections of childhood: A study of the retrospective method. *Monographs of the Society for Research in Child Development* 35, No. 5.

ZUCKER, R. A., and GOMBERG, E. S. L. (1986) Etiology of alcoholism reconsidered. *American Psychologist* 41, 783–793.

5

Improving Episodic Memory Performance of Survey Respondents

ROBERT T. CROYLE
and ELIZABETH F. LOFTUS

Many surveys challenge the cognitive abilities of respondents by asking them to recall the date, frequency, or characteristics of personal events. According to Tulving's (1983) framework, this is a task of episodic memory retrieval. Chapter 4 of this volume demonstrates the inherent difficulties of this task. Individuals can adopt a number of different strategies in order to recall the distant past, and these efforts are frequently characterized by bias and error. The following contributions in chapters 6 to 8 describe recent investigations of methods for improving the episodic memory performance of survey respondents. Two of the contributions examine reports of health behavior, whereas the third presents findings concerning reports of voting.

Health surveys comprise a major segment of the data-collection efforts of the federal government. The National Health Interview Survey is but one example. For this reason, public health policymakers are justifiably concerned about the accuracy of the data collected in these massive efforts. More recently, the academic public health research community has displayed a growing concern about the validity of health-related self-reports. Surveys are widely relied upon as a means for evaluating the impact of large clinical interventions. Primary prevention trials, which often include cognitive and behavioral endpoints, are especially vulnerable to errors in memory-based self-reports. As the emphasis on early detection and tracking of behavioral risk factors continues to grow, the need for developing methods to reduce memory-related errors among survey respondents will increase accordingly.

Voting surveys serve a variety of critical functions in all of the Western democracies. The media, political parties, and public-opinion experts rely on these data to gain an understanding of voters' candidate preferences. Even more fundamental, however, are the data concerning the frequency of voting itself. Some would argue that the electoral survey is as important an indicator of the political health of a nation as the health survey is of its physical health. Given the low turnout in recent presidential elections in the United States, there is a growing interest in testing competing explanations for nonparticipation. The expense of this kind of research could be greatly reduced if retrospective self-reports of voting could be improved sufficiently to be used.

Verification of Self-Reports

A major roadblock faced by many survey researchers investigating the validity of self-reports is the scarcity of reliable verification data. Theoretically oriented research on survey methods has tended to focus on nonhealth subject matter for good practical reasons. Voting records present a less daunting challenge to beleaguered graduate assistants when compared with medical records. Many phenomena of interest to health-behavioral scientists are unlikely to be documented in any form. In those cases where documentation of health-related events has occurred, the record may be limited in scope and difficult to interpret. The use of medical records for research purposes also raises special confidentiality concerns that are unique to the health domain. On the other hand, erroneous conclusions drawn from an unverified case control study survey can have widespread and damaging consequences for the health and safety of an entire population.

A study conducted by Crespi and Swinehart (1982) illustrates the most common approach to the verification issue. In their study, survey respondents were asked to recall whether or not they had performed a particular health behavior within the previous two months. Verification data were not obtained. Instead, the investigators carefully examined response patterns in order to identify the most likely instances of overreporting and underreporting. Crespi and Swinehart then demonstrated the significant impact of a relatively simple intervention on apparent overreporting. In two surveys, before being asked if a behavior occurred during the past two months, half of the participants were first asked to report whether or not the behavior occurred within the previous six months. The relative reduction in reporting in response to the two-month question produced by this introductory question was the focus of the Crespi and Swinehart discussion. The authors described additional analyses of their data, however, that yield findings relevant to the accuracy issue. When they compared the results obtained from the groups using only the two-month interval with the six-month reports of the experimental groups, the reported rates of health behaviors were strikingly similar. The authors argued that this pattern indicated overreporting among participants in the two-month group. In addition, they cited evidence suggesting that the kinds of socially desirable behaviors they studied usually are overreported.

The contributions in this part illustrate three other strategies for addressing the verification issue. The Loftus, Smith, Klinger, and Fiedler study (chapter 6) utilizes medical records for verification purposes, focusing on those elements of the record that are most reliable, yet are also amenable to survey data collection. One frequently overlooked constraint on the use of surveys as a substitute for record audits is the fact that much of the information contained in medical records is never communicated to the patient. Loftus et al. overcome this problem by limiting the focus of study to health visits and to procedures requiring patient participation.

Nutritional epidemiologists have more reasons than most health researchers to be concerned about the validity of health surveys that rely on human memory. For many years the primary tool of their trade, the food frequency questionnaire, has provided the raw data for many of our most well-known dietary recommendations. Epidemiologists and nutrition scientists have grappled with a wide variety of nutrition and dietary behavior assessment methods including the twenty-four-hour recall, the four-day diet record, and numerous versions of the food frequency questionnaire (Block, 1989). To date, the problem of memory error has been addressed through the use of large study samples and, in some cases, the use of multiple measures. These solutions are inadequate and are based on the mistaken assumption that memory errors are random rather than systematic. The problem of systematic memory error has only recently attracted significant attention among nutritional epidemiologists (e.g., Dwyer, Krall, and Coleman, 1987; Raphael, 1987). Although many publications have appeared in the last decade that document the reliability of dietary behavior and nutrition assessment methods, research employing direct and objective verification (that is, observations of food consumption) is sorely lacking (for a recent exception, see Myers et al., 1988). Fisher and Quigley (chapter 8) address this need by utilizing an observational verification strategy in their study of dietary behavior recall.

Abelson, Loftus, and Greenwald (chapter 7) address the verification issue by using voting records. Although recordkeeping practices vary from state to state, voting records are generally superior to medical records in their simplicity, accessibility, and accuracy. Furthermore, by using an especially comprehensive data bank in the state of Washington, the investigators are able to examine the role of temporal voting patterns as a determinant of self-report accuracy.

Cognition, Memory,
and the Enhancement of Self-Reports

Only a small proportion of the research on survey methods has examined cognitive factors; only a small proportion of this has included objective verification. Given this state of the art, it should not be surprising that studies designed to test ways of reducing cognitive sources of error in surveys are only now emerging. Investigators who are not survey experts but who use surveys as a tool for their own research have shown substantial interest in developing ways of reducing cognitive errors. Clearly, however, any attempt to improve cognitive performance must be informed by cognitive theory and a basic familiarity with research on human memory.

When discussing these issues with public-health scientists, for example, we have found it useful to distinguish between episodic and semantic memory. A simple way to convey the distinction is to use Tulving's (1989) illustration of recollecting (episodic) versus knowing (semantic). We know many impersonal facts about the world that we don't remember learning. But the recollection of a life event is characterized by a particular time, location, personal relevance, and, in many cases, emotion. For the survey context this often means that the semantic system is automatically relied upon as the respondent interprets the question, but the episodic system is required to locate and describe an event (e.g., a child's illness) that the question refers to. The anatomical basis of the two systems is illustrated dramatically by the case of K.C., a brain-injured man who cannot remember any personal events, yet knows a great deal about the world around him (see Tulving, Schacter, McLachlan, and Moscovitch, 1988).

An understanding of the dynamics and features of episodic memory supplies the survey researcher with a menu of variables to target. The temporal quality of personal memories suggests that more salient life events, or "landmarks," serve to delineate between periods that are less eventful. To the extent that individuals lack natural boundaries around time periods of interest to the survey investigator, dating errors are more likely to occur. Research suggests that supplying the respondent with useful landmarks can reduce telescoping and, consequently, increase accuracy (Loftus and Marburger, 1983). This leads us to a more general point: that in order to help the respondent sort through his or her memory, we can only be helpful to the extent that we know how that memory is organized. Only a friend who is familiar with the floor plan of our house can provide useful suggestions on how to find our lost set of keys.

The three contributions in this part describe different methodologies for testing the utility of cognitively informed survey methods. Loftus et al. test a number of different strategies independently, whereas Fisher and Quigley incorporate several principles within one strategy and compare the results with a control group. Abelson et al. present a converging set of experiments and analyses designed to explain the phenomenon of overreporting. All three research programs yield promising results. Loftus et al. first document different types of error that occur in response to two types of questions. Medical visits are underreported, whereas procedures within those visits are overreported. In each case the preferred recall strategies of the respondents are documented, and the investigators demonstrate ways to reduce the errors produced by those strategies.

Abelson et al. replicate earlier findings showing that voting is overreported. Surprisingly, they find that the two-time-frame procedure that reduces overreporting of medical visits is ineffective in the voting context. The story becomes even more complex when they find that overreporting is also resistant to a preamble that provides excuses for nonvoting. One key to the solution appears to lie within voters' histories of participation in previous elections. Habitual voters err in the direction of overreporting, whereas habitual nonvoters tend to underreport participation.

Fisher and Quigley discuss an intriguing application of the "cognitive interview," a method that has also been tested in the domain of eyewitness testimony. After describing the cognitive principles that serve as the foundation for this method, they report data from a study of eating behavior. The subjects were provided an opportunity to select and consume several foods while their selections were recorded by the researchers. Later, their memory of food consumption was tested through either the cognitive interview or through more straightforward, traditional means. The cognitive interview produced more accurate responses, with the improvement greater for recall than for recognition.

These studies demonstrate the practical importance of research concerning cognition and survey methods. The Loftus et al. findings are directly applicable to the large-scale evaluation surveys typical of health services research. Fisher and Quigley's study provides a means of tracing the source of an outbreak of food poisoning. Abelson et al.'s data show that despite the apparent apathy of the American electorate, the tendency to overreport voting is robust. Their analysis suggests not only memory confusion produced by frequent elections, but also an underlying persistence of social norms supporting participation. Studies of this kind provide a bridge between the laboratory of the experimental psychologist and the practical concerns of policymakers. They also illustrate the diverse range of application for basic research on human memory.

Further research on improving episodic memory among survey respondents is needed to address a number of issues that are largely unexplored. Little is known about the cognitive dynamics of proxy reporting, a method that may be more widely used as the proportion of the population who is elderly increases. The role of emotion in memory, which has been the subject of substantial debate and investigation during the past two decades (Bower, 1981; Isen, 1984) has yet to be investigated systematically within the context of health surveys. More work is needed on how health-related experience is represented in memory, especially symptoms and illness episodes (Skelton and Croyle, 1991). The identification of effective recall cues that can be utilized in health surveys will depend in large part on the progress made by scientists who conduct basic research on human memory.

Research on improving episodic memory performance among survey respondents may be most cost-effective when it employs a two-stage strategy. First, less costly methods can be utilized to document the relative effects of a wide variety of theoretically plausible memory aids. Once the techniques with the greatest effects have been identified, they can then be tested in more costly studies that include a verification of accuracy. Finally, psychologists need to develop more creative experimental paradigms that involve real or simulated health-related events that can later be used to verify the accuracy of long-term recall. Such a strategy would allow investigators to study episodic memory and survey methodology in a more controlled and cost-efficient manner than is now attainable.

The authors would like to acknowledge the support of grants HS 05521 and Health Care Technology Assessment and HS 06660 from the National Center for Health Services Research from the Agency for Health Care Policy and Research.

References

BLOCK, G. (1989) Human dietary assessment: Methods and issues. *Preventive Medicine* 18, 653–660.

BOWER, G. H. (1981) Mood and memory. *American Psychologist* 36, 129–148.

CRESPI, I., and SWINEHART, J. W. (1982) Some effects of sequenced questions using different time intervals on behavioral self-reports: A field experiment. Paper presented at the annual conference of the American Association for Public Opinion Research, May.

DWYER, J. T., KRALL, E. A., and COLEMAN, K. A. (1987) The problem of memory in nutritional epidemiology research. *Journal of the American Dietetic Association* 87, 1509–1512.

ISEN, A. M. (1984) Toward an understanding of the role of affect in cognition. In WYER, R. S., and SRULL, T. K. (eds.). *Handbook of Social Cognition*, vol. 3. Hillsdale, NJ: Erlbaum, pp. 179–236.

LOFTUS, E. F., and MARBURGER, W. (1983) Since the eruption of Mt. St. Helens did anyone beat you up? Improving the accuracy of retrospective reports with landmark events. *Memory and Cognition* 11, 114–120.

MYERS, R. J., KLESGES, R. C., ECK, L. H., HANSON, C. L., and KLEM, M. L. (1988) Accuracy of self-reports of food intake in obese and normal-weight individuals: Effects of obesity on self-reports of dietary intake in adult females. *American Journal of Clinical Nutrition* 48, 1248–1251.

RAPHAEL, K. (1987) Recall bias: A proposal for assessment and control. *International Journal of Epidemiology* 16, 167–170.

SKELTON, J. A., and CROYLE, R. T., eds. 1991 *Mental Representation in Health and Illness*. New York: Springer-Verlag.

TULVING, E. (1983) *Elements of Episodic Memory*. New York: Oxford University Press.

———— (1989) Remembering and knowing the past. *American Scientist* 77, 361–367.

TULVING, E., SCHACTER, D. L., MCLACHLAN, D. R., and MOSCOVITCH, M. (1988) Priming of semantic autobiographical memory: A case study of retrograde amnesia. *Brain and Cognition* 8, 3–20.

6

Memory and Mismemory for Health Events

ELIZABETH F. LOFTUS,
KYLE D. SMITH, MARK R. KLINGER
and JUDITH FIEDLER

"During the past 12 months, about how many times did you see or talk to a medical doctor?" This question is one of many posed to respondents who participate in the National Health Interview Survey, a major government-sponsored sample survey designed to obtain information on the health of Americans. In this survey 50,000 people are asked each year to recall the occurrence of health-related conditions and their consequences, such as days lost from work. The resulting survey estimates of health problems and the utilization of healthcare services are used to formulate legislation relating to health programs. But surveys are not the only time when people have to recall health-related experiences from their recent past. Such recall is routinely required of patients by their doctors. A major concern of the current research is how accurately people remember and report to interviewers health incidents that have happened to them.

Not only does research on memory for health experiences have practical importance, but it also relates to a body of psychological literature on autobiographical memory. In autobiographical-memory studies people are typically asked about their own past personal experiences. Interest centers around the issue of how such memories are organized, and how, over time, they distort or change (Rubin, 1986). Some researchers are content to try to understand the structure and retrieval of autobiographical memories without worrying about how that structure relates to past reality. It is "more important that our memories seem real than that they be real" (Rubin, p. 4). Other researchers insist that we cannot really understand autobiographical memories unless we know precisely what initial events led to those memories. Since our current work does involve verification of past memories, and we are concerned not only with what seems real but what is real, our results are informative to both classes of researchers.

Health-Related Memories

There are numerous studies of memory for health experiences in which the researcher did not assess the accuracy of the memories. For example, Crespi and Swinehart (1982) asked people questions like, "In the last two months have you had an eye exam?" The data of interest were the percentage of people who said yes, but the researchers had no means of determining whether these yes responses were accurate or not. Another example is Fathi, Schooler, and Loftus (1984), in which people were asked, "In the last 12 months, how many times have you gone to a doctor, or a dentist, or a hospital, or utilized any health-care specialist or facility?" Interest was not in the accuracy of recollection, since this was not assessed, but was in processes that people use to retrieve this type of information. Fathi et al. found that people tended to retrieve their health experiences in a forward direction, that is, starting with the most temporally distant memories and proceeding toward the more recent events. Although we can potentially gain valuable information about retrieval strategies from these types of studies, we cannot learn precisely how accurate the memories are because the verification of memories was not done.

More ambitious studies of memory for health experiences involve an attempt to verify the accuracy of memory. For example, in one study of people's ability to report their own hospitalizations ("Reporting of Hospitalization," 1965), respondents were 1,500 people who had been discharged from a hospital during the previous year. Nearly all people remembered the hospitalization if asked about it within ten weeks of the discharge date, but the percentage dropped over time, so that less than 90% remembered it if asked a year later. In another study of women's ability to report on their pregnancy history (Tilley, Barnes, Bergstralh, Labarthe, Noller, Colton, and Adam, 1985), respondents were several thousand women who had given birth to a daughter at least ten years before. In general there was good agreement when mothers' recall of personal history (such as past miscarriages) was compared with their records; however, for medical interventions such as drugs, agreement with medical records was poor. This is an example of a long line of studies in which records and recall of health conditions have been investigated (e.g., Bean, Leeper, and Wallace, 1979; Corwin, Krober, and Roth, 1971).

Another approach to the study of memory for health experiences is to explore ways of improving the information obtained (Means and Loftus, 1991). Means conducted in-depth interviews (1.5 hours) with 40 members of a health maintenance organization, asking them to describe all of the occasions during the past twelve months on which they had seen a health plan staff member concerning their physical health. Reported incidents were compared with medical records, revealing relatively poor memory for events of a recurring nature (e.g., three or more visits for the same condition). Two techniques, Decomposition and Time Line, were successful in enhancing memory for recurring events. Although the interventions significantly improved memory, they were quite time-consuming, thus impractical to use in many situations.

In the present research we explored the accuracy of health memories by comparing memories to information obtained from medical records. Our interest was in the kinds of errors that people make. Unlike the Means and Loftus research, which involved in-depth interviews (1.5 hours) with a relatively small number of people (40), our research involved shorter (.5 hour) telephone interviews with a large sample of respondents (approximately 1,000). We also explored ways of improving the accuracy of memory. The particular techniques that we studied were ones that would not be especially time-consuming, and thus could be used with large samples of rememberers, or when time is of the essence. Our basic procedure involved first gathering memories from people and then comparing those memories to information obtained from medical records. As will become clear, we found that some types of health information are overreported, whereas other types are underreported. Thus, improving memory sometimes means increasing reports, whereas other times it means reducing reports.

One technique we tested involved instructing people to recall their visits to a health clinic over the previous year, using one of several retrieval orders. Some people recalled in a forward (chronological) direction, others in a backward (reverse chronological) direction, and still others were left free to recall in any order they wished. As we shall see, people preferred one order but performed slightly better when they used another order.

A second technique we tested involved requesting information from two separate time frames versus a single time frame. All respondents were asked, for example, to report whether they had had their blood pressure checked in the previous two months. However, some were first asked about the previous six months. As we shall see, people responded differently to the two-month question when it was asked first rather than second.

Overview of Method

Our research was carried out in collaboration with Group Health Cooperative (GHC) of Puget Sound, the largest consumer-governed health maintenance organization in the United States. The Center for Health Studies at GHC conducts telephone surveys of Group Health clientele on a regular basis, using standardized questionnaires from which interviewers read. By selectively manipulating the item content within one such survey, we conducted several experiments. Each subject participated in one or two of the individual experiments. For ease of exposition, we first present an overview of the subject sample and methods. Then the specific studies incorporated into the survey are described separately, as if they were independently conducted studies.

Subjects

Prospective survey participants were randomly selected by computer from GHC membership rolls. Letters were mailed to 1,199 members asking for their participation in a consumer survey. Of these, 249 either could not be contacted or refused to participate or did not complete the survey. This left 950 members who completed the survey, yielding a completion rate of 79.2% of those who were sent letters requesting their participation. The sample was randomly drawn within stratified geographical regions.

Of the 950 members who participated in the survey, 94% (893 people) gave permission for their medical records to be reviewed. Of those who participated in the survey, 37% were males and 62% females (1% unknown).

Of the 950, 9% had 11 or fewer years of education, 27% had a high school degree, 29% had some college, 16% had a college degree, and 18% had post-college education (2% unknown). Of the 950, 85% were Caucasian, 4% were black, 4% were Asian (7% unknown or very rare). Of the 950, 8% were never married, 70% were married or living as married, 3% were separated, 8% divorced, 4% widowed, 5% were adolescents (2% unknown).

The participants who were interviewed ranged in age from 14 to 82, with a mean of 42.5 years; 15% were over 65. Adults and young people aged 14 to 17 responded for themselves. Data for children aged 2 to 13 years were obtained by interviewing parents as proxies for the children, and 19.3% of the sample consisted of parental proxy reports.

Procedure

The respondents for all experiments except one were interviewed during March 1986. Respondents in the landmark study (experiment 3) were interviewed near November 1, 1986. Each respondent who agreed to participate was telephoned and asked a series of approximately fifty questions (some of which had subquestions). The questions were part of a routine consumer opinion survey conducted by GHC to gather opinions and evaluations of GHC services and to provide information to assist in the planning of healthcare programs and facilities. The survey lasted approximately a half-hour. Specific questions pertinent to this research project were embedded in the beginning of this questionnaire. In order to incorporate the manipulations of item content required by the various experiments, we constructed twenty different versions of the survey questionnaire. Participants were randomly assigned to versions.

All versions of the survey began in the same way. The members were asked how many years they had been enrolled at GHC for healthcare, and the specific medical center to which they usually went. After a few more preliminary questions, they were asked the critical questions that constituted the experiment(s) in which they were participating.

When the survey was finished, respondents were asked whether they would grant permission to have their medical records checked. The following wording was used: "We would like to consult your GHC records to obtain some additional information about your recent visits to GHC for healthcare. All of the information will be held in confidence as provided by law, and used only for research in health services. May I have your permission for this record review? Thank you." Of those asked, 94% granted permission.

Analysis of Medical Records

The first step in the medical-record check was to order the charts of the respondents who had granted permission to have their records checked. For this research, abstracting of charts was done by research assistants who were trained by GHC. For each subject, two types of information were pulled from the medical record. First, all visits within the previous two years were listed by date. (Initially, we also listed the name of the physician. However, in an excessive number of cases, the handwriting of the physician was so poor that it could not be read, leading to a fivefold increase in the time needed to abstract the chart. We soon dropped the physician's name as an item to be extracted from the record.)

The second type of information obtained from the medical records was on several specific procedures (e.g., blood pressure reading) that the subject had had during the previous six months. This information was generally found in laboratory reports, radiology reports, or other parts of the medical chart. The abstracters recorded whether the respondent did or did not have each procedure. For each procedure found, the date was also noted.

Once we had the survey- and medical-record data, they were matched by a complex set of procedures. We describe these procedures in more detail in connection with our discussion of the specific experiments.

Experiment 1: Order of Retrieval

Introduction

When a person tries to retrieve multiple memories, there are different orders in which they can be retrieved. Several studies show a tendency to recall in a forward direction, that is, starting with the most temporally distant memories and proceeding toward the more recent (e.g., Fathi, Schooler, and Loftus, 1984; King and Pontious, 1969). In the Fathi et al. research, students were asked to recall all the times in the preceding twelve months when they had visited a healthcare professional or facility. Subjects had to "think out loud" as they responded, and their comments were tape-recorded. Analysis of the response protocols showed that for those who recalled more than one health event recall tended to be in a forward direction: Subjects would typically start with the most temporally distant instance, then the second most distant, and so on. The accuracy of their recall was not established.

In two experiments in which accuracy was established, students recalled information about exams they had taken in an introductory psychology course (Loftus and Fathi, 1985). In the first experiment they were instructed to recall either in a forward, a backward, or a free-recall order. Forward search led to less accurate recollection than did backward search and free recall. In the second experiment backward and forward search were compared, and backward search produced more accurate recollections.

There are problems in comparing the health-memory study, in which people preferred the forward order, to the exam-memory study, in which people performed better with a backward search. Just because people perform better with backward retrieval of exams does not mean that they will perform better with backward retrieval of health events. There may be classes of tasks in which people tend to retrieve more accurately in a forward direction, and other classes in which the backward order is better. In retrieving exam information, for example, since exams are fairly independent events, people might well begin by retrieving the most recent (that is, most available) instance. This would explain the benefits of backward search in the exam domain. With health events, on the other hand, there may be a causal relationship between various visits that might lead subjects to retrieve in a forward direction, following the chain of causality (e.g., "I had an eye infection and so I went to an ophthalmologist and returned for several follow-up visits.").

In experiment 1 respondents were asked to recall health events over the previous year. Furthermore, respondents were instructed to recall their visits, using either a forward, a backward, or a free-recall order. The experiment produced data bearing on two issues: the order that people prefer to use when they are free to choose; and the order, if any, that produces the most accurate remembering of health events.

Method

SUBJECTS.   A total of 373 GHC members participated in this experiment.

PROCEDURE.   Participants received one of three versions of the questionnaire asking them to recall their visits to GHC over the previous year. The three versions differed in the order in which respondents were asked to retrieve their visits. In the forward version respondents ($n = 125$) were asked:

> I'd like to ask you about the visits you have made to GHC for healthcare over the past 12 months. Starting with the first visit you made in the past 12 months, and then coming forward to the next one, and so on, will you tell me the month of each visit, and the provider you saw?

In the backward version respondents ($n = 128$) were asked:

> I'd like to ask you about the visits you made to GHC for healthcare over the past 12 months. Starting with the most recent visit, and then going back to the next one before that, and so on, will you tell me the month of each visit, and which provider you saw?

In the free-recall version respondents ($n = 120$) were asked:

> I'd like to ask you about the visits you have made to GHC for healthcare over the past 12 months. Will you tell me the month of each one, and the provider you saw?

Regardless of version, when the subject had finished providing the list of specific visits, he or she was asked, "In all, how many visits did you make to GHC for healthcare during the past 12 months?" Thus it was possible for a subject to recall, say, two specific visits, but to estimate that in all there were more than two visits actually made.

Results

Of the 373 people who participated in this experiment, 365 gave permission to have their records reviewed. For several reasons, we were able to verify information from the records of only 329 of these individuals. (We made several attempts to obtain the records of the other 36 but were unable to get those records.) All analyses described in this section pertain, then, only to the 329 verified cases.

NUMBER OF ACTUAL VISITS AND RECOLLECTIONS. The participants in this experiment actually had a range of visits, from a low of 0 to a high of 98. Of these participants, 114 were in the forward (chronological) group, 112 were in the backward (reverse chronological) group, and 103 were free to recall their visits in any order they wished. Table 1 shows the mean number of actual visits, the mean number of visits that could be recalled and dated, and the recall estimate of total visits.

In looking at table 1, first notice that random assignment to conditions was effective. There were, on average, approximately five visits per person in each of the three conditions, and the mean numbers of visits across conditions were not significantly different, $F(2,326) < 1$, $MSe = 22.8$.

Next, notice that in all three conditions the mean number of visits recalled and dated was lower than the actual number of visits. Overall, respondents specifically recalled an average of 2.23 visits, which was only 45% of their actual visits. The forward order produced the lowest number of visits (2.0) and the backward order the highest (2.38). An analysis of variance did not reveal a significant overall effect due to recall strategy, $F(2,326) = 1.06$, $MSe = 4.4$, $p > .05$.

After listing the specific visits, respondents provided an estimate of the total number of visits they had made, and these data are also included in table 1. Notice that the estimate was, on the average, 4.26 visits, which is somewhat lower than (87%) the actual number of visits. The estimated total was lowest for those in the forward condition, although not significantly so, $F(2,326) < 1$, $MSe = 32.0$.

These results reveal several things. First, when people have to estimate their total number of visits, the mean estimate is somewhat lower than the actual number of visits. Moreover, when people must specifically recall and try to date their visits, they underreport by a substantial amount. Second, the order of retrieval had a very slight, but not significant, effect on performance. Fewer visits were recalled and dated and fewer were estimated in the forward-recall condition.

Table 1 Experiment 1: Order of Retrieval: Mean Actual, Recalled, and Estimated Visits.

	Forward	Backward	Free Recall	Mean
Actual Visits	4.74	5.13	4.90	4.92
Recalled and Dated Visits	2.00	2.38	2.33	2.23
Recalled Estimate of Visits	3.75	4.44	4.62	4.26
N	114	112	103	329

At first glance it may appear as if we have found that people are failing to specifically remember a substantial number of their visits and that order of retrieval matters little. In fact, the omission problem may be even worse than we think. The specifically remembered visits could conceivably include a number of false alarms (recall of nonexistent visits), thereby erroneously raising the number of specifically recalled visits. To determine whether order of retrieval influences the likelihood of producing false alarms, as well as the precise likelihood that actual visits are omitted from recall, further analyses are required.

COMPLETENESS OF RECALL.   Based upon the simple analysis conducted above, we estimated that people were specifically remembering 44% of their actual visits. However, as noted, the omissions might actually be higher because of false alarms. By matching dates of actual visits with dates of recalled visits, we can circumvent the false-alarm problem and simultaneously reduce any bias in our estimate based upon unequal numbers of actual visits. (That is, a single subject who had fifty visits but recalled only one of them could dramatically influence the estimate.)

To determine completeness of recall, we calculated a completeness score for each subject. These scores involve the specifically remembered visits, not the estimated total. The completeness score was the ratio of the number of correctly recalled visits (hits) to the total number of actual visits (hits plus misses). This can be thought of as the percentage of visits that were specifically recalled for each individual.

A major challenge was how to define a hit. How do we determine from limited reported information whether a recollection corresponds to an actual visit, and which visit it corresponds to? For each visit recalled, respondents gave us a recalled date. The strictest way to define a hit is to include only cases in which the month and year of a recalled visit exactly matched the month and year of an actual visit. By this criterion, only 22% of actual visits were hits. This is substantially less than the 44% estimated from looking at the ratio of mean specifically recalled visits to mean actual visits. On the other hand, this criterion is extremely strict, especially given the fact that people are not particularly good at dating visits. Suppose we loosen the criterion to define a hit as including all cases in which the month and year of a recalled visit came within a month of the actual visit. This adds 10% to the estimated hits, for a total of 32% of actual visits being hits. Suppose we further loosen the criterion to define a hit as including all cases in which the month and year of a recalled visit came within two months of the actual visit. This adds 4% to the estimated hits, for a total of 36%. Table 2 presents all the data from which these calculations can be made. In table 2 we present the percentage of actual visits that are exactly recalled, off by one month, off by two months, and so on.

Table 2   Experiment 1: Order of Retrieval: Completeness of Recall (percentages of actual visits correctly recalled).

		Forward	Backward	Free Recall	Mean
Difference in Months	0 Months (exact)	24	22	19	22
Between	1 Month	8	12	11	10
Actual and	2 Months	3	4	5	4
Recalled	3 Months	2	2	4	3
Visits	Total	37	40	39	39

To make life easier for our readers, here is what we conclude about completeness from these data. By a strict criterion, respondents specifically recall 22% of their actual visits. By a looser criterion of, say, recalling a visit and accurately dating it within three months of an actual visit, respondents recall 39% of their visits. The completeness scores do not differ as a function of retrieval strategy, $F(2,326) < 1$, MSe $= .14$. (Our conclusions here and throughout this section remained when nonparametric tests were performed.)

It is of interest to ask about what is forgotten. About 60% of actual visits were not specifically remembered. It is natural to expect that these would tend to be the older visits, rather than the recent ones. Of the forgotten events, 27% of them were visits from the most recent four-month period, 33% of them were visits from five to eight months earlier, and 40% of them were visits from nine to twelve months earlier. These results are not surprising, for they represent a standard forgetting curve in which people are increasingly likely not to remember events as the time increases since those events happened.

ACCURACY OF RECALL.   The above analyses tell us that people are failing to remember roughly 60% of their actual visits. But the analyses tell us nothing about how often what they do remember corresponds to an actual visit. We wanted to calculate an accuracy score for each subject. To do this, we needed to calculate the ratio of correctly recalled visits to the total number of visits recalled. This would give us the percentage of recalled visits that were actual visits. Once again we had the problem of how to define a hit, and our definition depended on how much precision of dating we required. We calculated the percentage of recalled visits that were accurately recalled, defining accuracy as within three months of an actual visit. Given this definition of a hit, 58% of recalled visits were accurate. Put another way, 42%

of recalled visits were either false alarms or poorly dated visits. The effect of order of retrieval on accuracy scores was not significant, $F(2,326) < 1$, MSe $= .23$, although the hit rate was somewhat higher in the backward group (63%) than the other two groups (forward, 56%; free, 56%). The pattern was not different when strict definitions of a hit were used.

ACTUAL ORDERS USED.   We found order of retrieval mattered very little. Respondents were slightly, but not significantly, more accurate and complete when they were instructed to recall in a backward order. The lack of statistical significance raises the possibility that respondents did not follow our instructions. To examine this, we calculated the percentage of respondents in each condition who used each strategy, and these data are presented in table 3. As table 3 shows, just over half of respondents specifically recalled only 0 or 1 visit, and thus could not be classified as using a forward or backward strategy. From table 3 we see that of those instructed to go forward, 79% of those with more than one recalled visit did recall in the forward order (30/38). Of those instructed to go backward, 76% of those with more than one recalled visit did recall in the backward order (41/54). So at least three-quarters of respondents were following our instructions when they could. However, it should be kept in mind that, in the final analysis, only 35 people were instructed to go forward and did so, and only 46 people were instructed to go backward and did so. These relatively small numbers may be partially responsible for the lack of statistical significance. Certainly, with greater power, the 7% advantage in accuracy for backward respondents could well be significant.

As for those in the free-recall condition, 44% of those with more than one visit used a forward order, whereas 22% of them used a backward order. Thus, there was a preference in this group for the forward order.

Table 3   Experiment 1: Order of Retrieval: Actual Strategy Used (in percentages).

	Too Few Visits Recalled (0 or 1)	No Systematic Order	Forward Order	Backward Order
Instructed to Use:				
Forward order	63	6	30	2
Backward order	46	8	5	41
Free recall	54	15	20	10
Total	54	10	18	18

TELESCOPING OF EVENTS.   It is to be expected that respondents who recall an actual visit misremember its date. When this error occurs, does the event appear to have occurred more, or less, recently? Studies involving other sorts of "important" memories, such as crime victimization, show that forward telescoping (the event is remembered as occurring more recently) is the more common error (Garofalo and Hindelang, 1977; Sudman and Bradburn, 1973).

To identify the relative prevalence of forward versus backward telescoping errors, we examined the number of times each error occurred. We found that the bulk of the errors were errors of misdating by a single month (65% of misdating errors). In terms of all misdating errors, approximately two-thirds represented a forward telescoping error.

INDIVIDUAL DIFFERENCES.   We first examined gender differences in recall. Over the course of the year, women had more visits than men did (5.39 versus 4.24 visits, $F(1,327) = 4.39$, MSe = 22.8, $p < .05$). Yet women and men recalled approximately the same number of visits (2.24 versus 2.18 visits, $F < 1$). This might lead one to expect that men were being more accurate since, relative to women, their actual number of visits matched more closely their recalled number. However, this is not necessarily the case, since men might be producing a larger number of false alarms than women.

Our matching process permitted a better description of the completeness and accuracy of females versus males. When we matched the dates of actual visits with dates of recalled visits, we found that the percentage of true visits that were recalled was higher for women than men (.39 versus .30, $F(1,327) = 4.37$, MSe = .14, $p < .05$). Thus the recall of women was more complete than that of men. To assess relative accuracy, we calculated the percentage of recalled visits that were accurate. This figure was higher for women than men (.59 versus .46, $F(1,327) = 5.43$, MSe = .22, $p < .05$). Thus, the recall of women was more accurate than that of men.

We next examined differences in recall as a function of age. These data are shown in table 4. Age was related to the number of actual visits in a predictable way, $F(5,323) = 3.70$, MSe = 80.7, $p < .01$. The oldest age groups had more actual visits than the youngest age group. However, age was unrelated to both completeness and accuracy scores, both F's < 1.

We next examined differences in recall as a function of education. Level of education did not affect recall in any significant way. It had no effect on number of actual visits, $F(4,324) < 1$. It had no effect on number of visits recalled, $F < 1$. The overall completeness score was independent of level of education, $F < 1$. Finally, the overall accuracy score was independent of level of education, $F < 1$. Thus, the memories of health matters obtained from those who were highly educated were not better than the memories of those who were less educated.

Table 4   Experiment 1: Order of Retrieval: Age and Recall of Visits.

	Age in Years				
	25 or Less	25–39	40–59	60 or More	Mean
Actual Visits	4.32	4.72	5.18	5.42	4.92
Recalled and Dated Visits	2.06	2.20	2.06	2.75	2.23
Recalled Estimate of Visits	3.76	4.27	4.55	4.00	4.26
Percentage of Actual Visits Correctly Recalled	49	34	33	40	36
Percentage of Recalled Visits That Were Accurate	57	54	53	61	55
N	34	147	96	52	329

The questionnaire asked respondents to give a subjective rating of their health, using a scale with four response categories: excellent, good, fair, and poor. We obtained ratings from 326 of the respondents in this experiment. We examined the data to see if subjective health rating was related to memory for health events. We found that people rarely rated their health as "poor"; only 1.2% did so. The most common rating was "excellent," given by 50.6% (good = 38.4%, fair = 9.8%). Completeness and accuracy scores were independent of subjective health rating.

Discussion

We found that when people provide an estimate of the number of visits they made over the previous year, their mean estimate is somewhat lower than the actual number of visits. For this sample that was 87% of actual visits. We also found that when people must specifically remember their visits, only about 39% of actual visits are specifically recalled. Obviously, there is a substantial difference between the 39% of visits that respondents were able to specifically remember and the 87% of total visits that they estimated. This means that respondents know they made more visits than the ones they can specifically remember. This finding is reminiscent of the work of Hasher and Zacks (1984), showing that people are sensitive to frequency of occurrence information. People have a good idea about how many times certain events happened in their lives, even if they cannot specifically recall each instance.

There is underreporting in all three retrieval conditions. Only about 58% of specifically recalled visits were accurately recalled, and the instruction about the order to use had very little effect. There was a slight preference for using the forward order when people were free to use any order, but the instruction to go backward led to a slight advantage. This is another example of a common occurrence: Simply because people tend to perform a task in a given way does not mean that it is the most efficient way. Another, more trivial, example is the observation that most people button their shirts or blouses from top to bottom, although it is actually more efficient to button them from bottom to top (Gilbreth and Carey, 1948).

A word of caution is in order in interpreting the absolute magnitude of the figures reported here. When we talk about false alarms or misses as errors in recollection, we must acknowledge that it is possible that some of these "errors" could be due to problems in the medical records (Martin, 1987). Analyses of medical records have shown the occasional inaccurate or missing piece of information. Whereas GHC has an exceptionally advanced method of recordkeeping, it still cannot be assumed that all discrepancies between the recollections and the medical records are errors of memory. Additionally, another possible source of error is in the abstracting of information from the medical records. The documents that our abstracters faced were complicated, and some mistakes could have occurred.

Experiment 2:
Order of Retrieval and Proxy Recall

Introduction

An important interest to cognitive psychologists and survey researchers is the ability of people to store and retrieve information about themselves versus another person. In many national surveys respondents are sometimes asked to retrieve information not only about themselves but also about other individuals. An individual might be asked to recall the doctor visits of a spouse or child, for example. In fact, in some cases one adult is permitted to respond for all those in the household who are not available at the time of the interview or not wishing to respond for themselves (Jabine, 1985). It is natural to wonder about the accuracy of these proxy responses, and whether techniques can be found to improve proxy memory.

Numerous studies have demonstrated that knowledge about oneself is more accessible in memory than knowledge about others (e.g., Kuiper and Rogers, 1979). Self-related information is apparently more affect-laden, more familiar, more robust, more complex, and more likely to be stored in a verbal rather than visual fashion (Fiske and Taylor, 1984). Even if the rememberer has actually observed or participated in the episodes of another individual, it cannot be expected that the retrieval of those other-related episodes will be accomplished in a fashion similar to the retrieval of one's own personal episodes (Thompson, 1982). Self-memory has been shown to be more accurate than proxy memory in the reporting of chronic conditions (Feldman, 1960), and it is likely that other self-health-related experiences would also be better remembered than the health experiences of another.

These ideas motivated experiment 2. We recognize that there already exists evidence that proxy reporting sometimes produces poorer information (White and Massey, 1981), but little is known about the mechanisms of proxy reporting, in part because few studies with validation have been done. If we are ever to develop a technique to improve proxy reporting, such information is essential.

Method

SUBJECTS. A total of 170 people participated in this experiment. These individuals were persons who had participated in experiment 1 and also indicated that they were married and had been living with their spouses for the past 12 months.

PROCEDURE. After respondents were asked to recall their own visits to GHC over the previous year, they were asked to recall the visits made by their spouses. Respondents received one of three versions of the questionnaire asking them to recall their spouses' visits. They were instructed to use the same order of retrieval that they had used for themselves. In the forward version respondents were asked:

> Now, I'd like to ask you about the visits your (wife/husband) has made to GHC for healthcare over the past 12 months. Starting again with the first visit during the past 12 months, and then coming forward to the next one, and so on, will you tell me the month of each visit, and which provider he or she saw?

The backward and free-recall instructions were comparable to those described in connection with experiment 1. Regardless of version, when the subject had finished providing the list of specific visits, he or she was asked, "In all, how many visits did your (wife/husband) make to GHC for healthcare during the past 12 months?" Again, it was possible for a subject to recall, say, two specific visits for his or her spouse, but to estimate that in all there were more than two visits actually made.

Results

Of the 170 people who participated in this study, 56 had spouses who did not belong to GHC. In the remaining 114 cases, spouses were contacted to gain their permission to check their medical records. In all, 90 spouses granted permission, but for only 69 of these people were we able to obtain medical records and complete the verification process. All analyses described here pertain only to the 69 interviewed members and their spouses.

NUMBER OF ACTUAL VISITS AND RECOLLECTIONS. Of the participants in this experiment, 24 were in the forward condition, 20 were in the backward condition, and 25 were in the free-recall condition. Table 5 shows the mean number of actual visits, the mean number of visits that could be recalled and dated, and the recall estimate of total visits. These data are presented separately for the respondents' own visits and for the spouses' visits.

In looking at table 5, first notice that the backward group had somewhat more actual self-visits and actual proxy visits than the other groups. Two analyses of variance showed that the retrieval order was not significantly related to actual self-visits, $F(2,66) = 1.52$, MSe = 22.6, $p > .2$, but was significantly related to actual proxy visits, $F(2,66) = 4.15$, MSe = 11.9, $p = .02$.

Next, notice that the mean number of proxy visits specifically recalled was lower than the actual number of self-visits. Overall, respondents recalled an average of 1.7 of their own visits, or 35% of their actual visits. When respondents recalled spouse visits, they recalled 37% of actual spouse visits.

After listing the specific visits, respondents provided an estimate of the total number of visits that their spouses had made. These data are also included in table 5. Overall, respondents estimated a mean of 3.6 total visits

Table 5 Experiment 2: Order of Retrieval and Proxy Recall: Mean Actual, Recalled, and Estimated Visits.

	Forward	Backward	Free Recall	Mean
Self: Actual Visits	4.6	6.3	3.8	4.8
Recalled and dated visits	1.5	2.1	1.7	1.7
Recalled estimate of visits	3.2	5.2	2.6	3.6
Proxy: Actual Visits	4.0	6.2	3.2	4.3
Recalled and dated visits	1.3	2.4	1.3	1.6
Recalled estimate of visits	3.2	6.9	2.1	3.9
N	24	20	25	69

for themselves, or 75% of their actual visits. When respondents estimated the total spouse visits, they estimated 91% of actual spouse visits.

These results reveal several things. First, when people have to estimate the total number of visits made by their spouses, they underreport just slightly. When they must specifically recall and try to date the visits, the underreporting is much greater. The backward group estimated and also specifically recalled somewhat more visits than the other two groups, but this could be due simply to the fact that they had more visits to recall. In order to reduce recall bias due to differences in actual visits, we needed to use the completeness and accuracy scores described earlier.

COMPLETENESS OF RECALL. To determine the completeness of recall, we calculated two completeness scores for each subject, one for self-recall and one for proxy recall. The completeness score was the ratio of the number of correctly recalled visits (hits) over the total number of actual visits. This can be thought of as the percentage of actual visits that were recalled.

In table 6 we report the completeness scores. The numbers reported are the percentage of actual visits that were recalled, and as can be seen, respondents reported more of their own visits (44%) than their spouses' visits (30%). We used a very liberal criterion for a hit (the recalled visit occurred within six months of the actual visit). Respondents in the backward group had the highest completeness scores for spouses' visits and recalled nearly as many of their spouses' visits as their own visits. In the forward group, respondents recalled a smaller percentage of their spouses' visits than their own visits. Although the backward completeness score for proxy recall is the highest, the three completeness scores do not differ significantly, $F(2,67) = 1.39$, MSe = .13, $p > .2$.

ACCURACY OF RECALL. We now turn to the issue of how often the visits that are recalled are actual visits. These results are presented in table 7. Here we present the percentage of recalled visits that were accurately recalled,

Table 6 Experiment 2: Order of Retrieval and Proxy Recall: Completeness of Recall (percentages of actual visits that were recalled).

	Forward	Backward	Free Recall	Mean
Self-Visits	44	42	44	44
Spouse Visits	21	40	30	30
Difference (advantage for self-recall)	23	2	14	14

Table 7   Experiment 2: Order of Retrieval and Proxy Recall: Accuracy of Recall (percentages of recalled visits that were correct).

	Forward	Backward	Free Recall	Mean
Self-Visits	63	68	60	63
Spouse Visits	32	68	46	47
Difference (advantage for self-recall)	31	0	14	16

defining accuracy as within six months of an actual visit. As we can see, given this definition of a hit, 63% of recalled self-visits were accurate, whereas only 47% of recalled proxy visits were accurate. The accuracy figure for the backward group recalling proxy visits is significantly higher than the other two groups, $F(2,67) = 3.17$, MSe = .2, $p < .05$.

SUMMARY.   Again we found underreporting of health-related visits in all three retrieval conditions for the subsample of 70 respondents in this study. Using a very liberal criterion for a hit, respondents reported only 44% of their own actual visits. When reporting for their spouses, performance was even less complete: 30% of actual spouse visits were recalled. In terms of accuracy, again people were more accurate when reporting their own rather than their spouses' visits. Of the visits reported, 63% of their own, and 47% of their spouses' visits were accurate. If any retrieval strategy produced better performance it was the backward strategy. Use of the backward strategy significantly increased the accuracy of reports of spouse visits.

INDIVIDUAL DIFFERENCES.   We examined gender differences in proxy recall. In the self versus proxy study, 39 females and 31 males participated. Table 8

Table 8   Experiment 2: Order of Retrieval and Proxy Recall: Completeness and Accuracy for Males and Females.

	Completeness		Accuracy	
	Male	Female	Male	Female
Self-Recall	46	42	60	66
Proxy Recall	21	36	38	54
Difference (advantage for self-recall)	25	6	22	12

permits us to see how females and males differ in performance when reporting for themselves and for their spouses. Compared to males, females were marginally more complete (36% versus 21%) when reporting on their spouses' visits, $F(1,68) = 3.44$, MSe = .13, p < .07. They also were slightly more accurate (54% versus 38%) when reporting on their spouses' visits, $F(1,68) = 2.11$, MSe = .24, p = .15. No other individual difference variables (e.g., age, educational level) were significantly related to proxy recall.

Experiment 3: Landmarks

Introduction

Past work has shown that the use of landmarks, or highly salient events, can improve people's ability to date events from the past (Baddeley, 1979; Loftus and Marburger, 1983). Landmarks have been shown to mark effectively the beginning of the reference period and reduce the incidence of *forward telescoping*. Forward telescoping is a memory distortion in which events that occurred prior to the beginning of the reference period are telescoped forward into the reference period. Thus, an event that happened fifteen months ago might be recalled as having occurred in the last year. In experiment 1 two-thirds of all dating errors were forward-telescoping errors.

When people are asked to recall all visits from, say, the last year, obviously forward telescoping operates to inflate the estimated number of events that are reported as occurring in the reference period. In one study (Loftus and Marburger, 1983) the introduction of a landmark event significantly reduced the tendency of respondents to remember an event as having occurred more recently than it actually did. Not only did unique public landmarks have this effect, more regular public landmarks (New Year's Day) as well as private landmarks also reduced forward telescoping, resulting in more accurate reporting. Thus, the use of landmarks appears to be a promising way to improve memory.

Initially we had intended to use a six-month reference period, which would have required respondents to be run on July 1, 1986. However, the initial sample of respondents was exhausted prior to this date. In order to remedy this situation, a new sample of 211 respondents was surveyed approximately on November 1, 1986, about their visits over the previous ten months.

Method

SUBJECTS. A total of 211 GHC members participated in this experiment.

PROCEDURE. Respondents received one of two versions of the survey questions, asking them to recall their visits over the preceding ten months. In the control (ten-month) condition, respondents ($n = 104$) were asked, "How many visits have you made to GHC for healthcare during the past ten months?" In the landmark condition, respondents ($n = 107$) were asked, "How many visits have you made to GHC for healthcare since New Year's Day, January 1st?"

Results

Of the 211 people who participated in this experiment, we received permission and were able to verify information from 186 (93 in each condition). Three respondents were removed because of extreme recollections. One recalled 58 and two recalled 60 visits. In actuality they had 22, 24, and 26 visits. We calculated the mean number of actual visits for the remaining 183 respondents as well as the mean recall estimate of total visits for each of the two conditions.

Unfortunately, that random assignment was not as effective as we would have hoped. There was a mean of 4.02 actual visits in the ten-month condition, but 5.34 visits in the landmark condition, $t(68) = 1.58$, $p > .1$. As far as the recalled estimate is concerned, the ten-month and landmark respondents recalled an equivalent number, that is, about four visits (ten-month = 3.86, landmark = 4.07). This means that the underreporting problem occurred in the landmark condition but not in the ten-month condition.

Because the two groups differed in terms of their actual visits, we conducted an analysis of covariance. Equating for the actual number of visits, would the landmark versus ten-month instruction produce a different recalled estimate? The answer to this question is no. The analysis of covariance was not significant, $F(1,180) = 1.10$, $MSe = 11.5$.

Discussion

We found that, overall, respondents underreport the healthcare visits they made over the previous ten months. Underreporting was greater for respondents in the landmark condition than in the ten-month condition. However, the landmark respondents had more visits, complicating our interpretation of results. Nonetheless, we speculate about why the use of a landmark, which should reduce errors, may produce problems of other kinds.

The recall estimate presumably is made up of actual visits from within the reference period, plus other visits that are telescoped from a prior period. If the landmark minimizes the telescoping problem, then the recall estimate in the landmark condition will be reduced. In terms of obtaining an accurate estimate, the minimizing of telescoping may actually produce a poorer estimate. Put another way, if forgetting of actual visits is compensated for in part by the telescoping of earlier visits, then an estimate that contains telescoped errors is an estimate that is closer to reality.

In retrospect the ten-month reference period was probably not a good reference period to use, if one wants to compare performance to a landmark condition. Ten months may convey to the respondent a certain requirement for precision that is not conveyed when, say, a year or six months is used instead. A landmark technique might show a benefit over the six-month or one-year reference period but not over a ten-month reference period.

It is worth mentioning that there are numerous theoretical papers that discuss the mechanisms by which humans and other organisms time events from the past (e.g., Crowder and Greene, 1987; Killeen and Fetterman, 1988; Parker and Glover, 1987). Much of this work is not directly relevant to discussions of telescoping, although in some cases the ideas could contribute to our understanding of the phenomenon and the potential therapy for the phenomenon. For example, Crowder and Greene make the point that events in the near past are distinguished more by their time of occurrence than events in the distant past. This notion suggests that telescoping problems may be different if we are dealing with recent versus distant events. Future investigators who wish to devise experiments on telescoping should take account of these notions when determining the reference periods to use in their research and the ways of interpreting their data.

Experiment 4: Two-Time Frames

Introduction

An intriguing technique for potentially reducing forward telescoping was reported by Crespi and Swinehart (1982). Respondents were asked which of several actions (had blood pressure checked, had physical exam, had eye exam, etc.) they had taken in the past two months. Other respondents were first asked whether they had engaged in each behavior during the past six months, and then were asked the two-month question. When the six-month question was asked first, affirmative responses to the two-month question averaged 12% less than when the two-month question was asked alone. For example, when asked the six-month question first, 11% claimed to have had an eye exam in the last two months, 32% claimed to have had their blood pressure checked, 20% claimed to have had a physical exam. However, if the two-month question was asked alone, these figures were higher: 23%, 48%, and 32%, respectively. In short, the two-time-frame questioning procedure produced quite different estimates of the extent to which respondents engaged in the various health-related activities.

While the two-time-frame procedure reduced the number of affirmative responses, did it lead to more accurate reporting? Crespi and Swinehart did not verify respondents' reports, but they had several reasons for believing that the lower reports were more accurate. Nonetheless, they appealed to future researchers to reinvestigate their method with personal memories that could be verified.

It is natural to ask why people report fewer activities within a two-month period if they are first asked about activities within six months. There are a number of hypotheses. First, it is possible that events from three and four months ago are "captured" by the six-month question and thus do not need to be reported in response to the two-month question. Forward telescoping due to response bias factors is prevented by the six-month question. Second, the need to demonstrate a socially desirable concern for health matters can be satisfied when respondents answer the six-month question and do not need to demonstrate this concern again for the two-month question. Finally, it is possible that the two-time-frame procedure conveys that the interviewer wants greater precision in dating than the single-time-frame question might imply.

Experiment 4 was designed in part to explore the two-time-frame procedure as a potentially useful means of increasing the accuracy of reported memories. In addition, we hoped to learn something about why people were reporting fewer activities when asked two questions rather than one. Crespi and Swinehart showed that people reported fewer activities in the two-month-period when asked about a longer reference period first. Would people also report fewer activities when asked about a shorter reference period first? If the percentage reporting an activity were reduced when a shorter reference period came first, what explanations could account for this result? The precision hypothesis would predict that respondents who were first asked about one month and then about two months might sense a greater demand for precision and respond more accurately to the two-month question than respondents asked only about two months. The telescoping and social-desirability explanations for the two-time-frame effect would predict that asking about a shorter reference period first would not improve accuracy over a single-time-frame question. (A more detailed report of this study can be found in Loftus, Klinger, Smith, and Fiedler, 1990).

Method

SUBJECTS. A total of 739 members participated in this experiment.

PROCEDURE. Respondents received one of three versions of the questionnaire asking them whether they had any of a list of procedures (e.g., blood pressure reading) done under their GHC coverage. Several of the procedures on this list were routine, whereas others were ones that the GHC staff were particularly interested in. The three versions differed in terms of the reference period about which respondents were asked. In the 2-6 condition, respondents were first asked about procedures utilized over the previous two months and then about procedures over the previous six months. Because respondents could not anticipate the sequence of questions, responses to the two-month question appearing first in the 2-6 sequence may be considered equivalent to responses to a two-month question asked alone. Adult respondents who were over 18 years ($n = 180$) were asked about seven different procedures:

> During the past 2 months, since (date), have you had any of the following procedures done under your GHC coverage?
>
> Blood pressure reading?
>
> Test of blood in your stool?
>
> Mammogram—x-ray of breast only (asked only of women over 40 years)?
>
> Pneumococcus vaccine—flu vaccine (asked only of people over 65 years)?
>
> Breast exam by a doctor or nurse (asked of women only)?
>
> Pap smear test for cancer (asked of women only)?
>
> Had a new prescription filled at a GHC pharmacy?

Next, the respondent was asked, "During the past 6 months, since (date), have you had any of these procedures at GHC?" and the procedures were repeated to them.

Adolescents between the ages of 14 and 17 were asked a different set of questions; also parents responding for their children below age 13 were asked this set of "child" questions ($n = 62$).

> During the past 2 months, since (date), have you (has your child) had any of the following procedures at GHC?
>
> Physical examination?
>
> Urine test?
>
> Vision test?
>
> Hearing test?
>
> Had a new prescription filled at a GHC pharmacy?

Next, the respondent was asked, "During the past 6 months, since (date), have you (has she/he) had any of these procedures at GHC?" and the relevant procedures were repeated to them.

In the 6-2 condition, respondents were first asked about procedures utilized over the previous six months and then about procedures over the previous two months. Adult respondents who were over 18 years ($n = 180$) were asked about the seven adult procedures, listed earlier, using the six-month reference period. Next, if they answered yes, they were asked about the relevant procedures using the two-month reference period. Adolescents who were 14 to 17 and parents reporting for their young children ($n = 73$) were asked about the five child procedures, listed earlier, using first the six-month and then the two-month reference period.

In the 1-2 condition, respondents were first asked about procedures utilized over the previous month and then about procedures over the previous two months. Adult respondents who were over 18 years ($n = 188$) were asked about the seven adult procedures, using the one-month and then the two-month reference period. Adolescents aged 14 to 17 and parents reporting for their young children ($n = 56$) were asked about the five child procedures, using first the one-month and then the two-month reference period.

Results

For this analysis we considered responses to the two-month question appearing first in the 2-6 condition to be equivalent to responses to a two-month probe alone. We then compared these responses to those received from the 6-2 and from the 1-2 respondents in terms of their recollections of the two-month reference period.

NUMBER OF PROCEDURES REMEMBERED.   Do people report more procedures when asked about a single time frame (e.g., two months) than when asked about that same frame preceded by another time frame (e.g., six months, then two months)? One answer to this question can be found in table 9, showing the percentage of respondents who reported a procedure within the last two months.

First, compare the 2-6 condition to the 6-2 condition. For nine out of twelve separate procedures, there were fewer visits reported in the 6-2 condition. That is, for nine out of the twelve procedures, asking the six-month question first reduced the reporting of visits that had occurred in the previous two months, as Crespi and Swinehart had shown.

Next compare the 2-6 condition to the 1-2 condition. There is no consistent pattern showing fewer reports in the 1-2 condition, that is, when a shorter time frame precedes the time frame of interest.

**Table 9   Experiment 4: Two-Time Frame: Percentage Reporting a
Procedure in the Last Two Months.**

	Condition		
	6-2	2-6	1-2
Blood Pressure Reading	31.8	29.8	32.1
Colon Cancer Test	5.1	5.6	7.1
Mammogram (women over 40)	17.1	5.0	0.0
Pneumococcus Vaccine (over 65)	5.0	0.0	0.0
Breast Exam (women)	18.3	18.7	12.0
Pap Smear (women)	8.3	15.6	12.0
Rx Filled	24.5	30.4	33.9
Child Physical Exam	9.8	15.3	13.7
Child Urine Test	6.7	12.3	5.9
Child Vision Test	0.0	6.9	11.8
Child Hearing Test	0.0	7.0	7.8
Child Rx Filled	22.6	28.6	28.6

Another comparison can be made to shed light on whether a sequencing
effect would appear when a shorter time frame precedes the time frame of
interest. We can compare the responses to the six-month question in the 2-6
condition to the responses to the six-month question when the six-month
question is asked first (as it is in the 6-2 condition). The percentage of
respondents who reported a procedure within the last six months is shown in
table 10.

Compare the 6-2 to the 2-6 condition. For all twelve procedures, the 2-6
condition led to fewer reported visits during the six-month reference period.
Thus, we have another instance in which having respondents report activities
in two-time frames reduces the proportion reporting the activity in the
second time frame.

In sum there appears to be a modest reduction in the percentage who
report a visit over a two-month period when these respondents are first asked
about a six-month period. As for whether a shorter reference period
preceding the critical one has a similar effect, the results are mixed.
Answering about a two-month period first reduced reporting in a six-month
reference period; however, answering about a one-month period first did not
have a reliable effect on answers for a two-month reference period.

One problem with these data is that we have no guarantee that the actual
numbers of visits are the same in the three conditions. To determine more
meaningfully whether one condition leads to more overreporting than
another, we must examine reports that can be verified.

Table 10   Experiment 4: Two-Time Frame: Percentage Reporting a Procedure in the Last Six Months.

	Condition	
	6-2	2-6
Blood Pressure Reading	61.9	57.3
Colon Cancer Test	21.2	17.6
Mammogram (women over 40)	23.8	9.5
Pneumococcus Vaccine (over 65)	30.0	25.0
Breast Exam (women)	36.9	35.2
Pap Smear (women)	29.8	28.4
Rx Filled	49.1	47.2
Child Physical Exam	43.5	32.8
Child Urine Test	23.3	17.5
Child Vision Test	15.9	12.3
Child Hearing Test	14.8	11.1
Child Rx Filled	48.3	44.4

ACCURACY OF RECALL.   Of the 739 persons who participated in this experiment, we were able to verify medical information of 660 people. The analyses described in this section pertain only to the 660 verified cases.

For ten of the twelve procedures, we computed three scores. From the medical records, we found the percentage of people who actually had the procedure during the previous two months. We compared this to the percentage who reported having the procedure during the previous two months. We then calculated the extent of overreporting by subtracting actual procedures from recalled procedures. These computations are shown in table 11 for respondents who recalled over the two-month reference period. The n's refer to the number of people who were asked about the procedure and for whom verification could be obtained.

The data in table 11 reveal consistent overreporting. It ranges from 2% for the flu vaccine to over 6% for the breast exam and blood pressure check. The median amount of overreporting across procedures was 3.7%. In table 12 the same data are presented for the six-month reference period. Here even more massive overreporting is apparent. Overreporting ranges from a low of about 7% for the mammogram to a high of nearly 20% for the flu vaccine. The median amount of overreporting across procedures was 12.5%.

Notice that the prescription data are not included in the above analyses. They were deliberately omitted because of the following problem. The respondents were asked whether they had filled a *new* prescription (for themselves or their child) during the reference period. In retrospect this

Table 11   Experiment 4: Two-Time Frame: Overreporting for Two Months.

	n	Percent Recalled	Percent Actual	Overreporting Difference	Over-reporting Ratio
Blood Pressure Reading	486	31.3	25.1	6.2	1.25
Colon Cancer Test	487	6.0	2.1	3.9	2.86
Mammogram (women over 40)	119	7.6	3.4	4.2	2.24
Pneumococcus Vaccine (over 65)	49	2.0	0.0	2.0	—
Breast Exam (women)	265	16.2	9.8	6.4	1.65
Pap Smear (women)	266	12.0	7.1	4.9	1.69
Child Physical Exam	171	13.0	10.1	2.9	1.29
Child Urine Test	168	8.2	4.7	3.5	1.75
Child Vision Test	171	5.8	2.3	3.5	2.52
Child Hearing Test	170	4.7	1.2	3.5	3.92

wording was unfortunate. Suppose a respondent got a prescription that could be refilled once. If the doctor reissued the prescription, should it be classified as *new* or not? A second problem arose with the medical record data. The medical record data provided dates on which prescriptions were filled but did not distinguish between old and new prescriptions. This meant that we had numerous instances in which respondents told us that they had not had a new prescription filled, but the records told us that prescriptions had been filled, leading to massive but misleading underreporting. Given these problems, the only sensible thing to do was to ignore the prescription data.

For all other procedures we found massive overreporting. We now can ask whether the overreporting problem is different as a function of being asked about a single-time frame versus two-time frames. To see how our analyses were done consider the blood pressure check, for which we provide complete data for the two-month reference period in table 13. In the 2-6 condition, 29.8% recalled having a blood pressure check, which was quite close to the percentages recalling this procedure in the other two conditions (31.8% in the 6-2 condition and 32.1% in the 1-2 condition). However, when one subtracts the actual percentages from the recalled percentages in each of the three conditions, it becomes evident that overreporting is a more serious problem

Table 12 Experiment 4: Two-Time Frame: Overreporting for Six Months.

	n	Percent Recalled	Percent Actual	Overreporting Difference	Over-reporting Ratio
Blood Pressure Reading	312	59.6	44.6	15.0	1.34
Colon Cancer Test	315	19.4	7.0	12.4	2.77
Mammogram (women over 40)	84	16.7	9.5	7.2	1.76
Pneumococcus Vaccine (over 65)	36	27.8	8.3	19.5	3.35
Breast Exam (women)	172	36.0	17.4	18.6	2.07
Pap Smear (women)	173	28.9	16.2	12.7	1.78
Child Physical Exam	117	38.5	26.5	12.0	1.45
Child Urine Test	119	21.0	10.9	10.1	1.93
Child Vision Test	121	14.0	6.6	7.4	2.12
Child Hearing Test	118	13.6	5.9	7.7	2.31

in the 2-6 condition than in the other two conditions. In the 2-6 condition the overreporting of blood pressure checks is 10.5% (29.8% − 19.3%), whereas in the 6-2 condition it is only 3.1% and in the 1-2 condition it is 4.7%. Thus, there is overreporting in all three conditions, but it is greatest when the two-month reference period is asked about first.

Another observation from table 13 concerns the false alarms, that is, cases in which people recalled having their blood pressure checked, but their record did not confirm this. The false-alarm rate was 50% in the 2-6 condition, but it was lower when another question preceded the one about the two-month reference period (32% in the 6-2 condition and 29.6% in the 1-2 condition). In short, false alarms occurred much less often with the two-time-frame approach.

In contrast to false alarms, the pattern for misses was different. Misses occurred when people had had their blood pressure checked in the previous two months but claimed they had not. In the 2-6 condition 22.6% of actual blood pressure checks were not recalled by respondents, as compared with a somewhat higher number in the 6-2 condition (24.4%) and a slightly lower number in the 1-2 condition (17.4%). Thus, misses were unaffected by the use of the two-time-frame approach.

Table 13   Blood Pressure Check—Two Months.

| Two-Month Question First | Medical Records | | |
	Had Test	Did Not	Total
Participants' Response:			
Yes, I had my B.P. checked	24	24	48
		50.0%	29.8%
No, I did not	7	106	113
	22.6%		70.2%
Total	31	130	161
	19.3%	80.7%	100.0%

| Two-Month Question Following Six-Month Question | Medical Records | | |
	Had Test	Did Not	Total
Participants' Response:			
Yes, I had my B.P. checked	34	16	50
		32.0%	31.8%
No, I did not	11	96	107
	24.4%		68.2%
Total	45	112	157
	28.7%	71.3%	100.0%

| Two-Month Question Following One-Month Question | Medical Records | | |
	Had Test	Did Not	Total
Participants' Response:			
Yes, I had my B.P. checked	38	16	54
		29.6%	32.1%
No, I did not	8	106	114
	17.4%		67.9%
Total	46	122	168
	27.4%	72.6%	100.0%

The blood pressure data for the six-month reference period are shown in table 14. Here we compare the 6-2 condition to the 2-6 condition, the condition in which a shorter reference period is asked about first. Notice that the two-time-frame condition (2-6) led to almost 9% more false alarms but about 4% fewer misses than the 6-2 condition. A similar pattern can be easily seen in the breast exam data. In the two-month condition overreporting was 6.4%. All three conditions show overreporting for a breast exam during the

Table 14   Blood Pressure Check—Six Months.

	Medical Records		
Six-Month Question First	Had Test	Did Not	Total
Participants' Response:			
Yes, I had my B.P. checked	66	30	96
		31.2%	61.9%
No, I did not	12	47	59
	15.4%		38.1%
Total	78	77	155
	50.3%	49.7%	100.0%

	Medical Records		
Six-Month Question Following Two-Month Question:	Had Test	Did Not	Total
Participants' Response:			
Yes, I had my B.P. checked	54	36	90
		40.0%	57.3%
No, I did not	7	60	67
	11.5%		42.7%
Total	61	96	157
	38.9%	61.1%	100.0%

two-month reference period. However, the overreporting is greater when the two-month reference period is asked about first (11% overreporting), compared to when it is asked about second (7.3% overreporting for the 6-2 condition and 1.1% overreporting for the 1-2 condition). The false-alarm rate was high in all conditions. Of those who claimed to have had a breast exam, 77% were false alarms in the 2-6 condition, whereas this figure was lower in the 6-2 condition (53%) and in the 1-2 condition (36%). Misses were lower than false alarms. Of those who actually had a breast exam, 43% failed to report it in the 2-6 condition, whereas the miss rate was lower in the two-time-frame conditions (22% in the 6-2 condition and 30% in the 1-2 condition). In sum, overreporting occurred in all conditions, but it was highest when the two-month reference period was asked about first. This condition also led to a higher false-alarm and miss rate than the other two conditions in which the two-month reference period was preceded by an earlier question.

For most of the procedures we inquired about, there were so few individuals who had actually had them or who recalled them that it became meaningless to discuss differences in overreporting as a function of one- versus two-time frames. Consider the pneumococcus (flu) vaccine question asked of individuals over the age of 65. Only 36 individuals provided verified data for the six-month reference period and 49 individuals provided verified data for the two-month reference period. No one in the sample actually had the procedure in the previous two months, thus the one positive response is a false alarm. It happened to occur in the 6-2 condition, which produced a high false-alarm rate in this condition, relative to the 2-6 or 1-2 conditions, where it was zero. The false-alarm rate would then be 100% in the 6-2 condition and 0% in the other two conditions, but a report of these percentages would be highly misleading.

Discussion

When it comes to answering a question about a specific procedure that a person had in the recent past, overreporting occurs. It is more extensive over a six-month reference period than a two-month reference period. Yet, even after only two months, the extent of overreporting was 4% (across all procedures).

Can we do anything to reduce the overreporting that occurs in the two-month reference period? Crespi and Swinehart showed that asking first about a six-month reference period reduces overreporting. They never verified reporting to determine whether the lower reporting meant more accurate reporting. We did. We found that when it came to blood pressure checks and breast exams, the 6-2 condition led to far less overreporting than the 2-6 condition. There are several possible reasons for the beneficial effect of the 6-2 condition. The reason we favor is that it conveys to the respondent that the interviewer desires greater precision in responding. The precision hypothesis derives support from the observation that the 1-2 condition also produced more accurate responding.

One difference between our procedure and that of Crespi and Swinehart is that we gave respondents a date that marked the beginning of the reference period. The date was given once, at the beginning of the list of procedures inquired about, and thus may have been ignored or forgotten by some respondents. Those who did not keep the date in mind while working through the list of procedures may have not sensed that the question was demanding precision. The two-time-frame procedure might have worked only for this subgroup. This train of thought leads to the speculation that the beneficial effect of the two-time-frame procedure would have been even greater if the date had not been included.

General Discussion

Recollections about health events were obtained in this study, and these were compared to information gathered from medical records. Before we can even begin to talk about improving health memories, we need to know something about how accurate and complete these memories are.

The Errors People Make

We found that the errors that people make when they recall health events—that is, whether they under- or overreport—depend on exactly what people are being asked to recall. If asked to recall specific visits made over the previous year, people dramatically underreport. In experiment 1 fewer than 40% of actual visits were specifically recalled. If asked to estimate the number of visits made over the previous year, without specifically remembering each one, people still underreport, but to a lesser degree. In experiment 1 the estimate of visits made was 87% of actual visits. A similar pattern of underreporting was observed when people recalled their spouses' visits over the previous year.

By contrast, when people are asked whether they had a specific procedure (e.g., flu shot) in the recent past, they overreport. In experiment 4 the median amount of overreporting for the procedures we asked about in the six-month reference period was approximately 13%. For many procedures, two to three times as many people reported having had a procedure done as actually did.

Why do people underreport when asked about visits over the previous year and overreport when asked about a specific procedure? One possible explanation concerns the details inherent in the question and the amount of information required in the answer. Underreporting occurred when people were asked to report their visits and to give specific information (e.g., date, provider) about each one. This could have created a cautious criterion for responding. Also no specific cues as to type of visit were provided that might have helped guide the search. It also appears that simple forgetting of visits can explain some of the underreporting.

As noted earlier, underreporting still occurred when people estimated their total number of visits. However, it should be kept in mind that the estimate was produced after people tried to recall specific visits. Although we know there were instances of respondents being aware that there were more visits in their past than could be specifically produced, the recall of the specific visits may have influenced the estimate in another way; namely, after producing, say, two specific visits, the respondent may feel constrained not to report more, or at least not many more, visits in order to remain consistent.

Put another way, the production of specific visits may have anchored the estimate. A future study in which estimates are produced without a prior listing would be useful for resolving this issue.

In contrast, overreporting occurred when people were asked about a specific procedure (e.g., flu shot) in the recent past. In this case the cue inherent in the question was very detailed and could be used to guide the search (Norman and Bobrow, 1979; Tulving, 1983). Moreover, specific information about the visit was not required; the response was either yes or no. The cue could have caused some respondents to decide that the procedure was done and that, even if they were uncertain about a date, a yes response was appropriate.

Social desirability may also contribute to the underreporting of visits and overreporting of procedures that we observed here. If a respondent sees a report of many visits (nature unspecified) over the course of a year as a tacit admission of poor health, social-desirability concerns lead to underreporting. On the other hand, many questions about recent procedures (e.g., blood pressure check) imply a concern about health maintenance, a concern with preventive practices, and thus may carry with them a positive social-desirability component. Therefore, these questions create pressure to provide an affirmative response.

Reducing Errors

Given the amount of underreporting of visits and overreporting of procedures that we observed, it becomes worth our while to devise means of correcting these errors. This was, of course, the goal of experiments 1 to 4.

To reduce error in the reporting of visits, we manipulated the order in which respondents were asked to retrieve their visits (experiments 1 and 2). We found that if respondents were allowed to recall visits in any order they wished, they preferred the chronological (forward) order. However, when they were instructed to retrieve visits in a reverse chronological (backward) order, their responding was more accurate (significantly so when a spouse's visits were recalled). The backward order may be beneficial because it permits respondents to retrieve successfully a recent event that then provides cues to other events.

The advantage for the backward order resembles the advantages that we discussed earlier in the recollection of college exams (Loftus and Fathi, 1985). However, we should note that one other study involving memory for health visits did not find an advantage for the backward order but rather found a marginal advantage for the free order (Jobe, White, Kelley, Mingay, Sanchez, and Loftus, 1990). Several differences between the studies could potentially be responsible for the differing results. One difference concerns the type of patients included in the study. The Jobe et al. subjects generally received care from independent providers and thus received bills for services that could have served as memory reminders. Our subjects were members of an HMO and did not receive bills.

To reduce error in the reporting of procedures, we asked about procedures in either a single-time frame or two-time frames (experiment 4). We found that if respondents first answered about, say, a six-month reference period and then a two-month reference period, the overreporting problem was less severe than if we asked the two-month question first. The two-time-frame procedure may be beneficial because it conveys to the respondent a greater need for precision in answering. The two-time-frame procedure may also work for social-desirability reasons. If a respondent has the opportunity to mention a health maintenance procedure as having occurred during the longer reference period, the need to give a socially desirable response has been satisfied, and he or she does not need to mention it again during the shorter reference period. This specific social-desirability hypothesis does not explain the benefits of having a shorter reference period first. However, there is no reason why the short-first versus long-first approaches should necessarily be beneficial for exactly the same reasons.

Practical Implications

The methods studied here showed modest reductions in the errors of under- and overreporting of health events. Despite the use of these methods, however, many errors were still made. This means that new techniques—yet to be discovered—could do a better job of eliciting more accurate recollections of past health events. Two methods for improving health memory were studied by Means and Loftus (1991): the Decomposition method and the Time Line method. These were extraordinarily successful in improving memory, but they were also very time-consuming. What is needed now is the development of methods that are as efficient and economical as the ones studied here but with increased power to improve memory. A further collaboration between survey researchers and cognitive psychologists could profitably work toward this goal (Fienberg, Loftus, and Tanur, 1985).

This research was supported by Grant Number HS 05521 from the National Center for Health Services Research and Health Care Technology Assessment. We thank Peggy Schnell for her invaluable assistance in chart abstracting, and Don Johnson for his many hours of assistance with data analysis. Liz Fries provided important support throughout many phases of this project. Without our tireless student research assistants, this project would have taken three times as long, and for this help we thank LeAnn Davis, Jackie DuBois, Jeff Joyce, Marla Levin, Kris Morgan, Curt Small.

References

BADDELEY, A. (1979) The limitations of human memory: Implications for the design of retrospective surveys. In Moss, L., and GOLDSTEIN, H. (eds.). *The Recall Method in Social Surveys*. London: University of London Institute of Education.

BEAN, J. A., LEEPER, J. D., and WALLACE, R. B. (1979) Variations in the reporting ofmenstrual histories. *American Journal of Epidemiology* 109, 181–185.

CORWIN, R. G., KROBER, M., and ROTH, H. P. (1971) Patients' accuracy in reporting their past medical history: A study of 90 patients with peptic ulcer. *Journal of Chronic Disease* 23, 875–879.

CRESPI, I., and SWINEHART, J. W. (1982) Some effects of sequenced questions using different time intervals on behavioral self-reports: A field experiment. Paper presented at the annual conference of the American Association for Public Opinion Research, May.

CROWDER, R. G., and GREENE, R. L. (1987) On the remembrance of times past: The irregular list technique. *Journal of Experimental Psychology: General* 116, 265–278.

FATHI, D., SCHOOLER, J., and LOFTUS, E. (1984) Moving survey problems into the cognitive psychology laboratory. *Proceedings of the Survey Research Section, American Statistical Association*. Washington DC: American Statistical Association, pp. 19–21.

FELDMAN, J. J. (1960) The household interview survey as a technique for the collection of morbidity data. *Journal of Chronic Diseases* 11, 535–557.

FIENBERG, S. E., LOFTUS, E. F., and TANUR, J. M. (1985) Cognitive aspects of health surveys for public information and policy. *Milbank Memorial Fund Quarterly/Health and Society* 63, 598–614.

FISKE, S. T., and TAYLOR, S. E. (1984) *Social Cognition*, Reading, MA: Addison-Wesley.

GAROFALO, J., and HINDELANG, M. J. (1977) *An Introduction to the National Crime Survey*. Washington, DC: U.S. Department of Justice.

GILBRETH, F.,.B., and CAREY, E. G. (1948) *Cheaper by the Dozen*. New York: Crowell.

HASHER, L., and ZACKS, R. T. (1984) Automatic processing of fundamental information: A case of frequency of occurrence. *American Psychologist* 39, 1372–1388.

JABINE, T. B. (1985) Reporting chronic conditions in the national health interview survey: A review of findings from evaluation studies and methodological tests. Manuscript. Washington, DC: Department of Health and Human Services.

JOBE, J. B., WHITE, A. A., KELLEY, C. L., MINGAY, D. J., SANCHEZ, M. J., and LOFTUS, E. F. (1990) Recall strategies and memory for health care visits. *Milbank Memorial Fund Quarterly/Health and Society* 68, 171–189.

KILLEEN, P. R., and FETTERMAN, J. G. (1988) A behavioral theory of timing. *Psychological Review* 95, 274–295.

KING, D. L., and PONTIUS, R. H. (1969) Time relations in the recall of events of the day. *Psychonomic Science* 17, 339–340.

KUIPER, N. A., and ROGERS, T. B. (1979) Encoding of personal information: Self-other differences. *Journal of Personality and Social Psychology* 37, 499–514.

LOFTUS, E. F., and FATHI, D. C. (1985) Retrieving multiple autobiographical memories. *Social Cognition* 3, 280–295.

LOFTUS, E. F., KLINGER, M. R., SMITH, K. D., and FIEDLER, J. (1990) A tale of two questions: Benefits of asking more than one question. *Public Opinion Quarterly* 54, 330–345.

LOFTUS, E. F., and MARBURGER, W. (1983) Since the eruption of Mt. St. Helens, has anyone beaten you up? Improving the accuracy of retrospective reports with landmark events. *Memory and Cognition* 11, 114–120.

MARTIN, C. J. (1987) Monitoring maternity services by postal questionnaire: Congruity between mothers' reports and their obstetric records. *Statistics in Medicine* 6, 613–627.

MEANS, B., and LOFTUS, E. F. (1991) When personal history repeats itself: Decomposing memories for recurring events. *Applied Cognitive Psychology*.

NORMAN, D. A., and BOBROW, D. G. (1979) Descriptions: An intermediate stage in memory retrieval. *Cognitive Psychology* 11, 107–123.

PARKER, B. K., and GLOVER, R. L. (1987) Event duration memory: The effects of delay-interval illumination and instructional cuing. *Animal Learning and Behavior* 15, 241–248.

Reporting of hospitalization in the health interview survey. (1965) (Public Health Service, DHEW-HSM Publication No 73-1261.) Washington DC: U.S. Government Printing Office, July.

RUBIN, D. C., ed. (1986) *Autobiographical Memory*. Cambridge, England: Cambridge University Press.

SUDMAN, S., and BRADBURN, N. M. (1973) Effects of time and memory factors on response in surveys. *Journal of the American Statistical Association* 68, 805–815.

THOMPSON, C. P. (1982) Memory for unique personal events: The roommate study. *Memory and Cognition* 10, 324–332.

TILLEY, B. C., BARNES, A. B., BERGSTRALH, E., LABARTHE, D., NOLLER, K. L., COLTON, T., and ADAM, E. (1985) A comparison of pregnancy history recall and medical records. *American Journal of Epidemiology* 121, 269–281.

TULVING, E. (1983) *Elements of Episodic Memory*. New York: Oxford University Press.

WHITE, A. A., and MASSEY, J. T. (1981) Selective reduction of response bias in a household interview survey. *American Statistical Association Proceedings*, Social Statistics Section, 211–216.

7

Attempts to Improve the Accuracy of Self-Reports of Voting

ROBERT P. ABELSON, ELIZABETH F. LOFTUS, and ANTHONY G. GREENWALD

An important self-reported behavior for which survey data are beset with inaccuracies is that of voting. Comparisons of actual vote counts with retrospective answers to the question, "Did you vote?" consistently find a tendency toward overreporting of voting. This is the case both in studies that simply compare aggregate real voting percentages with aggregate claimed voting percentages and in studies that validate voting claims separately for each individual survey respondent. The latter procedure is troublesome to carry out, necessitating a good deal of search of public records, but it yields more sensitive information. In this chapter we shall confine our attention to this more sensitive type of study.

The rate of vote misses in reporting—the percentage among those actually voting who report that they hadn't—is small, typically less than 5%. By contrast, the rate of false alarms—the percentage among those who didn't vote but say that they had—is sizable, often as high as 25% or 30%. Specifically, checks of the voting records of respondents on the National Election Surveys (NES) found the following percentages of false alarms: 27% in 1964, 31% in 1976, 23% in 1978, and 27% in 1980 (Silver, Anderson, and Abramson, 1986). (High rates have been maintained in more recent elections, as we will detail below.)

The consequences of these errors are potentially serious for analyses of the correlates of vote turnout. Vote-validation checks are too expensive to be carried out for every election one might want to study. Reports of preelection intention to vote are untrustworthy, and the cheapest and most straightforward way to identify actual voters would therefore seem to be to tap respondents' memories of having voted. The overreporting tendency, however, pollutes the pool of apparent voters with impostors whose characteristics may well be different from those of true voters. Understanding why vote overreporting occurs, and how to diminish it, could serve a double purpose: It would lead to cleaner analyses of the correlates of voting behavior and, beyond that, would contribute toward a general model of how to improve answers to questions that rely on reconstructive memory.

Vote overreporting, we should note, is not typically attributed to failure of memory. Postelection reports are usually gathered within several days, or at most within two or three weeks, of the election. Unlike sporadic events, such as visits to doctors six months ago, it does not seem plausible that one would readily get confused in the short run over whether one had participated in the distinctive communal event of going to the voting booth on Election Day.

Rather, the assumption has been that false reports of voting are given for reasons of social desirability. (See Presser, 1990, for a representative statement of this assumption.) Voting is widely touted as an act of good citizenship, and it is not hard to imagine that many nonvoters want to avoid the unflattering attribution that they are bad citizens. Indeed, Silver, Anderson, and Abramson (1986) found that potential voters who endorse norms of political participation are more likely to falsely report voting. Silver, Abramson, and Anderson (1986), in a related analysis, reported that among nonvoters, those who before the election had claimed an *intention* to vote were more likely to claim afterward that they had actually voted. Also, when a social group is stimulated to vote in greater numbers, its members have an increased tendency to tell interviewers they have voted even when they haven't (Anderson, Silver, and Abramson, 1988). Finally, other self-flattering social and political acts, such as donating to the community chest (Parry and Crossley, 1950) or having voted for a winner rather than a loser (Clausen, 1968), are also typically overreported.

The potential social-desirability artifact in self-reports of voting was indeed recognized long ago by the writers of the NES vote report question, who included the following prophylactic preamble:

> In talking to people about elections, we often find that a lot of people were not able to vote because they weren't registered, they were sick, or they just didn't have time. How about you—did you vote in the elections this November?

The intention of this preamble is to make nonvoting seem socially permissible, but overreporting has not been forestalled by this manipulation of question wording.

In the hope that some alternative way of posing the vote report question would be less susceptible to overreporting, we conducted wording experiments on three surveys for which vote validation records were available. Two of these experiments involved a variation of the two-time-frame procedure discussed in the previous chapter. We first describe the results of the experimental manipulations; then we treat other aspects of our data; and we conclude with a discussion of the probable roles of social desirability and faulty memory on vote overreporting.

Applying the Two-Time-Frame Procedure: Experiment 1

Consider a respondent who is asked, "Did you vote in the Congressional elections of 1986?" and falsely replies yes. Two explanations for this bias are memory confusion and social desirability. If the question is asked shortly after the election, memory confusion seems unlikely, but in our experiment 1 the key survey was taken in May 1987. This was six and a half months after the elections, and it is conceivable that some respondents might have telescoped remembered voting behavior forward from 1984, or even 1982. As we have seen with health-related behaviors, one method for inhibiting forward telescoping is to insert, prior to the target question, an introductory question with a broader time frame. This is what we did for a random half of the respondents on the 1987 NES pilot study. The introductory question, which we label (ME) for "multiple elections," was:

> (ME)   Thinking back over the last four national elections, that is, the Presidential elections of 1980 and 1984, and the Congressional elections of 1982 and 1986, did you vote in any of these elections?

For the remaining half of the respondents, this introductory question was omitted. All respondents were then asked the target question (TQ) of whether they had voted in the most recent particular election of 1986.

In order to maintain comparability with past NES data, the introductory sentence offering excuses for nonvoting was retained. Putting these ingredients together, two forms of vote-self-report questions were created. Form 1 is the single-time-frame condition and form 2 is the two-time-frame condition.

> (Form 1)   In talking to people about elections, we often find that a lot of people were not able to vote because they weren't registered, they were sick, or they just didn't have time. How about you—

(TQ1)   Did you vote in the 1986 elections for United States Congress last November?

(Form 2) In talking to people about elections, we often find that a lot of people were not able to vote because they weren't registered, they were sick, or they just didn't have time. How about you—

(ME)   Thinking back over the last four national elections, that is, the Presidential elections of 1980 and 1984, and the Congressional elections of 1982 and 1986, did you vote in any of these elections?

(TQ2)   Did you vote in the 1986 elections for United States Congress last November?

Our thinking was that there might be diminished overreporting on (TQ2) compared to (TQ1), because the (ME) question could stimulate veridical memories of actually having voted in an earlier election instead of the one in 1986. But what about the social-desirability factor? Would the two-time-frame procedure encourage more truthful reporting on the target question? Our hypothesis was that it would, because respondents could say yes, they had voted in one or more of the set of past elections, satisfying a minimal norm of good citizenship, and thus decreasing the pressure to misrepresent their 1986 vote.

Table 1 presents the results for registered voters for whom it could be clearly established whether or not they had actually voted. It is important in analyses of overreporting to give the complete data set, lest different ways of summarizing error percentages create confusion (for a case in point, see

Table 1   Voting Report Accuracy by Experimental Condition: Experiment 1.

Form 1 (N = 144) (TQ only)	Six to Seven Months After Election Self-Report	
	I Voted	I Didn't
Actually Voted	95	4
Actually Didn't	17	28
Form 2 (N = 165) (TQ after ME)	Self-Report	
	I Voted	I Didn't
Actually Voted	108	4
Actually Didn't	22	31

Cahalan, 1968). Our table, therefore, gives the cross-tabulation of frequencies of actual vote by reported vote by question form. The results are disappointing. Of nonvoters in the form 1, single-time-frame condition, we found that $17/(17 + 28) = 17/45$, or 37.8%, claimed to have voted; in the form 2, two-time-frame condition, $22/53$, or 41.5%, made such a claim. The difference between these two percentages is nowhere near statistically significant and is in the wrong direction anyway. Of note also is the fact that question form makes no difference either in the rate of vote misses: In the control condition, 4 out of 99 actual voters (4.0%) report that they had not voted, compared to 4 out of 112 (3.6%) in the experimental condition.

Applying a Modified Two-Time-Frame Procedure: Experiment 2

Our assumption had been that saying yes to a query about voting in any of the past four elections would relieve the respondent of the pressure to appear virtuous by claiming participation in the most recent election. The prequestion indeed elicited yeses—in fact, in 95% of the relevant cases—but this did not diminish the proclivity to overstate voting in the target 1986 election. Why not? Perhaps our judgment of the respondents' tendencies is flawed. Perhaps saying yes to the prequestion serves in many people to increase, not decrease, the salience of norms of good citizenship. In other words, many citizens might think, "If it's good to vote in some elections, it's good to have voted in this particular one." In our second and third experiments, we tried to turn this around to the notion, "If you can't vote in all elections, maybe it's all right not to have voted in this one."

Experiment 2, conducted in Seattle, Washington, in 1988–1989, was designed with several purposes in mind. Publicly available voting records in the state of Washington are extraordinarily well organized, summarizing by voter's name and place(s) of residence his or her vote participation in every national, state, and local election in the 1980s. This offered a unique opportunity for empirical exploration of a potential memory-confusion factor: if false reports of voting are the result of memory intrusions from earlier acts of voting, then people who have more frequently voted would be more likely to commit such errors. (This conjectured type of error was dubbed a "persistence forecast" by Cahalan, 1968).

Experiment 2 also included a variation on the two-time-frame procedure. We describe this procedure now, and return later to an analysis of the effects of the vote-frequency factor. The target vote question concerned a senatorial primary election in September 1988. Voting in this primary was potentially confusable with the later presidential vote of November 1988 as well as with primary and regular election votes from prior years. A random sample in the Seattle area was contacted by telephone in December 1988, and a second random sample in May 1989. Each sample was subdivided into two conditions.

In the experimental two-time-frame condition, the target question was preceded by a question asking whether the respondent had voted in *both* the September primary and the regular November election. The purpose of this prequestion was to encourage people to consider a negative response, on the grounds that one shouldn't be expected to vote all the time. We thought that this induced tilt toward saying no might reduce false alarms on the target question.

The exact wordings of the two conditions were as follows (form 1 is the single-time-frame condition):

(Form 1)   There were two elections last fall—the primary election on September 20th and the Presidential election on November 8th. In talking to people about elections we often find that a lot of people were not able to vote because they weren't registered, they were sick, or they just didn't have the time. How about you—

(Target)   Specifically, did you vote in the primary election last September 20th?

(Form 2)   There were two elections last fall—the primary election on September 20th and the Presidential election on November 8th. Most people aren't able to get to vote in every election. How about you—

("Both")   Did you vote in BOTH the September and November elections? . . . Let me make sure I haven't confused you—

(Target)   Specifically, did you vote in the primary election last September 20th?

We first analyze this two-time-frame manipulation by looking separately at data from December 1988 (three months after the target election), and from May 1989 (eight months after the target election). Table 2 displays the results for registered voters for whom vote validation data were available.

Note that the rates of false alarms are quite high: three months after the target election the proportions of nonvoters claiming to have voted are 21/64, or 32.8%, for the single-question condition and 21/69, or 30.4%, for the two-question condition; eight months after election the false-alarm proportions are 25/41, or 61.0%, for the single- and 27/50, or 54.0%, for the two-question condition. The rates are lower in the respective two-question

Table 2   Voting Report Accuracy by Experimental Condition: Experiment 2.

	Three Months After Election Self-Report	
Form 1 (N = 161) (Target only)	I Voted	I Didn't
Actually Voted	93	4
Actually Didn't	21	43
Form 2 (N = 160) (Target + prequestion)	Self-Report	
	I Voted	I Didn't
Actually Voted	87	4
Actually Didn't	21	48
	Eight Months After Election Self-Report	
Form 1 (N = 111) (Target only)	I Voted	I Didn't
Actually Voted	69	1
Actually Didn't	25	16
Form 2 (N = 124) (Target + prequestion)	Self-Report	
	I Voted	I Didn't
Actually Voted	66	8
Actually Didn't	27	23

groups, but nonsignificantly. Moreover, the rate of vote *misses* is (nonsignificantly) *higher* with the two-question form: after a three-month delay, 4.1% for the control versus 4.4% for the two-question condition; after eight months, 1.4% for the control versus 10.8% for the experimental condition. Thus, if any systematic question condition difference were to be attributed to the data, it would be that the two-question procedure encourages lower claims of having voted in the target election among actual voters and nonvoters alike. Even if the "both elections" prequestion tends to make voting claims a bit more modest, as expected, it does not make them more accurate.

Anyway, none of these hinted condition effects in the data are statistically reliable. A four-way log-linear analysis (Wickens, 1989) on the frequencies in table 2 yields as a clearly best-fitting model one in which question condition is unrelated to the other three factors: The model [Q][SVD], where Q is question form, S is self-report, V is actual vote, and D is time delay, has a 7 d.f. likelihood ratio chi-square of 7.87 (p > .25). We will discuss the interpretation of the effects of time delay on vote report accuracy in a later section, after concluding our pursuit of question form effects.

A Further Try at a Wording Variation

In a third experiment we made one further try at a wording variation that might diminish overreporting. Abandoning the two-time-frame idea, we tried a direct attack on a major puzzle underlying the whole phenomenon; namely, the failure of the carefully crafted preamble that tries to make nonvoting permissible (". . . people were not able to vote because they weren't registered, they were sick, or they just didn't have time").

A possible flaw in this preamble is that it flows awkwardly into the target question. After giving three reasons why a possible voter might *not* be able to vote, the text then proceeds to the question, "*Did* you vote?" Instead, a more natural sequel might concern the respondent's *inability* to vote, worded, for example, in terms of "missing out" on voting. Posing the question in the miss-out form has the virtue not only of being syntactically more natural, but also turns an excuse for *non*voting into an affirmative yes response. If yeasaying reinforces social desirability in the "Did you vote?" form, this reinforcement should be removed in the "Did you miss out?" form.

The vehicle for experiment 3 was the 1989 NES pilot study on a national sample of respondents whose 1988 voting records had been validated. The interviews were conducted in July 1989. The control condition, applied to a random half of the sample, was the standard NES vote question with the preamble (see form 1 of experiment 1). In the experimental condition the preamble was the same, but "Did you vote in the elections last November?" was replaced with, "Did you miss out on voting in the elections last November?" Table 3 displays the results for registered voters.

Once more the wording manipulation made no significant difference. The false-alarm rates are 31/55, or 56.4%, for the standard question form and 28/48, or 58.3%, for the miss-out form. These rates are quite high, compara-

Table 3   Voting Report Accuracy by Experimental Condition: Experiment 3.

Form 1 (N = 262) (Did you vote?)	Eight Months After Election Self-Report	
	I Voted	I Didn't
Actually Voted	202	5
Actually Didn't	31	24
Form 2 (N = 242) (Did you miss out?)	Self-Report	
	No Miss	Missed
Actually Voted	192	2
Actually Didn't	28	20

ble to those in the eight-month-delay conditions of experiment 2 (although we shall see later that overreporting of 1988 voting was high even with shorter delay). To add insult to experimental injury, the direction of the minuscule difference in false-alarm rates between the two conditions is opposite to hypothesis, with the miss-out wording leading to (nonsignificantly) more overclaiming. We postpone possible explanations of why our question manipulations were consistently ineffective until we have looked at other aspects of our data.

The Effect of Time Delay on Accuracy of Reporting

Setting aside question manipulation as ineffective in experiments 1 to 3, we can proceed to look at other aspects of the data. All three studies permit inspection of the effects of time delay on the tendency to overreport voting. Table 2 from experiment 2 above has already given some evidence that overreporting gets worse with longer delay. For experiments 1 and 3 we displayed only the data pertinent to our question-wording experiments, which were run six or eight months after election. But data are also available from NES on earlier self-reports by the same subjects from postelection telephone surveys approximately two weeks after the vote. (These data did not include a wording manipulation).

Table 4a gives the false-alarm percentages at each delay for each experiment. (The data were collapsed over the statistically insignificant question-wording conditions in all the relevant cases). We see that overreporting increases with delay in all three studies, though in experiment 3—conducted in a presidential year—false alarming was extraordinarily high right after the election and increased only trivially eight months later. Experiments 1 and 3 involved the same subjects across the two-time delays, thus introducing correlated proportions, and experiment 2 involved different subjects, entailing independent proportions. Applying the respectively appropriate significance tests for the effects of delay on false alarming, we obtain critical ratios

Table 4a False-Alarm Rates by Time Delay Since the Designated Election (numbers of nonvoters in parentheses).

Expt. 1 (Nov. 1986)		Expt. 2 (Sept. 1988)		Expt. 3 (Nov. 1988)	
.5 mos.	6.5 mos.	3 mos.	8 mos.	.5 mos.	8 mos.
16.3%	40.0%	31.6%	57.1%	54.4%	57.3%
(98)	(98)	(133)	(91)	(103)	(103)

Table 4b   Miss Rates (failures to report actual votes) by Time Delay (numbers of nonvoters in parentheses).

Expt. 1 (Nov. 1986)		Expt. 2 (Sept. 1988)		Expt. 3 (Nov. 1988)	
.5 mos.	6.5 mos.	3 mos.	8 mos.	.5 mos.	8 mos.
.9%	3.8%	4.8%	6.3%	.5%	1.7%
(211)	(211)	(168)	(144)	(401)	(401)

$z = 3.77$, 3.81, and 0.69 for the three experiments. The average z is 2.76, $p < .01$ by the Stouffer test (Rosenthal, 1984).

Before it be hastily concluded that because overreporting increases with time delay, the social desirability of voting grows with greater distance from an election (an implausible result on the face of it), it is necessary to consider the effects of delay on the opposite type of error: actual voters reporting that they didn't vote. Table 4b gives these miss rates. Here, again, there are increases in error with longer delay, consistent over the three studies. The absolute sizes of the percentage increases are smaller than those for false alarms, but the *relative* increases are larger in two of the three studies. The statistical significance tests of the respective delay effects, calculated in the same fashion as for the false alarms, yield $z = 2.12$, 0.58, and 1.89, with an average of 1.53, $p < .01$ by the Stouffer test.

The significance tests for the two types of errors yield similar assessments: greater delay appears to induce both more false alarms and more misses, rather than simply more false alarms. In other words, long delay promotes *general inaccuracy*. It would be misleading to say instead that long delay enhances only the tendency to claim having voted. If delay simply promotes social-desirability bias, failures to report actual voting should decline over time, not increase.

The appropriate interpretation of delay effects is captured most clearly by log-linear analysis (Wickens, 1989), which copes with the great disparities in absolute frequencies by referring them to a logarithmic scale. Because of the differences in design, experiments 1 and 3 have to be handled differently from experiment 2. The latter is easiest to explain, as follows: We fit the saturated [VSD] model (V = vote, S = self-report, D = delay), and then inspect the log-linear parameters (lambdas) for the three-variable interaction and for the simple self-report by delay interaction. The question at issue is whether the three-way data can be completely explained by a general degradation in accuracy with greater delay, or whether there is also a greater net tendency with longer delay to claim to have voted. Applying the [VSD] model to the data of table 2 collapsed over question form, the estimate of the lambda parameter for the three-way interaction of actual vote by self-report by delay is .169, which is 2.35 times its standard error. The simple interaction of self-report by delay yields a lambda of .097, which is only 1.35 times its standard error—in other words, not significantly different from zero.

In experiments 1 and 3, both panel studies, the categorical variables are actual vote, V; early self-report, E; and late self-report, L. In each data set, all three variables are pairwise associated; that is, the model [VE][VL][EL] fits. The question here is whether the estimated lambda parameter for the association of vote with late report is significantly lower than the estimated lambda for the association of vote with early report. These estimates are correlated, and the details tricky. We applied Haberman's (1979) FREQ program to the case at hand, and the outcome is a clearly significant difference in the direction of declining general accuracy over time for experiment 1, and a similar, albeit nonsignificant, trend for experiment 3. The competitive data interpretation is that the main effect lambdas for E and L are significantly different, with self-reports of voting becoming more frequent at the later time, but the evidence for this is nil. There is no difference whatever in experiment 1, and in experiment 3 the difference is (nonsignificantly) in the wrong direction.

Thus, the results of the log-linear analyses are clear: In all three studies, accuracy of report declines with greater delay, significantly so except in experiment 3. The odds ratios associated with accurate reporting are very high (primarily due to the large number of actual voters giving true reports), but these odd ratios decline over the (roughly) half-year delays in the three studies by factors of at least 4 and as much as 13. As we know already, there is a general bias in the direction of higher reported than actual voting, but *it is a consistent result of the three studies that the overreporting bias, as such, does not significantly increase with delay*,[1] and the sizes of these nonsignificant bias changes are not even suggestive, netting out to a virtual zero over the three studies.

Voting Habits
as Sources of Reporting Inaccuracy

On the hypothesis that inaccuracy of vote reporting might be partly accounted for by past voting habits, a vote-rate variable was calculated for each respondent in experiment 2. The record included irregular (non-November)

---

1. In one of many alternative analyses of the data from experiment 2, a five-way log-linear analysis, including actual vote, self-report, delay, and two voting habit variables (see next section), the self-report by delay interaction attained the .03 level. We are not inclined to attach importance to this one exception, in view of the general failure to find this interaction in other analyses or data sets.

votes, such as primaries, as well as regular biennial votes. Vote-rate was calculated as the number of pre-September 1988 votes in the record divided by the number of years in the interval from the oldest vote in the record to September 1988; for example, if there were three pre-September 1988 votes and the oldest was in November 1984, the VOTERATE variable would be (3/3.83) = .78. A separate, dichotomous variable was created to index whether or not the respondent had ever voted in an irregular election. This variable, denoted IRR_VOTR, was included on the grounds that people might use as a memory aid in vote report the self-concept, "I only vote in November elections."

In separate analyses of December 1988 and May 1989 data, we used self-report as the (dichotomous) criterion variable, and three predictor variables: actual vote in September 1988 (REALVOTE); VOTERATE; and IRR_VOTR. For clarity of interpretation, we ran ordinary multiple regressions with data pooled over the ineffective question manipulation. The results are displayed in Table 5.

This analysis establishes that past voting habits have statistically significant predictive value for vote-self-reports, over and above the accurate contribution of the actual vote. In other words, past habits (as indexed by typical voting rate and by the proclivity to vote in non-November elections) help predict *errors* in self-reports: the habitual voter is more apt falsely to claim having voted, and the habitual nonvoter tends to deny a true vote. These effects are small but occur for delays of both three months and eight months. (Incidentally, not shown in table 5 is the variable NOVEMVOT, the record of whether the respondent voted in the November 1988 presidential election. It is a weak and insignificant predictor of the reported September 1988 vote, by itself or in combination with the other predictors). It is the case, as previously noted,

Table 5   Self-Report Regressed on Real Vote, Vote-Rate, and Irregular Vote: Experiment 2 (September 1988).

Variable	Self-Report in December 1988 (N = 301)				Self-Report in May 1989 (N = 235)			
	B†	SE	t	R-sq.°	B†	SE	t	R-sq.°
REALVOTE	.577	.045	12.95	.471	.311	.055	5.69	.208
VOTERATE	.090	.039	2.31	.485	.126	.050	2.53	.241
IRR_VOTE	.145	.073	2.00	.492	.208	.103	2.01	.255

†Regression coefficients are unstandardized.
°The values given for multiple R-squared are the cumulative values when the variables are entered stepwise, up to and including the indicated variable. The regression coefficients, on the other hand, are given for the final step, including all three predictors.

that accuracy falls off rather precipitously with the longer delay (*R*-squared for REALVOTE alone is .208 at eight months as opposed to .471 at three months).

We have also run analyses with the more sophisticated alternative of logistic regression, instead of ordinary multiple regression. The conclusions remain the same.

Discussion of Results

The major phenomenon with which we started this research is the persistent bias toward vote overreporting, and it is again strongly manifest in our three data sets. The tendency of a large fraction of registered respondents who haven't voted to report that they have is apparently a very hardy artifact. Three sets of facts are noteworthy:

1. In contrast to the overreporting of medical visits, vote overreporting is not diminished by the two-time-frame procedure, as embodied with a prequestion about voting in *any* of the past four elections or a prequestion about voting in *both* of the past two elections. Consistent with these negative results, Presser (1990) has recently found that asking about voting in *most* elections fails to decrease overreporting on a subsequent target question.

2. Vote overreporting survives a preamble that attempts to provide excuses for nonvoting, and a question change that forces people actively to reject those excuses in order to overreport.

3. With increasing time delay since the election, the bias toward overreporting remains and, in addition, there is an increase in reporting errors of both kinds: claiming a nonvote and denying an actual vote. In part, these inaccuracies are associated with typical past history as a voter or nonvoter.

If vote overreporting is primarily a social-desirability artifact, it is clear that the two-time-frame procedure and other "did you/didn't you" wording variants are of no help in reducing the bias. Nor is the two-time-frame technique a cure for the forward telescoping of fuzzy memories of voting, an error source implied in paragraph 3 above.

Why should the norm of being a voter loom so large in the interview situation when, in actual behavior, voting is not so desirable as to produce overwhelming turnouts? Indeed, in American culture there are many expressions of the alienated counternorm of staying away from the polls because the parties don't differ, politicians are sleazy, or the political process fails to address serious problems.

One way to explain this discrepancy is by the situational context of the survey interview. Almost invariably when vote-self-reports are elicited, many of the other questions concern preferences for candidates and attitudes toward political issues. Even without survey content manifestly addressed to the politically active citizen, the mere presentation of the interviewer as a representative of democracy's establishment may be sufficient to activate norms of citizen duty and suppress cynical counternorms. If the interview context makes citizen duty very salient, this might override the attempted influence of the question-framing manipulations.

While this explanation has a ring of plausibility to it, we would do well to consider some other factors. Individual differences among voters should not be overlooked: Confirmed cynics may freely admit that they have not voted; indeed, Silver, Anderson, and Abramson (1986) have found that those who do not explicitly endorse good citizenship norms are less prone to overreport their votes. Although the recognition of individual differences reduces the apparent tension between the norm of voting and the counternorm of scorning the political process, we are still left with some puzzlement as to why the tendency toward vote overreporting is quite so high, and as to what to do about it. Subtle wording changes have persistently failed; perhaps only a blunt approach such as the interviewer pointedly mentioning the intention to check the respondent's report with the actual voting records could succeed.

Let us take one more look at memory failure as an explanation for overreporting. Another relevant characteristic of voting behavior is that at fixed intervals a window of opportunity arrives, and one either does or doesn't act. Perhaps it is easier to remember accurately that one *did* do something (a positive instance), than that one *did not* do something (a negative instance), reminiscent of the well-known superiority of positive over negative instances in concept formation (Hunt, 1962). Given that voting is a private—and infrequent—action, and that discussions of voting behavior by the general public are probably perfunctory and short-lived, there is very little residue of experienced consequences by which one might retrieve the fact of *not* having voted in a given election. It is interesting to consider other actions that are appropriate only at widely separated fixed intervals and that leave hardly a clue for a memory search to seize upon. For example, suppose respondents were asked in February or March, "Did you leave a Christmas bonus for the mail carrier?" or asked in November, "Did you request the optional annual inspection of your furnace last spring?" Such questions, we conjecture, might be subject to the same overreporting bias as is voting behavior. The respondent who did leave the bonus or request the inspection might well remember some detail of the action, enabling an accurate yes response, whereas the respondent who didn't take action might have to fall back on thinking, "Well, I don't specifically remember, but that's the appropriate thing to have done, and I usually do, so I must have."

This line of speculation could also explain the apparent intrusion of past voting habits into present voting reports (in experiment 2), without any diminution of such a tendency under the two-time-frame procedure. In the domain of medical visits, what the time-frame prequestion presumably does is to help the respondent locate an actual visit and its sequelae more accurately on the time line, inhibiting the natural tendency to forward telescope. In the voting context, however, people who failed to vote in the target election may have only a vague general impression of having gone to the polls at some past time, but be unable to retrieve the specifics that would permit them to identify a vote as having been an old one rather than the recent one. It might seem an implausible hypothesis to politically concerned academics that the general public has difficulty distinguishing most acts of voting one from another, but this would not be inconsistent with the low information level and limited attention span characteristic of mass public opinion (Kinder and Sears, 1985, pp. 661–664).

To the extent that vote misreporting is a memory problem over and above the social-desirability problem, and that the memory difficulty stems largely from the indistinguishability of one election from another, a corrective strategy that suggests itself is to ask questions that *dwell upon the mundane details of particular acts of voting*. The interviewer might announce an interest in whether polling places were more crowded this election than in the past, whether the *particular* candidates had posters near the polls, whether the poll watchers were as courteous as usual, and so on. Then the respondent, forewarned and warmed up, could be asked whether he or she had voted, and what the specific details were. It is no good merely asking the respondent to name the location of the polling place, as tried unsuccessfully by Presser (1990), since this is a piece of general knowledge independent of particular elections. Rather, properties that might distinguish between elections, and help the respondent to generate an image of the scene for the vote in question, would be ideal. This suggestion is consistent with the "Cognitive Interview" technique proposed by Fisher and Quigley (chapter 8 in this volume). In any event, vote misreporting remains one of the most intriguing research challenges in the survey field.

We thank the Board of Overseers of the National Election Studies of the Center for Political Studies, University of Michigan, for including our items in their pilot studies, and Santa Traugott, the Project Manager, for her help in expediting data handling.

References

ANDERSON, B. A., SILVER, B. D., and ABRAMSON, P. R. (1988) Interviewer race and black voter participation. *Public Opinion Quarterly* 52, 53–83.

CAHALAN, D. (1968) Correlates of respondent accuracy in the Denver validity study. *Public Opinion Quarterly* 32, 607–633.

CLAUSEN, A. (1968) Response validity: Vote report. *Public Opinion Quarterly* 32, 588–606.

HABERMAN, S. J. (1979) *Analysis of Qualitative Data, Vol. 2: New Developments*. New York: Academic Press.

HUNT, E. B. (1962) *Concept Learning: An Information Processing Problem*. New York: Wiley.

KINDER, D. R., and SEARS, D. O. (1985) Public Opinion. In LINDZEY, G., and ARONSON, E. (eds.). *Handbook of Social Psychology*, vol. 2. New York: Random House, pp. 659–741.

PARRY, H. J., and CROSSLEY, H. M. (1950) Validity of responses to survey questions. *Public Opinion Quarterly* 14, 61–80.

PRESSER, S. (1990) Can context changes reduce vote overreporting? *Public Opinion Quarterly* 54, 586–593.

ROSENTHAL, R. (1984) *Meta-Analytic Procedures for Social Research*. Beverly Hills, CA: Sage.

SILVER, B. D., ABRAMSON, P. R., and ANDERSON, B. A. (1986) The presence of others and overreporting of voting in American national elections. *Public Opinion Quarterly* 50, 228–239.

SILVER, B. D., ANDERSON, B. A., and ABRAMSON, P. R. (1986). Who overreports voting? *American Political Science Review* 80, 613–624.

WICKENS, T. (1989) *Multiway Contingency Tables Analysis for the Social Sciences*. Hillsdale, NJ: Erlbaum.

8

Applying Cognitive Theory in Public Health Investigations: Enhancing Food Recall with the Cognitive Interview

RONALD P. FISHER
and KATHRYN L. QUIGLEY

Public-health epidemiologists rely heavily on histories of food consumption to investigate foodborne outbreaks. Those histories, usually obtained between two to seven days after the suspect meal, are used to identify specific foods consumed by ill and well persons present at the implicated meal, to determine which foods are associated with the illness (Bryan, 1973). If a laboratory examination of the foods served at the meal is impossible or inadequate, the food-consumption histories may be the only source of information available to link a foodborne outbreak with a specific food (Mann, 1981). In such cases it is particularly important to obtain accurate food-consumption histories. The few studies conducted to examine the accuracy of such histories, however, indicate that errors in food-consumption recall are frequent (Decker, Booth, Dewey, Fricker, Hutcheson, and Schaffner, 1986; Mann, 1981). Furthermore, it has been suggested that there is little evidence or optimism that these food-consumption histories can be improved by employing various interview techniques (Decker et al., 1986).

The goal of the current research was to improve food-consumption histories by applying a variant of the *cognitive interview*, a technique that has been found to enhance respondent recollection in another discipline: eyewitness memory for the details of a crime (e.g., Fisher, Geiselman, Raymond, Jurkevich, and Warhaftig, 1987; Fisher, Geiselman, and Raymond, 1987; Geiselman, Fisher, MacKinnon, and Holland, 1985). The cognitive interview is based on principles of memory retrieval, cognition,

154

and communication, as gathered from laboratory research in cognitive psychology and from extensive analysis of tape-recorded interviews conducted in the field (Fisher, Geiselman, and Raymond, 1987). Although the cognitive interview was developed initially to enhance witness recollection in criminal investigations, with minor modifications it should be applicable to other types of investigative interviewing, since it is based primarily on general principles of cognition. The present study examined the efficacy of the technique to obtain more extensive and accurate food-consumption histories in a simulated foodborne-outbreak investigation.

The theoretical framework of the cognitive interview, as applied to eliciting food-consumption histories, is based on five general principles of cognition and memory retrieval: context reinstatement, focused retrieval, extensive retrieval, varied retrieval, and multiple representations. Below we provide a simple conceptual description of each principle. A more detailed, concrete, step-by-step description for conducting investigative interviews is provided elsewhere (Fisher and Geiselman, in press).

The principle of context reinstatement suggests that an event will be better recalled if the rememberer is in the same psychological environment as when the event occurred originally (Tulving and Thomson, 1973). Thus, the interviewer encourages the respondent to think about the environmental context (e.g., dining-room arrangement, lighting conditions) and the relevant psychological context (e.g., why the respondent selected specific foods) at the time of the original meal. The principle of focused retrieval is based on the concept that memory retrieval, especially for details, requires mental concentration (e.g., Kahneman, 1973). Any distractions from this mental concentration, whether physical (e.g., extraneous noise) or psychological (e.g., interrupting the respondent's narration to ask a question), will disrupt memory retrieval. The principle of extensive retrieval states that the more retrieval attempts one makes, the more successful recall will be (Roediger and Payne, 1982). In practice this principle is fulfilled by encouraging respondents to search through memory even if they indicate that they have recalled as much as possible. It is important to note that when the respondent is encouraged to make additional searches through memory, the interviewer cannot simply ask the same question as posed originally. Such an approach often leads the respondent to indicate, "I already told you, I don't know." The interviewer must vary the form of the question, at least superficially, so that the respondent is induced to make another search through memory. The concept of varied retrieval is based on the notion that memories not activated by one retrieval probe may be accessed with another probe (Anderson and Pichert, 1978). Thus, a respondent who cannot recall a fact when asked a direct question (e.g., "Did you eat any vegetables?") may provide the answer when asked a different question ("What foods did you select last?"). In general changing the dimension of the question (e.g., from categorical to temporal) is likely to elicit new information. The final principle, multiple representations, suggests that the event to be remembered is stored in several forms (Fisher and Chandler, 1984). For example, the foods eaten are stored in several "mental images." There may be one image of the food while on the plate, another image of the food being served by the waiter, a third image of the food being carried away after the meal, and so on. Each of these images should be evoked and probed separately, exploiting all of the contents before probing other images (Fisher and Quigley, 1988). In order to be aware of the respondent's multiple representations of the meal, at the beginning of the interview, the interviewer should encourage the respondent to provide an open-ended description of all of the events related to the meal in question. During this initial narration the interviewer should note the various mental representations the respondent has of the meal and probe them later.

In a pilot study of food recall, more accurate food-consumption histories were obtained by using the cognitive interview than simply asking participants to recall the foods they had eaten at an earlier meal. In that study, nine students were encouraged to sample party foods (e.g., chips, beverages, cookies) from a buffet spread containing seventeen items. The students were told that they were participating in a study about how people eat and were not made aware of a forthcoming memory test. Two to seven days later, the students were interviewed for their recollections of the foods they had eaten. Four students were given a "standard" interview and were asked to recall the foods they had selected and also those not selected, but which were available from the table. The remaining five students were given the cognitive interview.

The cognitive interview elicited approximately 20% to 25% more correct information than did the standard interview. This advantage held both for foods eaten and those available but not eaten. Furthermore, the cognitive interview generated fewer incorrectly recalled foods. Although the sample was too small to produce conventional levels of statistical reliability, the magnitude of the effect was approximately the same as that found in the earlier eyewitness studies. The present study was conducted, in part, to extend the results of the pilot study to a larger sample of participants.

In foodborne-outbreak investigations, a menu of the items served at the suspect meal is occasionally available for review to facilitate the respondent's recollection. Does the presence of a menu nullify the advantage conferred by the cognitive interview? As a check on this possibility, and to increase the ecological validity of the research, the current study employed a recognition test (comparable to selecting from a menu) in addition to the recall task (generating the foods).

Method

Subjects

Twenty-six undergraduate students from Florida International University participated voluntarily in the experiment. The subjects were assigned randomly to one of two conditions, resulting in thirteen subjects per condition.

Procedure

Shortly after completing an in-class examination, the students were invited to another classroom to eat party foods. Those students who wished to participate voluntarily arrived at the "dining room" at various times, depending upon when they finished the examination. Upon arrival the students were encouraged to sample from the foods available. Thirty-four different foods (soft beverages, chips, pretzels, nuts, crackers, cheeses, fruits, raw vegetables, dips, pickles, olives, cookies, and candies) were displayed on two adjacent buffet tables. Plates and utensils were provided and seating was available in the "dining room," so the subjects could sit and converse casually with one another while eating. The subjects were permitted to return to the tables to select additional foods as often as they desired. Unlimited time was available for subjects to eat as much as they wished before leaving. Typical eating times were fifteen to twenty minutes.

Two video cameras were set up in the room to record the foods selected by each subject. The subjects were told that we were observing people's behavior while waiting in lines. No mention was made about any later memory test of the foods.

Four to fourteen days after the foods were eaten, subjects were interviewed individually with either a standard (no mnemonic instructions) interview or the cognitive interview. The retention intervals were approximately the same for the two conditions. For the no-instruction condition, the retention intervals ranged from 4 to 14 days, with a mean of 7.77 days; for the cognitive interview condition, the retention intervals ranged from 4 to 14 days with a mean of 7.15 days.

All interviews began by asking the subjects to describe all of the foods in as much detail as possible. In the no-instruction interview, subjects were asked to recall the foods that they had selected and also the other foods that were on the table, but which they did not select. Other than this open-ended request, no additional cues were provided to assist the subjects in their recall. After completing their responses, the subjects were asked if there were any more foods they could remember.

In the cognitive interview, subjects were asked initially to re-create the context (environmental and psychological) of the previous eating session and then to generate a complete description of all the foods they remembered, indicating whether they were selected or not. Subjects were asked to recall the items in sequential order, beginning at one end of the table, and then to recall the foods in reverse order by beginning at the other end of the table (varied retrieval). They were asked to take someone else's perspective, such as the person next to them in line, and attempt additional recall from that perspective (extensive recall). Subjects were asked to think about the foods when they initially selected them and also when they sat down to eat (multiple representations). During the interview, subjects were instructed that memory requires intense concentration and that the experimenter expected them to work diligently at the task (focused retrieval). If subjects gave a nondiscriminating response (e.g., "I drank some soda"), they were asked to describe it in more detail. The subjects were encouraged to go through several mental operations (e.g., context reinstatement, multiple representations) to facilitate this process. A model interview is presented in the Appendix to exemplify the principles outlined above. The interview presented was formed by excerpting parts of two interviews conducted during the actual study. For economy and readability, noninformative comments have been edited out of the model interview and the language has been stylized.

Immediately following the interview, subjects were given a list (menu) of fifty-four foods, of which thirty-four were presented at the original meal. The remaining twenty were foils, foods not presented at the meal. Of the foils fifteen were in the same food categories as the presented items (e.g., other beverages, other cheeses) and five were from nonpresented food categories (meats, fish). The test foods were ordered randomly on the sheet. The subjects were asked to respond to each test food, identifying it as either a food that (a) they selected, (b) was available, but which they did not select, or (c) was not available. If unsure, subjects indicated "don't know."

After the final test, subjects were debriefed about the purpose of the experiment and were asked about their reactions. None of the subjects reported that they had suspected a later memory test.

Results

The interviews were audiotape-recorded and later scored for accuracy of recall by comparing the subjects' responses with the videotape of the original meal. All interviews were scored for recall of (a) foods selected[1] (b) foods

1. We refer to the named foods as "selected," as opposed to "eaten," because our videotapes allow us to examine only which foods were selected, not which were actually eaten. Our observations of the subjects' eating behavior suggest that most subjects ate all of the foods selected.

available but not selected, and (c) intrusions (foods not included in the experiment, but which were reported). Responses were scored using both a stringent and a lenient criterion. With the stringent criterion, responses were considered correct only when sufficient detail was provided to discriminate the specific item from all of the other foods available. For example, as there were both green and red grapes, the response, "I ate some red grapes," was considered correct, but "I ate some grapes" was not. However, since there was only one type of olive (green), the response, "I ate some olives," was considered correct. With the lenient criterion, responses that lacked discriminating detail, but which referred to the general class of food (e.g., "some grapes"), were considered correct. Since the patterns of results were similar for the two criteria, we report the results of only the stringent criterion.

In actual field investigations, public-health officials typically conduct food-consumption histories about the suspect meal two to seven days after the meal, shortly after the symptoms are noticed. The retention intervals in the present study, however, ranged from four to fourteen days. In order to examine whether our longer retention intervals might have biased the results, we conducted an initial test to compare the results of those subjects interviewed within the first seven days with those interviewed between eight and fourteen days after the meal. The patterns of results were almost identical for the two groups, other than a slight overall reduction of scores for the longer retention interval. The presented results, therefore, reflect all of the collected data, collapsed across retention interval.

As seen in table 1, more than twice as many foods were recalled with the cognitive interview (12.22) than were with the no-instruction interview (5.92), $F(1, 24) = 24.51, MSe = 5.276, p < .01$. This held equally for selected and available-but-unselected foods; the interaction of interview and food type was not statistically significant, $F(1, 24) = .81, MSe = 4.673, p > .05$.

Although subjects were assigned randomly to the two groups, those in the cognitive interview group selected slightly more foods (8.15) than did those in the no-instruction group (6.00). As a result, there were potentially more selected foods to be recalled for the cognitive interview group than for the

Table 1   **Number of Selected and Available-but-Unselected Foods Recalled.**

	Interview	
Food	Cognitive	No-Instruction
Selected	5.30	2.69
Available-But-Unselected	6.92	3.23
Total	12.22	5.92

no-instruction group. It is unlikely that this accounts for much of the superiority of the cognitive interview group, since they also recalled more of the available-but-unselected foods, even though they had concomitantly fewer of these foods (25.85) than did the no-instruction group (28.00). A second way to circumvent the problem is to score the data in terms of proportion of selected foods that were recalled. The results are similar to the absolute number recalled. The cognitive interview group remembered a greater proportion of the selected foods (.65) than did the no-instruction group (.45) and also a greater proportion of the available-but-unselected foods (.27 versus .12).

There were forty-five cases in which the subjects recalled inappropriate foods (intrusions). Of these, eight were intraexperimental intrusions, in which subjects indicated that they had selected foods that were available, but which they had not actually selected. The bulk of the intrusion errors ($N = 37$) were extraexperimental, recalling foods that were not available in the experiment. Of these thirty-seven, all were categorical intrusions, recalling foods from food groups that were represented in the experiment (e.g., recalling "mozzarella," as there were other cheeses available). There were no noncategorical intrusions (recalling foods from food groups that were not represented, e.g., saying "salami," given that there were no meat products in the experiment). The average number of intrusions was approximately the same for the cognitive interview (1.77) as for the no-instruction group (1.69), $t(24) = .16$, $SE = .335$, $p > .05$. If anything, given that more responses were generated with the cognitive interview, the intrusion *rate* was slightly lower for the cognitive interview (13%) than for the no-instruction group (23%).

The recognition responses (indicating which of the menu items were selected, available but not selected, not available, or "don't know") were scored as follows. A response was scored as a *hit* if the subject indicated that a selected test food was, in fact, selected. A *miss* was scored if any other response (available-but-unselected, not available, or "don't know"[2]) was given. The hit rate was slightly higher for the cognitive interview group (.83) than for the no-instruction group (.79); however, the difference was not statistically significant, $t(24) = .14$, $MSE = .042$, $p > .05$. It is likely that this lack of difference was caused by the contribution of a few subjects in the no-instruction group who selected very few foods,[3] as the recognition task

2. "I don't know" responses were scored as if the subject had responded that the food was not available. In a secondary, unreported analysis we omitted these test items and scored only those items to which the subject made a positive response ("selected," "available-but-unselected," or "not available"). The pattern of results was unchanged.

3. In the no-instruction group one person selected only one food, one selected two foods, two people selected three foods, and two selected four foods. In the cognitive interview group only one person selected fewer than five foods.

becomes easier when there are fewer foods to remember. To circumvent this problem, we reanalyzed the data, this time including only those subjects who selected at least five foods. The reanalysis compares seven subjects in the no-instruction group (mean number of foods selected = 8.57) with twelve subjects in the cognitive interview group (mean = 8.58). The difference in hit rates is now somewhat larger, with the cognitive interview group (.83)[4] being marginally greater than the no-instruction group (.75), $t(17) = 1.37$, $SE = .044, .05 < p < .10$.

One possible explanation for the higher hit rate is that the cognitive interview may simply have lowered people's threshold for saying "selected" to anything, whether or not the food was actually selected. In order to examine this possibility, we also scored the data for false alarms, saying "selected" to nontarget foods (either available-but-unselected or unavailable). The false-alarm rate (likelihood of saying "selected" to a nontarget) was, if anything, slightly lower in the cognitive interview group (.03) than in the no-instruction group (.05). Thus, the cognitive interview group correctly recognized more selected foods and made fewer errors on the nonselected foods.

One method to combine the hit and false-alarm rates into one score, which better reflects overall recognition performance, is to use a signal-detection analysis (Murdock, 1982). When all of the subjects in the two groups were compared, the resulting d' score was slightly, although nonsignificantly, higher for the cognitive interview group (mean $d' = 3.30$) than for the no instruction group ($d' = 3.10$), $t(24) = .45$, $SE = .314, p > .05$.[5] When the scores were reanalyzed using only those subjects who selected at least five foods, the differences were larger (mean d's for cognitive interview and no-instruction groups were 3.34 and 2.39, respectively) and attained conventional levels of statistical significance, $t(17) = 2.01$, $SE = .284, p < .05$.

The cognitive interview took considerably longer to conduct (15.2 minutes) than did the no-instruction interview (1.5 minutes). To what degree was the superiority of the cognitive interview group due simply to their taking more time to recall the foods? It is difficult to separate the effects of instructions from interview time in the present experiment, as they were so highly correlated with one another ($r_{xy} = .809, p < .01$). Nevertheless, there are some suggestive data from the present experiment that lead us to believe that time itself was not the critical difference between the cognitive and no-instruction groups. First, there was little correlation between interview

4. The group means are weighted scores, so that deleting the data for one subject who selected only three foods had a negligible effect on the group mean.

5. Signal-detection analysis does not permit probabilities of 1.0 or .0; therefore, we used the accepted practice of assigning values of .99 for those subjects who recognized all ($p = 1.0$) of the selected foods and .01 for those who made no false alarms ($p = .0$).

time and number of correctly recalled foods within each of the cognitive interview and no-instruction conditions (r_{xy} = .297 and .332, respectively, both ps > .20), although note that these low correlations may reflect restricted ranges of interview times within each group. Second, all interviews were terminated when the subjects indicated that they could not recall any more foods, that is, when additional time would be of no value. We defer additional thoughts about the role of interview time until the discussion.

Discussion

The results clearly demonstrate the effectiveness of the cognitive interview as a memory enhancer. More than twice as many foods were recalled with the cognitive interview than with the no-instruction interview, with no more intrusion errors. Comparable, although not as large, effects were found with the recognition test (selecting from a menu). There were more positive identifications (hits) of foods selected and fewer incorrect identifications (false alarms). In summary the cognitive interview supports better recollection with no obvious cost, except for the additional time. Decker et al.'s (1986) pessimism about the unlikelihood of improving food-consumption histories with better interviewing procedures, fortunately, seems to be unfounded.

It is important to note that the cognitive interview is made up of several component principles (e.g., context reinstatement, focused retrieval, multiple representations), each of which is effected by a variety of interviewing techniques. For example, focused retrieval is effected by (a) asking open-ended questions, (b) not interrupting respondents during a response, (c) minimizing extraneous noises, and so on. Because all of these techniques were used as a package in the cognitive interview, we cannot isolate the effect of any one specific technique. It may be that in the present experiment the entire benefit of the cognitive interview was due to only one of the cognitive principles or only one of the various interviewing techniques. Perhaps the superiority of the cognitive interview reflects only that subjects were encouraged to retrieve the events in different ways. Similarly, one can argue that perhaps the entire effect was due to the context reinstatement component. A similar argument can be made about any of the individual components, either at the level of cognitive principles or specific interviewing techniques. We cannot refute this argument on the basis of the present study, because, technically, all of the component cognitive principles and interviewing techniques were confounded within the package of the cognitive interview. We have reason to believe from other studies, however, that each of the component principles enhances recollection. For example, the effect of context reinstatement has been demonstrated by Tulving and Thomson (1973), and of varied retrieval by Anderson and Pichert (1978). It seems reasonable that the relative value of each of the component techniques will vary from one interviewing situation to the next, for instance, from recall to recognition, or from mail surveys to face-to-face interviews. We encourage other interested researchers to explore these interactions by parsing the cognitive interview into its component techniques and examining their relative value as the information-processing requirements of the task change (Fisher, Geiselman, and Amador, 1989).

How valuable is the cognitive interview compared to simply conducting a recognition test? On the surface it appears that the recognition task elicited more information from the no-instruction group than did the recall task for the cognitive interview group. Subjects in the no-instruction condition recognized approximately 79% of all the selected foods; by comparison, subjects in the cognitive interview group recalled only 65% of the selected foods. These numbers are somewhat misleading for three reasons. First, in the present study the recognition test always followed a recall test. Such a double-testing procedure elevates performance on the second (recognition) test, since the earlier attempt to recall strengthens the information (see Richardson, 1985, for a review). A true recognition score, one not preceded by the recall test, would likely have been lower than that observed here. Second, there were many more false recognitions (2.31 false alarms per subject in the no-instruction group) than false recalls (1.77 intrusions per subject in the cognitive interview group), so that the recognition task generated more misleading clues than did the cognitive interview. Third, and most important from the practical aspect, in order to construct a comprehensive recognition test, with all of the target items present, one would have to know the target items prior to constructing the test. In the laboratory this does not present a problem, since the experimenter knows the target items. In the field, however, where the interviewer does not know the target items prior to the interview, it would be difficult to construct such a comprehensive recognition test.

In the present experiment the cognitive interview took considerably longer to conduct than the no-instruction interview. To what extent does this extra time account for the superiority of the cognitive interview? An implicit assumption behind this question is that time, per se, affects recollection; that is, the more time one spends in retrieval, the better will be recollection. We are not aware of any empirical evidence to support this claim. The most relevant study is one by Roediger and Thorpe (1978), who showed in a free-recall task that subjects generated more correct responses as the allotted response time increased; however, this came at the expense of increased intrusions. Thus, the additional response time did not enhance recall as much as it lowered the threshold for responding. Note that in the present study the increase in number of correct items recalled by the cognitive interview group was not accompanied by an increase in the error rate. On the contrary, the intrusion rate was, if anything, lower in the cognitive interview group (13%) than in the no-instruction group (23%). Second, in the present study, length and type of interview were highly correlated, thereby effectively precluding a separation of the two factors. Other studies, however, have shown that the superiority of the cognitive interview is not attributable to its greater length. In a recent laboratory study by Fisher and Layton (1990), interview time was experimentally controlled. Nevertheless, recall of subject-performed actions was better when tested with the cognitive interview than with a no-instruction format. In the one field test documenting the technique's effectiveness, police detectives took no longer to conduct the cognitive interview than a standard police interview (Fisher, Geiselman, and Amador, 1989). We are confident, therefore, that the cognitive interview enhances recall because of the mental operations it promotes, not because of the additional time that may be required.

Assuming it does take somewhat longer to conduct the cognitive interview, how impractical is that for survey researchers? That depends in part on the time demands of the particular survey. If a very large number of respondents must be interviewed and there are stringent time constraints, then the additional time may preclude using the cognitive interview. If the number of respondents is relatively small, however, as in the outbreak of legionnaires' disease, then the extra time associated with the cognitive interview is not extremely debilitating. Some surveys with large numbers of respondents proceed in two stages. In the first stage an intensive face-to-face interview is conducted with a few target individuals to determine the range of potential responses. For example, if a foodborne outbreak occurred in a large hotel, intensive interviews might be conducted with some of the waiters, chefs, or other kitchen personnel to determine the range of foods that were available at the target meal. In the second stage of the investigation, the named foods would then be presented in a recognition format to all of the hotel's guests to determine who ate which foods. In such cases the cognitive interview would be most appropriate for the first stage, where ample time is available for a few intensive interviews. The alternative, of eliminating the first stage and simply presenting a comprehensive list of foods for respondents to recognize, has the potential drawback of taxing the respondent with such a long list of choices that the questionnaire becomes unreliable.

It has been shown across a wide variety of surveys that not only the number but also the specific alternatives provided can alter the respondent's choice and the user's interpretation of the response (see Schwarz, 1990, for a review). Given the importance of selecting the appropriate set of alternatives when constructing the survey instrument, it may be worthwhile initially to conduct a few intensive interviews with a representative sample of individuals to determine the ultimate set of alternatives. Here, too, in the preliminary stages, when more intensive interviews can be conducted, the cognitive interview might be of greatest value.

Whereas the present study examined the effectiveness of the cognitive interview in recalling the details of an isolated event, many survey researchers are interested in recalling events that occur repeatedly, for instance, "How often did you visit a physician during the past year?" A recent study by the National Center for Health Statistics (1989) showed that an effective method to elicit such information is first to decompose the series of events into specific isolable events (e.g., the last) and probe for details of each specific event. In the second phase the respondent is encouraged to construct a personal time line to determine whether the recalled event falls within the specified limit (one year). We suspect that a modification of the presently described cognitive interview can be useful in the initial decomposition phase. For example, the respondent can be encouraged to use varied retrieval operations by probing along different dimensions. One can probe the various events temporally ("Can you remember any specific visits to the doctor during the afternoon? the morning?"), spatially ("Can you remember any examinations in the closest (farthest) examination room?"), proprioceptively ("Can you remember any appointments where you had to stand (sit) most of the time?"), emotionally ("Can you remember any examination in which you were particularly happy (upset) with the results?"), and so on. As a second suggestion, respondents can be encouraged to reconstruct their mental operations associated with specific appointments ("Think about speaking with the receptionist to make an appointment. Did you try to schedule your appointment around any other events? If so, which events?"). We leave it to other investigators to determine how the cognitive interview can be adapted to meet their specific needs.

One immediate application of the cognitive interview for public-health workers is in the investigation of sexually transmitted diseases, especially when respondents have had contact with many sexual partners, so that recollection becomes problematic. From a theoretical perspective, somewhat different memory processes may be used in investigating the two types of event, as the target information (names of foods versus action sequences) differs (see Cohen, Peterson, and Mantani-Atkinson, 1987). As such, the cognitive interview will have to be modified to accommodate the new task's demands. Nevertheless, it may serve as the basis of an effective interviewing technique.

How useful is a technique like the cognitive interview for improving survey research in general? We suspect that it depends in large part on the degree of direct interaction between the respondent and the questioner. At one extreme, the written mail survey, there is virtually no direct interaction between the questioner and the respondent; at the other extreme, the face-to-face interview, there is maximum interaction between the two; and in the middle, the telephone interview, there is an intermediate degree of interaction. Our experience is that the cognitive interview will be more effective as the degree of interaction increases between questioner and respondent. Some principles (e.g., context reinstatement) can be incorporated into interviews with minimal interaction, for example, by providing written instructions encouraging the respondent to re-create the original context. However, there is little guarantee that respondents will follow these written instructions without being monitored. Other principles are virtually impossible to implement in a noninteractive interview. For example, the principle of focused retrieval is implemented by the interviewer's controlling the interview environment to minimize distractions. Obviously, this is impossible to control in a mail survey and nearly impossible in a telephone interview. To make use of the principle of multiple representations, the interviewer should encourage the respondent to provide an initial open-ended description of the event, so that the interviewer can infer the respondent's various representations of the event. The interviewer probes these various mental representations during the remainder of the interview. This means that the interview questions cannot be predetermined as in a questionnaire. Rather, the interviewer must be flexible enough to tailor the interview to the specific mental representations of the individual respondent. In general we suspect that the cognitive interview will be of only limited value in written questionnaire surveys, but that it will be more valuable in telephone and face-to-face surveys.

The authors would like to thank David Tacher and Irene Praeger for assisting in the data collection. We would also like to thank David Mingay, Brian Cutler, and Paul Blake for their helpful comments on an earlier version of the manuscript.

References

ANDERSON, R. C., and PICHERT, J. W. (1978) Recall of previously unrecallable information following a shift in perspective. *Journal of Verbal Learning and Verbal Behavior* 17, 1–12.

BRYAN, F. L. (1973) *Guide for Investigating Foodborne Disease Outbreaks and Analyzing Surveillance Data*. Atlanta, GA: U.S. Department of Health and Human Services.

COHEN, R. L., PETERSON, M., and MANTANI-ATKINSON T. (1987) Interevent differences in event memory: Why are some events more recallable than others? *Memory and Cognition* 15, 109–118.

DECKER, M. D., BOOTH, A. L., DEWEY, M. J., FRICKER, R. S., HUTCHESON, R. H., and SCHAFFNER, W. (1986) Validity of food consumption histories in foodborne outbreak investigations. *American Journal of Epidemiology* 124, 859–862.

FISHER, R. P., and CHANDLER, C. C. (1984) Dissociations between temporally-cued and theme-cued recall. *Bulletin of the Psychonomic Society* 22, 395–397.

FISHER, R. P., and GEISELMAN, R. E. (in press) *Memory-Enhancement Techniques for Investigative Interviews: Increasing Eyewitness Recall with the Cognitive Interview.* Springfield, IL: Thomas.

FISHER, R. P., GEISELMAN, R. E., and AMADOR, M. (1989) Field test of the cognitive interview: Enhancing the recollection of actual victims and witnesses of crime. *Journal of Applied Psychology* 74, 722–727.

FISHER, R. P., GEISELMAN, R. E., and RAYMOND, D. S. (1987) Critical analysis of police interview techniques. *Journal of Police Science and Administration* 15, 177–185.

FISHER, R. P., GEISELMAN, R. E., RAYMOND, D. S., JURKEVICH, L., and WARHAFTIG, M. L. (1987) Enhancing enhanced eyewitness memory: Refining the cognitive interview. *Journal of Police Science and Administration* 15, 177–185.

FISHER, R. P., and LAYTON, R. (1990) Recall of subject-performed actions. Manuscript. Miami, FL: Florida International University.

FISHER, R. P., and QUIGLEY, K. L. (1988) The effect of question sequence on eyewitness recall. Manuscript. Miami, FL: Florida International University.

GEISELMAN, R. E., FISHER, R. P., MACKINNON, D. P., and HOLLAND, H. L. (1985) Eyewitness memory enhancement in the police interview: Cognitive retrieval mnemonics versus hypnosis. *Journal of Applied Psychology* 70, 401–412.

KAHNEMAN, D. (1973) *Attention and Effort.* Englewood Cliffs, NJ: Prentice-Hall.

MANN, J. A. (1981) A prospective study of response error in food history questionnaires. *American Journal of Public Health* 70, 401–412.

MURDOCK, B. B. (1982) Recognition memory. In PUFF, R. (ed.). *Handbook of Research Methods in Human Memory and Cognition.* New York: Academic Press, pp. 1–26.

NATIONAL CENTER FOR HEALTH STATISTICS: MEANS, B., NIGAM, A., ZARROW, M., LOFTUS, E. F., and DONALDSON, M. S. (1989) Autobiographical memory for health-related events. *Vital and Health Statistics,* series 6, no. 2. Public Health Service. Washington, DC: U.S. Government Printing Office.

RICHARDSON, J. T. (1985) The effects of retention tests on human learning and memory: An historical review and an experimental analysis. *Educational Psychology* 5, 85–114.

ROEDIGER, H. L., and PAYNE, D. G. (1982) Hypermnesia: The role of repeated testing. *Journal of Experimental Psychology: Learning, Memory, and Cognition* 8, 66–72.

ROEDIGER, H. L., and THORPE, L. A. (1978) The role of recall time in producing hypermnesia. *Memory and Cognition* 6, 296–305.

Schwarz, N. (1990) Assessing frequency reports of mundane behaviors: Contributions of cognitive psychology to questionnaire construction. In Hendrick, C., and Clark, M. S. (eds.). *Research Methods in Personality and Social Psychology*. Newbury Park, CA: Sage, pp. 98–119.

Tulving, E. (1974) Cue-dependent forgetting. *American Scientist* 62, 74–82.

Tulving, E., and Thomson, D. M. (1973) Encoding specificity and retrieval processes in episodic memory. *Psychological Review* 80, 352–373.

APPENDIX

Model Cognitive Interview between Interviewer (Int) and Respondent (Resp)

Note: New information is printed in UPPERCASE.

Int: I'd like you to try to put yourself back in the same frame of mind as the night when you walked into the room and tell me what you were thinking or feeling.

Resp: Well, we had just taken a test. . . . I think having the food was a nice way to end the evening after a difficult test.

Int: After you came into the room, what is the first thing you did?

Resp: I signed my name in the notebook that was there, then I looked at the video camera and said my name. Then I picked up a plate and started walking along the tables.

Int: Try to put yourself back to where you were standing at the beginning of the tables, holding your plate. Try to visualize the foods that were on the tables. It may help if you close your eyes . . . (pause) . . . Now, start with the first item on the table and work your way down the table, describing each item to me in as much detail as possible. Try not to leave anything out.

Resp: Next to the plates and utensils were some vegetables. I remember BROCCOLI, CUCUMBERS, TOMATOES, MUSHROOMS. . . . After the vegetables, there were some dips. I think there was a BLUE-CHEESE DIP. There were some NUTS. And I remember getting excited because there was chocolate, CHOCOLATE-COVERED PEANUTS . . .

Int: OK, let's go back to the beginning of the tables again. Close your eyes and try to remember any color of items you might have seen.

Resp: Well, the broccoli was green, the cucumbers were green, and I think there were some GREEN GRAPES. I also remember seeing something orange. It seems like there were some CARROTS.

Int: Let's take this from a different perspective. Can you start at the other end of the table and work in a backward direction? Again, please describe each item in as much detail as possible.

Resp: At the end of the table were two or three bottles of SODA with some cups and ice. Next to the sodas were the chocolates. I remember the chocolate-covered peanuts and M & M's, and I remember chocolate kisses, HERSHEY'S KISSES . . .

Int: After you selected the items from the buffet tables, what did you do?

Resp: I looked around the room and saw two girls from my class, so I walked over to where they were sitting and sat down and started to eat.

Int: Now, put yourself back in your seat. It may help if you close your eyes again and try to visualize your plate. Tell me everything you remember seeing on your plate.

Resp: Starting at 9:00, there was the broccoli. Next to the broccoli was the mushrooms, then the blue-cheese dip, then I think I had some CHEESE . . .

Int: Do you remember what type of cheese it was?

Resp: Yes I think it was CHEDDAR CHEESE . . . then next to the cheese was the chocolate-covered peanuts.

Int: Do you remember what anyone sitting near you was eating?

Resp: I think one of the girls sitting next to me was eating PRETZELS.

Int: Now I'm going to go over all of the items that you told me were on the tables. Try to visualize the tables again and tell me if I leave anything out or if you remember any other items as we go along. . . .

PART
IV

EXPRESSION:
THE CASE OF
ATTITUDE MEASUREMENT
IN SURVEYS

9

Opportunities
in Survey Measurement
of Attitudes

ROBERT P. ABELSON

A large proportion of the questions asked in surveys concern the attitudes of the respondents: attitudes toward controversial issues, political candidates, racial groups, consumer products, and so on. How attitudes relate to each other and how they depend on the demographic characteristics of the respondents are the stuff of much survey analysis. In laboratory studies, and in social psychology as well, attitude measures are often the dependent variables. The importance of the methodology of attitude measurement can hardly be exaggerated.

In the following two chapters in this part, two key problem areas in the survey measurement of attitudes are discussed, with emphasis on the exploitation of new or untapped opportunities for extracting more subtle and detailed information about attitudes than is typical of present survey practice.

One such area is that of *multiple measures* of a given attitude. For understandable reasons of conserving time and expense, survey interviews very often rely on a single question to tap each attitude topic in the survey. However, this corner-cutting practice clearly involves some loss of information. Consider the following comments, bracketing the sixty-year history of the field of attitude measurement, the first by its leading pioneer, the second by two codirectors of respected modern national survey organizations in the United States and Britain:

> One of the most frequent questions [about attitude measurement] is that a score on an attitude scale, let us say an attitude toward God, does not truly describe the person's attitude. There are so many complex factors involved in a

person's attitude on any social issue that it cannot be adequately described by simple numbers such as the score on some sort of test or scale. That is quite true, but it is also equally true of all measurements. . . . When the height of a table is measured, the whole table has not been described but only that attribute which was measured (Thurstone, 1931).

Questionnaires should ideally be made up of *groups* of questions, each group designed to cover a single dimension. This is just a similar sort of precaution to that taken by insurance companies when they re-insure, or by bookies when they lay off bets. Any single question—however careful the design process has been—may in the end turn out to be fatally flawed. . . . Answers to groups of questions on a single dimension should form a pattern. . . . Individual questions whose answers do not conform to the pattern are . . . suspect. In any event, since survey analysis consists largely of trying to decipher and make sense of patterns, it depends heavily on multiple measures. That is probably why virtually all influential survey results tend to travel in convoy (Davis and Jowell, 1989, p. 6).

In chapter 10 Jon Krosnick and I pursue one form of multiple-measure strategy, the analysis of the concept of attitude *strength*. The few empirical analyses that have been done of various possible indicators of strength (Abelson, 1988; Krosnick, 1989; Raden, 1985) agree that it is a multidimensional construct. For example, Abelson (1988) found that three factors—and usually more—were needed to characterize attitude conviction on any of a number of social issues. It is highly likely that different measures of attitude strength play differential roles in mediating the relationships between attitudes and resistance to persuasion on the attitude issue, or participation in relevant political activities, or various other dependent variables. Research evidence on these relationships is spotty, but we offer some preliminary guidance on the question of which measure(s) of attitude strength the interested investigator might choose.

One rather different new opportunity in survey measurement of attitudes arises from the concept of mode of attitude expression. The usual assumption is that the respondent has available a well-formed evaluative response to the attitude object, and merely needs to access this response and report it to the interviewer. In this view the attitude is accessible (Fazio, 1989) and the response is spontaneous. Beyond the problems of ambiguity of question meaning, discussed in part II of this book, there are at least two other major conditions under which this simple model of the attitude response process will fail: (1) the respondent has no strong prior attitude, and therefore must construct a response on the spot; (2) social norms inhibit the spontaneous expression of the subject's attitude, and the respondent tries to find a more permissible response. Both conditions imply a delay in response for further cognitive processing, and the response may be called deliberate rather than spontaneous. In case 1 there is the risk to the interpretation of the survey data that the deliberately constructed response is vacuous and transient—a nonattitude (Converse, 1970; Rosenberg, 1968). In case 2 there is the hazard that the deliberate response is biased in the socially desirable direction. This problem is especially evident in the area of racial prejudice, where many people respond with racial tolerance only under conditions when to do otherwise would invite the attribution that they are racists (Crosby, Bromley, and Saxe, 1980; Gaertner and Dovidio, 1986). Thus, if one is interested in "gut feelings" toward racial or ethnic out-groups, special procedures may be required to measure the accessibility of spontaneous attitudes. Of course, if the survey investigator is not primarily interested in gut attitudes, but rather in reasons, distinctions, explanations, considered preferences, or other products of cognitive work, then deliberate responses might be preferred to spontaneous responses. Sometimes the conjunction of both types of response is of interest. Devine (1989), for example, has argued that in the area of intergroup prejudice, many people are uncomfortable about their spontaneous negative feelings and undertake a self-conscious campaign to control or change such feelings.

The distinction between spontaneous and deliberate responses is discussed in detail in chapter 11 by John Dovidio and Russell Fazio. This dichotomy is akin to that between unintended thought and intended thought (Uleman and Bargh, 1989), and bears some relation to the distinctions between automatic and controlled responses (Shiffrin and Schneider, 1977), and between preferences and inferences (Zajonc, 1980).

How is the investigator to know if the respondent is being spontaneous or deliberate? Even more to the point, how can the investigator design the response task to encourage one mode or the other? In recent laboratory studies using reaction-time measures, it has been possible to tease apart these two different response modes, most notably in the delicate domain of racial attitudes (Dovidio and Gaertner, 1991). Indirect tasks are used that do not seem to respondents to be assessing their attitudes. The adaptation of these methods to survey practice poses technological challenges, and one line of solution involves laptop computers in face-to-face interviews. The Dovidio and Fazio chapter includes a brief discussion of the technical problems and opportunities associated with reaction-time measurement in field surveys.

Altogether, then, our task in these two chapters is to set forth a number of measures of attitudes in the two different modes of expression, and to try to do justice to their complexity. In chapter 10 Krosnick and Abelson discuss a variety of verbal measures of attitude strength, along with some of their relations to other variables, and offer preliminary advice in choosing among them. In chapter 11 Dovidio and Fazio amplify the spontaneous/deliberate dichotomy, and how it might affect established survey practice.

References

ABELSON, R. P. (1988) Conviction. *American Psychologist* 43, 267–275.

CONVERSE, P. E. (1970) Attitudes and nonattitudes: Continuation of a dialogue. In TUFTE, E. R. (ed.). *The Quantitative Analysis of Social Problems.* Reading, MA: Addison-Wesley, pp. 168–189.

CROSBY, F., BROMLEY, S., and SAXE, L. (1980) Recent unobtrusive studies of black and white discrimination and prejudice: A literature review. *Psychological Bulletin* 87, 546–563.

DAVIS, J. A., and JOWELL, R. (1989) Measuring national differences: An introduction to the International Social Survey Programme (ISSP). In JOWELL, R. (ed.). *British Social Attitudes: Special International Report.* London: Gower, pp. 1–10.

DEVINE, P. G. (1989) Stereotypes and prejudice: Their automatic and controlled components. *Journal of Personality and Social Psychology* 56, 5–18.

DOVIDIO, J. F., and GAERTNER, S. L. (1991) Changes in the nature and expression of racial prejudice. In KNOPKE, H., NORRELL, J., and ROGERS, R. (eds.). *Opening Doors: An Appraisal of Race Relations in Contemporary America.* Tuscaloosa, AL: University of Alabama Press, pp. 201–241.

FAZIO, R. H. (1989) On the power and functionality of attitudes: The role of attitude accessibility. In PRATKANIS, A. R., BRECKLER, S. J., and GREENWALD, A. G. (eds.). *Attitude Structure and Function.* Hillsdale, NJ: Erlbaum, pp. 153–179.

GAERTNER, S. L., and DOVIDIO, J. F. (1986) The aversive form of racism. In DOVIDIO, J. F., and GAERTNER, S. L. (eds.). *Prejudice, Discrimination, and Racism.* New York: Academic Press, pp. 61–89.

KROSNICK, J. A. (1989) Attitude importance and attitude accessibility. *Personality and Social Psychology Bulletin* 15, 297–308.

RADEN, D. (1985) Strength-related attitude dimensions. *Social Psychology Quarterly* 48, 312–330.

ROSENBERG, M. J. (1968) Hedonism, inauthenticity, and other goads toward expansion of a consistency theory. In ABELSON, R. P., ARONSON, E., McGUIRE, W. J., NEWCOMB, T. M., ROSENBERG, M. J., and TANNENBAUM, P. H. (eds.). *Theories of Cognitive Consistency: A Sourcebook.* Chicago: Rand McNally.

SHIFFRIN, R. M., and SCHNEIDER, W. (1977) Controlled and automatic human processing: II. Perceptual learning, automatic attending, and a general theory. *Psychological Review* 84, 127–190.

THURSTONE, L. L. (1931) The measurement of social attitudes. *Journal of Abnormal and Social Psychology* 26, 249–269.

ULEMAN, J. S., and BARGH, J. A., eds., (1989) *Unintended Thought.* New York: Guilford Press.

ZAJONC, R. B. (1980) Feeling and thinking: Preferences need no inferences. *American Psychologist* 35, 151–176.

10

The Case for Measuring
Attitude Strength
in Surveys

JON A. KROSNICK
and ROBERT P. ABELSON

Introduction

Attitude measurement is one of the most common goals of surveys. In the
news media, for example, we frequently read reports of survey results
revealing the proportions of Americans who approve and disapprove of the
president's performance in office, or the numbers of citizens who favor and
oppose legislation outlawing abortion, or the percentages of people who
prefer particular candidates running for public office. As this is true for the
popular press, so it is true for surveys conducted by academics and by
government. Many surveys are designed to measure behaviors as well, but
attitude assessment has been, since the earliest surveys, the primary focus of
research using the survey method (Converse, 1987). And, of course, the usual
purpose for attitude measurement is not so much to understand people's
preferences per se, but rather to understand the forces shaping individuals'
cognition and behavior.

Although it is very common to see attitudes measured in surveys, it is rare
for a survey to measure the strength of those attitudes. And yet it seems
patently obvious that not all attitudes are alike. Some are strong, in the sense
that they have profound effects on individuals' cognition and behavior, and
resist even the strongest pressures toward change. And other attitudes are
weak, vulnerable to situational pressures, and with little if any impact on an
individual's thinking or action. Thus, it would seem that any attempt to use
attitudes to understand cognition and behavior certainly ought to take into
account variation in strength across those attitudes. Yet, despite this obvious

rationale for doing so, the vast majority of surveys have not attempted to measure this attribute of attitudes at all. Instead, they have simply settled for measuring attitude direction—revealing the proportions of people who are pro or con, favorable or unfavorable, positive or negative.

To be sure, the research literature has not made it obvious exactly how one should measure attitude strength in surveys. For example, in his chapter "Attitude Measurement" in the *Handbook of Social Psychology*, William Scott (1968) described nine variable properties of attitudes that might be considered dimensions of attitude strength: magnitude, intensity, ambivalence, salience, affective salience, cognitive complexity, overtness, embeddedness, and flexibility. But Scott did not make clear which of these dimensions one should measure if forced to choose, or how to go about doing so. During the more than twenty years since Scott's chapter appeared, matters have gotten both more complicated and much clearer. Magnitude (or extremity), intensity, ambivalence (or certainty), and embeddedness have all been the subjects of extensive empirical research, whereas Scott's other properties have been largely ignored. In their places a number of other dimensions of attitude strength have been explored, including ego involvement, affective-cognitive consistency, accessibility, amount of attitude-relevant knowledge, personal relevance, and vested interest. As the result of this research, appropriate and practical measurement procedures have been developed and refined.

More important, the last thirty years have brought us a great deal of evidence attesting to why attitude strength should be measured. Specifically, numerous studies have shown that strong attitudes are in fact more firmly crystallized and have more impact on cognition and behavior than weak attitudes. However, this literature is scattered in the journals of a variety of disciplines and has yet to be widely recognized. A review article written by Raden (1985) a few years ago discussed some of this literature, and much relevant work done before and since helps to make the case for attitude-strength measurement even more powerfully. This, therefore, seems like an especially opportune time to take a careful look back at this literature.

In this chapter we set out to do so, but not without a goal in mind. In reviewing this literature we will do our best to make the case that attitude strength should be measured whenever attitude direction is measured in surveys. No matter what one's goal in measuring attitudes, we believe, it can be better achieved by measuring both attitude direction and attitude strength than by measuring direction alone.

In planning this review, we took into account both theoretical and practical considerations. Specifically, we recognized that the limitations on time and money that restrict all survey enterprises discourage the addition of numerous tagalong questions following each attitude measure. Therefore, rather than discussing all of Scott's (1968) dimensions of attitude strength and all of the others that have gained some attention, we will focus on just five of these dimensions. These five were selected because they possess three great virtues: they are the easiest to measure in surveys, they are the easiest to comprehend conceptually, and they are the most extensively validated as measures of the fixedness and consequentiality of attitudes.

We begin below by defining these five dimensions: extremity, intensity, certainty, importance, and knowledge. We also describe how each of these dimensions can easily be measured in surveys. Next, we clarify how these various dimensions are related to one another. And finally, we review the existing body of evidence, documenting that each of these dimensions is useful for understanding the dynamics of attitudes. All this will make clear, we hope, why including one or more of these measures of attitude strength in surveys will greatly help researchers to gauge and understand public opinion and social behavior.

Definitions and Measurement

Extremity

Attitude extremity is the degree of favorableness or unfavorableness of an individual's evaluation of a given object. The more extreme an individual's attitude is, the further it is from neutrality. Therefore, attitude extremity has typically been operationalized as the deviation of an individual's attitude rating from the midpoint of a pro-con dimension (Ewing, 1942; Judd and Johnson, 1981; Tannenbaum, 1956; Tesser, 1978; van der Pligt, Ester, and van der Linden, 1983). This seems straightforward enough on the surface, but as Abelson (1990) has recently pointed out, there are at least three different meanings of an "extreme" degree of favorability: The attitude object might attach to a number of strong values held by the individual; the attitude might be sweeping in its lack of qualification (e.g., "All research and commercial activity involving the incarceration of animals of any sort should be banned immediately"); or the attitude might be extreme because one deems it legitimate to go to great lengths to defend it—extremists in a political cause might endorse terrorism, for example. Despite this conceptual ambiguity, the assessment of extremity has been straightforward: departure from the neutral point of an attitude scale.

Intensity

Some attitudes involve strong, affective responses to objects, whereas other attitudes involve little or no emotional reaction. Attitude intensity is defined as the strength of an individual's feelings about an attitude object (Krosnick and Schuman, 1988; Schuman and Presser, 1981). Typically, it has been measured by asking people how strong or intense their feelings are toward a particular object (Cantril, 1944, 1946; Guttman and Suchman, 1947; Schuman and Presser, 1981; Stouffer, Guttman, Suchman, Lazarsfeld, Star, and Clausen, 1950).

Certainty

Attitude certainty refers to the degree to which an individual is certain that his or her attitude toward an object is correct. It has usually been measured by asking respondents how sure they are of their opinion, how easily their opinion could be changed, or how confident they are that their opinion is correct (Budd, 1986; Budd and Spencer, 1984; Cantril, 1944; Davidson, Yantis, Norwood, and Montano, 1985; Ewing, 1942; Holtz and Miller, 1985; Krosnick and Schuman, 1988; Lemon, 1968; Schuman and Presser, 1981; Tourangeau and Rasinski, 1990). Other studies have asked respondents how difficult they found it to report an opinion on an issue (Stouffer et al., 1950). A related construct is the degree of ambivalence (Schuman and Presser, 1981) or conflict (Tourangeau et al., 1989a, 1989b) evidenced by one's beliefs about an object.[1]

Importance

Attitude importance has been defined as the degree to which an individual considers an attitude to be personally important to him or her. Attitude importance has generally been measured by asking people how personally important their attitude or the attitude object is, how concerned they are about it, or how much they care about it (Cantril, 1944; Krosnick, 1988a, 1988b, 1989, 1990a; Madsen, 1978; Tourangeau, Rasinski, Bradburn, and D'Andrade, 1989a).[2]

---

1. Tourangeau and Rasinski (1990) recently demonstrated that certainty and conflict are only very weakly correlated with one another (r = .32 and .21 for two different issues), so they may not reflect the same underlying construct.

2. Some authors have referred to measures of attitude importance as assessing attitude centrality (e.g., Judd and Krosnick, 1982; Schuman and Presser, 1981). Given the other uses of the term *centrality* in social psychology over the years (Asch, 1946; Lewin, 1951; Newcomb, 1961), we now think it best to use this term to refer to the extent of connectedness between an attitude and other cognitive elements in memory, and to use the term *importance* to refer to the degree to which an individual is concerned about the attitude.

Knowledge

Some attitudes are accompanied in memory by relatively little information about the attitude object, whereas other attitudes are linked to large stores of beliefs about the object. Amount of attitude-relevant knowledge has usually been measured by asking respondents to list everything they know about an attitude object (Davidson, Yantis, Norwood, and Montano, 1985; Kallgren and Wood, 1986; Wood, 1982; Wood, Kallgren, and Preisler, 1985). This dimension has also been assessed simply by asking individuals to report how knowledgeable they feel they are about an issue (e.g., Chuang, 1988). In addition, knowledge has been gauged by the number of correct answers people give to quizlike questions (Iyengar, 1990; Wilson, Kraft, and Dunn, 1989).

Relations Between These Dimensions

In the simplest of worlds, these various dimensions of attitude strength would all be highly correlated with one another; that is, strong attitudes would be extreme, intense, held with great certainty, considered highly important, and bolstered by extensive knowledge. In contrast, weak attitudes would be moderate, would not involve intense feelings, would involve a great deal of ambivalence, would be unimportant to people, and would be bolstered by little or no knowledge. It would be very rare indeed to see an important attitude that was not extreme or an intense attitude that was not bolstered by lots of knowledge.

But the world is not so simple. Instead, a number of studies have documented low to moderate positive correlations between intensity and extremity (Cantril, 1946; Guttman and Suchman, 1947; Stouffer et al., 1950), intensity and certainty (Allport and Hartman, 1925; McCroskey, Prichard, and Arnold, 1967–1968; Raden, 1983; Stouffer et al., 1950), extremity and certainty (Allport and Hartman, 1925; Fazio and Zanna, 1978a; Johnson, 1940; McDill, 1959; Mehling, 1959; though see Lemon, 1968), importance and extremity (Borgida and Howard-Pitney, 1983; Brent and Granberg, 1982; Cialdini, Levy, Herman, Kozlowski, and Petty, 1976; Converse and Schuman, 1970; Granberg and Burlison, 1983; Howard-Pitney, Borgida, and Omoto, 1985; Knower, 1936; Krosnick and Telhami, 1990; Lemon, 1968; Rholes and Bailey, 1983; Smith, 1982), importance and intensity (Raden, 1983), importance and certainty (Raden, 1983; Tourangeau and Rasinski, 1990; though see Budd and Spencer, 1984), importance and knowledge (Bradburn and Caplovitz, 1965; Vallone, Ross, and Lepper, 1985; Wood, 1982), and certainty and knowledge (Davidson et al., 1985). Thus, it would seem at first blush that these dimensions are not all reflections of a single underlying, superordinate dimension that might be called attitude strength.

However, it is difficult to know exactly what to make of these zero-order correlations, because they are attenuated by random measurement error and inflated by shared systematic measurement error. Fortunately, the random measurement error problem can be overcome by using multiple measures of the dimensions, as Wilson, Hodges, and Pollack (1990) did. They found that the attitude-strength dimensions listed above are generally only weakly correlated with one another, and that strong correlations appear only very rarely. However, these analyses did not take into account correlated measurement error. This contamination with measurement error would most likely inflate correlations between measures using the same method and could depress correlations between measures using different methods.

One way to overcome this problem is via multiple indicator multitrait-multimethod analyses (e.g., Judd and Krosnick, 1982). Chuang (1988) did just this sort of analysis and reached a conclusion identical to that of Wilson, Hodges, and Pollack. Thus, it seems that these various dimensions are generally empirically quite separable from one another, so they should be viewed as distinct constructs.

This conclusion is further reinforced by a small body of evidence suggesting that these various dimensions of attitude strength each have unique causes. For example, Boninger, Krosnick, and Berent (1990) found that attitude importance is increased by perceptions of self-interest, social identification, and value relevance.[3] Fazio and Zanna (1978a, 1978b) showed that direct behavioral experience with an attitude object increases certainty about one's attitude toward it. And attitude extremity is increased by discussions among partisans favoring one side of the issue (Lamm and Myers, 1978), exposure to mixed evidence offering justifications both to support and to oppose a partisan position (Lord, Ross, and Lepper, 1979), thinking knowledgeably about the issue (Tesser, 1978), receiving insults during persuasion attempts (Abelson and Miller, 1967), and increased salience of group conflict on the issue (Price, 1989).[4]

Although these strength dimensions are clearly conceptually separable, it

3. Johnson and Eagly (1989) argued recently that self-interest and value relevance might produce attitudes with very different characteristics, thus suggesting that self-interest-based importance may be distinct from value-relevance-based importance. This debate is beyond the scope of our current enterprise.

4. Of course, it is plausible to hypothesize that many of the conditions that create greater attitude strength are themselves encouraged by strong attitudes, particularly in the context of attitude extremity and intergroup conflict (Abelson, 1990). For example, the increase in extremity following group discussion may make it more likely that some of the group's members will insult the out-group, or make more publicly salient the intergroup disagreement. These influences in

is useful to recognize the special conditions under which they do coexist at high levels, as Abelson (1988) illustrated. He conducted factor analyses of them on a number of different issues and consistently uncovered three general dimensions: cognitive elaboration, emotional commitment, and ego preoccupation.[5] Cognitive elaboration is similar to knowledge. Emotional commitment is a combination of intensity and certainty. Ego preoccupation involves concern about the attitude issue and the attachment of personal importance to the attitude object. These three dimensions were found to correlate only weakly in the general population, but Abelson (1988) argued that they could be viewed as components of attitudinal "conviction," with important consequences resulting from the simultaneous presence of all three. Consistent with this general perspective, Tourangeau, Rasinski, Bradburn, and D'Andrade, (1989a, 1989b) identified interactions among dimensions of strength.

Taken together, then, this body of evidence suggests that the various aspects of attitude strength that we discuss below do not all reflect a single underlying dimension. Rather, they are conceptually and empirically separable and may therefore have nonoverlapping effects.

The Evidence for Crystallization

Presumably, the most significant attribute of strong attitudes is that they are more resistant to change than weak attitudes. Therefore, if extremity, intensity, certainty, and knowledge are to be viewed as dimensions of attitude strength, we must first show that these dimensions differentiate crystallized attitudes from uncrystallized ones.

Fortunately, this claim has received support from four kinds of studies. The first type explored responsiveness to persuasive communications intended to change attitudes in laboratory settings. As would be expected, more extreme attitudes changed less (Ewing, 1942; Osgood and Tannenbaum, 1955; Osgood, Suci, and Tannenbaum, 1957; Sarat and Vidmar, 1976; Tannenbaum, 1956),[6] and attitudes that people considered more personally

---

turn may push the out-group more toward an extreme position, stimulate more heated thinking, and encourage new group discussions along partisan lines—leading to even further polarization. The possibility of such feedback loops, creating conflict escalation, is of considerable theoretical and practical importance.

5. Unfortunately, attitude extremity was not included in these analyses.

6. Note that this result is just the opposite of what would be expected based on "regression to the mean," whereby more extreme attitudes should change more than moderate ones (assuming that the mean attitude is moderate).

important changed less (Fine, 1957; Gorn, 1975; Knower, 1936; Powell, 1977; Rhine and Severance, 1970). Wood (1982) and Wood, Kallgren, and Preisler (1985) found that greater knowledge about an attitude object was associated with greater resistance to attitude change. And Marks and Kamins (1988) found greater attitude change among people low in attitudinal confidence.

A second approach to testing the resistance hypothesis involves examining people's responses to leading questions. Asking a leading question can induce people to generate cognitions consistent with the implications of the question and can thereby induce attitude change. If strong attitudes are more resistant to change, then these attitudes should prompt people to resist the persuasive impact of leading questions. As expected, Swann and colleagues found just this with regard to certainty: people who were more certain about their attitude were more resistant to influence in this fashion (Swann and Ely, 1984; Swann, Pelham, and Chidester, 1988).

However, Swann, Pelham, and Chidester (1988) did identify one type of leading question that induced more attitude change among high-certainty individuals than among low-certainty individuals. This involved asking people loaded questions that encouraged people to make statements that were consistent with, but more extreme than, their attitudes. Doing so led highly certain respondents' attitudes to become more moderate and had no effect on less certain respondents. Thus, resistance strategies that are usually effective can be turned on their heads.

A third set of studies has examined the impact of having people explain the reasons for their attitudes. This cognitive exercise can produce attitude change, and it would be expected to do so most among individuals with weak attitudes. Consistent with this notion, Wilson, Kraft, and Dunn (1989) showed that the disruptive effect of explaining attitudes is greatest among individuals with relatively little attitude-relevant knowledge (for a review of these and related studies, see Wilson, Dunn, Kraft, and Lisle, 1989).

The attitude-change hypothesis has also been tested via a fourth method: by assessing attitude stability over relatively long time periods during the course of everyday life. If stronger attitudes are indeed more resistant to change, they should show higher levels of stability. Consistent with this expectation, a number of studies have found that personally important attitudes are more stable over time than unimportant attitudes (Converse, 1964; Hahn, 1970; Kendall, 1954; Krosnick, 1988b; Schuman and Presser, 1981). High conviction enhances the stability of attitudes (Abelson, 1988), and high conflict is associated with lowered attitude stability (Tourangeau and Rasinski, 1990). Surprisingly, Schwartz (1978) found that more extreme attitudes were not more stable than moderate attitudes, but this result may be attributable to the confounding of less true attitude change with more regression to the mean among individuals with more extreme attitudes. Nonetheless, the general weight of the evidence here favors the hypothesis that stronger attitudes are more stable over time.

Additional studies have highlighted some of the likely mechanisms of the increased resistance of strong attitudes to change. First, Cialdini, Levy, Herman, Kozlowski, and Petty (1976) showed that in response to the news that individuals would be discussing an issue with someone with whom they disagreed, important attitudes became more polarized, whereas unimportant attitudes became more moderate. Thus, people presumably brace to protect important attitudes and prepare to be flexible when attitudes are unimportant. Second, a number of studies have illustrated that personally important attitudes are more likely to be consistent with other attitudes and with basic values than unimportant ones (Jackman, 1977; Judd and Krosnick, 1989; Krosnick, 1990b; Schuman and Presser, 1981; Smith, 1982). These other attitudes and values presumably lend stability to the target attitude in the face of attack. And finally, Howard-Pitney, Borgida, and Omoto (1986) demonstrated that people for whom an attitude is personally important are especially likely to generate challenging cognitive responses to counterattitudinal arguments. This tendency toward biased cognitive elaboration also presumably enhances resistance to change.

The Evidence for Greater Influence

It is all well and good to demonstrate that strong attitudes are more firmly crystallized than weak ones. But that is only the first step toward demonstrating that measuring attitude strength would be useful in surveys. In order to be fully convincing, we must produce evidence that strong attitudes also have greater influence on cognition and behavior than weak attitudes. Happily, there is a great deal of such evidence available, and it addresses many phenomena: the impact of attitudes on behavior and perceptions of others' attitudes, the impact of attitudinal similarity on social attraction, the impact of attitudes toward an object's individual attributes on attitudes toward the entire object, the impact of attitudes on memory for attitude-relevant information, the susceptibility of attitude reports to slight changes in a survey question, and a host of other miscellaneous findings. We review all this below.

Attitude-Behavior Consistency

One of the most important goals of surveys is to predict or explain individuals' behavior from reports of their attitudes. Although it is well known that the attitude-behavior relation is typically weak, it would seem likely that the relation would be strong in the case of strong attitudes and weak in the case of weak attitudes.

A number of studies have supported this assertion. For example, Fazio and Zanna (1978a, 1978b) found that more extreme attitudes and attitudes held with greater certainty were more consistent with behavior. Petersen and Dutton (1975) also found that greater attitude extremity was associated with increased attitude-behavior correspondence.[7] Sample and Warland (1973) and Davidson et al. (1985) also found greater attitude-behavior consistency for attitudes held with greater confidence. Krosnick (1988a), Schuman and Presser (1981), Jaccard and Becker (1985), and Rokeach and Kliejunas (1972) reported greater attitude-behavior consistency among people for whom the attitude was personally important than among people for whom the attitude was unimportant. Kallgren and Wood (1986) found greater attitude-behavior correspondence for attitudes accompanied by more relevant knowledge in memory. Finally, significantly greater numbers of people with high attitude conviction than those with low attitude conviction said they would volunteer to work once a month for a group supporting their attitude position (Abelson, 1987). Thus, this group of studies suggests that attitude strength does moderate the attitude-behavior relation.

This evidence would be especially significant for the typical survey researcher if it turned out that attitude strength varies across issues and attitude positions. In fact, this does appear to be the case sometimes. For example, Schuman and Presser (1981) showed that, in the late 1970s, Americans who were anti-gun control or antiabortion typically had stronger attitudes than those who were pro-gun control or proabortion. Similarly, Abelson (1987) found that, in the late 1980s, Connecticut residents with higher importance ratings and higher commitment scores alike tended to take the conservative side on each of two issues (antiabortion, pro-AIDS testing), whereas those with higher knowledge ratings tended to take the liberal sides. Furthermore, Abelson discovered that attitudes toward compulsory AIDS testing were of higher importance than attitudes toward the legality of abortion, but attitude intensity and clarity were higher on abortion than on AIDS. More data-snooping is required before it becomes clearer what types of issues in what stages of their history recruit what types of attitude strength, because attitude strength is sometimes completely independent of attitude position (e.g., Krosnick and Telhami, 1990).

---

7. Fazio's and Zanna's (1978a, 1978b) and Petersen's and Dutton's (1975) evidence could simply reflect the fact that more extreme attitudes are more variable and produce stronger correlations as a result (see Dawes and Smith, 1986, pp. 555–563).

Perceptions of Others' Attitudes

According to social judgment theory, actions and statements of attitudes are inherently ambiguous and require some degree of interpreting in order for a perceiver to specify precisely what another person's attitude is (Sherif and Hovland, 1961). This interpretation is accomplished partly through comparisons of the other person's behavior with one's own attitude, which acts as a perceptual anchor. And this comparative process is thought to bring about perceptual distortion: attitudes close to one's own are assimilated toward it, and attitudes clearly different are contrasted away from it.

Social judgment theory argues that stronger attitudes are more powerful anchors and therefore have more impact than weak attitudes on perceptual processes. Thus, individuals with strong attitudes are thought to see others as primarily falling into one of two groups: those with whom they agree (at one end of the attitude continuum) and those with whom they disagree sharply (at the other end of the continuum). People with weak attitudes would be expected to perceive others as falling more evenly across the attitude dimension.

This hypothesis has received support in Krosnick's (1986, 1988a) survey-based studies of attitude importance and political candidate perception. He found that voters who considered a political issue to be personally important perceived presidential candidates to take extreme, opposing stands on the issue. In contrast, voters for whom an issue was personally unimportant were more likely to perceive competing pairs of candidates as taking identical, moderate stands.

Judd and Johnson (1981) reported comparable findings, using a very different approach. They compared a group of women who were strongly pro-women's rights to a group who were only weakly so. Relative to the weakly-pro group, the strongly-pro group reported greater knowledge about the issue, attached greater personal importance to it, and showed greater attitude extremity. And as compared to the weakly-pro group, the strongly-pro group overestimated the proportions of people who were pro-women's rights and anti-women's rights (rather than being neutral) among a variety of social groups to which they did not belong. Similarly, van der Pligt, Ester, and van der Linden (1983) and Crano, Gorenflo, and Shackelford (1988) found that people with more extreme attitudes perceived a greater proportion of others to take their side on an issue. Consistent with this, Hurwitz (1986) found that people with more extreme attitudes judged attitude statements to be more extreme. And Allison and Messick (1988), who experimentally manipulated attitude extremity, showed that increased extremity heightens subjects' perceptions of the proportions of others who share their attitudes.

These studies indicate that greater perceptual distortion is associated with strong attitudes than with weak attitudes.[8]

Holtz and Miller (1985) found related evidence in their exploration of perceptions of the attitudes of social groups. Two kinds of groups were compared: those to which people did belong (in-groups), and those to which they did not belong and competed against for social status (out-groups). On issues people considered personally important, they exaggerated agreement with in-groups, and they exaggerated disagreement with out-groups. But on issues that were not personally important to people, no such exaggeration occurred.

Marks and Miller (1982) provided analogous evidence in a very different way. Rather than studying group membership, these investigators focused on the other person's attractiveness. On issues people considered personally important, they exaggerated perceived agreement between themselves and attractive others, and they exaggerated perceived disagreement between themselves and unattractive target others. No such effects appeared in the cases of issues that subjects considered personally unimportant, further indicating that strong attitudes have stronger effects on perception than do weak attitudes.

Only one study has reported results that are discordant with this literature. In Krosnick's (1991) study of the false-consensus effect, he did find the strength of the perceptual-distortion effect to vary depending upon the importance of the issue to people. Surprisingly, however, the false-consensus effect was weaker in the case of important attitudes than in the case of unimportant attitudes; that is, people generally tended to overestimate the proportion of others who shared their own opinions on an issue, but especially on issues they considered unimportant. This contradicts the expectation that more important attitudes would be more powerful instigators of the false-consensus effect.

However, this effect may be understandable in light of Dawes's (1989) analysis of the false-consensus effect. High-importance individuals presumably have more information about others' stands on an issue (Krosnick, 1990a), so they need not rely on their own stands to infer those of others. By contrast, low-importance individuals are presumably less well informed about the issue generally and are therefore forced to look to their own stands as information about where others may stand. Thus, the reduced false-consensus effect here may reflect greater issue-relevant knowledge among individuals whose attitudes on it are important to them.

---

8. We use the term *distortion* advisedly here. It is certainly conceivable that if we were to compare people's perceptions to measures of "truth," we would find that it is people with weak attitudes whose perceptions actually deviate more from truth than people with strong attitudes.

Taken together, then, this literature generally supports our expectation that more important attitudes have more impact on perceptions, and this finding highlights yet another reason why it is useful to distinguish strong attitudes from weak ones.

Similarity-Attraction Effect

Theories of cognitive consistency argue that people should be attracted to others who share their attitudes instead of others who hold attitudes that conflict with their own (e.g., Festinger, 1957; Heider, 1958). Consistent with this notion, a great deal of research has demonstrated that attitudinal similarity leads to interpersonal attraction (e.g., Byrne, 1961, 1971; Newcomb, 1961). If this is so, we would certainly expect it to be especially true in the case of strong attitudes as compared to weak ones.

There is much evidence in support of this expectation. A number of studies have shown greater correspondence between an individual's attitudes and his or her friends' attitudes when the individual's attitudes are extreme or highly important (Judd and Johnson, 1981; Tedin, 1974, 1980). Likewise, attitude similarity is a more powerful determinant of attraction to strangers (Byrne, London, and Griffitt, 1968; Clore and Baldridge, 1968) and to political candidates (Aldrich and McKelvey, 1977; Granberg and Holmberg, 1986; Krosnick, 1988b; 1990a; McGraw, Lodge, and Stroh, 1990; Rabinowitz, Prothro, and Jacoby, 1982; Schuman and Presser, 1981; Shapiro, 1969) when the attitude involved is personally important to the individual. Iyengar (1990) also reported a similar finding regarding attitude-relevant knowledge. The more an individual knew about a particular attitude, the more heavily he or she weighed self-other similarity involving that attitude when evaluating others.

Part-Whole Attitude Consistency

According to Fishbein and Ajzen's (1975; Ajzen and Fishbein, 1980) Theory of Reasoned Action, people's attitudes toward objects are derived from their beliefs about the attributes of the object and their attitudes toward those attributes. Fishbein and Ajzen assumed that attributes toward which an individual has stronger attitudes would have greater impact on the overall attitude toward the object. This enhanced impact is presumably reflected by a greater level of evaluative consistency between the overall attitude and the attitudes toward the attributes.

In line with this assumption, Budd (1986) showed that the attributes of cigarette smoking that individuals consider more important are also more strongly correlated with overall evaluations of smoking. Similarly, Watkins and Park (1972) and Rosen and Ross (1968) reported that attitudes toward one's own body parts are more strongly correlated with overall attitudes toward one's own body when attitudes toward the body parts are especially important. Analogously, an individual's self-esteem is more influenced by satisfaction with more personally important dimensions of self-evaluation (Hoelter, 1985; Kaplan, 1980; Marsh, 1986; Pelham and Swann, 1989; Rosenberg, 1965), and with dimensions that were evaluated with greater certainty (Pelham and Swann, 1989). And considerations of economic self-interest have more impact on presidential candidate preferences among people for whom economic issues are especially important (Young, Borgida, Sullivan, and Aldrich, 1987).

Memory for Attitude-Relevant Information

According to cognitive dissonance theory (Festinger, 1957), retaining information in memory that challenges one's attitude on an issue is uncomfortable. Therefore, people would be expected to be biased in favor of remembering attitude-consistent information and forgetting attitude-inconsistent information. This has been termed a "congeniality bias" in memory. Although investigators have found it very difficult to document this tendency reliably (Roberts, 1985), this may be because they have failed to differentiate strong attitudes from weak ones. Certainly, we would expect the effect to be stronger in the case of the former.

Consistent with this expectation, Berent (1990) showed recently that attitude importance does indeed regulate the strength of this effect. He examined memory for information acquired in two very different ways: reading sentences on computer screens in laboratory settings, and watching actual United States presidential debates when they were initially broadcast on television in people's own homes. As expected, individuals who considered an issue to be more important were more likely to remember attitude-consistent information and less likely to remember attitude-inconsistent information than people who considered the issue to be unimportant.

In contrast, Johnson and Judd (1983) found no greater congeniality bias in the case of committed activists on an issue, as compared to nonactivists. However, Johnson and Judd's memory measure was quite different from that used by Berent (1990). Instead of assessing recall of attitude-relevant statements that subjects had read, Johnson and Judd examined their subjects' recall of the hypothetical individuals who supposedly made each statement. Cognitive consistency theories do not offer such a strong rationale for a congeniality bias in this sort of memory task, so the failure to find an effect of activism is not especially disconcerting.

A second hypothesis involving attitude strength and memory has also received some support. This hypothesis proposes that people should attend more closely to and think more deeply about information relevant to stronger attitudes. As a result, this information should be better remembered than information relevant to weaker attitudes.

Howard-Pitney, Borgida, and Omoto (1986) failed to uncover evidence of such a relation in the case of attitude importance; and Crano, Gorenflo, and Shackelford (1988) failed to find an association in the case of attitude extremity. However, Iyengar (1990) did find that people who had more attitude-relevant knowledge stored in memory also had better recall of newly acquired attitude-relevant information. Similarly, Krosnick and Schuman (1985) and Berent (1990) found that attitude importance was associated with better memory for attitude-relevant information. Furthermore, Krosnick (1990a) found that perceptions of the directions of political candidates' stands on a political issue were more accurate among people who considered the issue more personally important. These individuals also evidenced greater accuracy in their perceptions of the directions of differences between political candidates' stands on an issue.

Berent (1990) showed that the correlation between attitude importance and memory for attitude-relevant information was not mediated by selective exposure to attitude-relevant information. Rather, attitude importance apparently induced deeper processing of such information, thus producing stronger memory traces. In addition, Krosnick and Schuman's (1985) evidence suggests that the association between attitude importance and memory appears when the recall task is performed days after information exposure, but not when it is performed only minutes after exposure. Thus, it seems that attitude strength is associated with differential decay of information in memory, not differential likelihood of storing a trace in memory initially.

Susceptibility to Survey Response Effects

The final area of research we shall consider is the most puzzling. This research has explored the magnitude of response effects: the impact on people's attitude self-reports of subtle changes in an attitude question's wording, format, or placement in a questionnaire. Since the earliest research in this area, researchers have assumed that respondents with strong attitudes would be less susceptible to such effects (Blankenship, 1940, p. 401; Cantril, 1944, pp. 34, 35, 45, 48–49; Converse, 1970, p. 177, 1974, p. 656; Erikson and Luttbeg, 1973, pp. 35–39; Gallup, 1941, p. 261; Kagay, 1988; Katz, 1940, p. 279; Payne, 1951, pp. 135, 179; Rosenberg, Verba, and Converse, 1970, pp. 24–25). Presumably, the notion was that a person who is strongly antiabortion, for example, will say so clearly and identically, regardless of how he or she is asked. In contrast, a person who is only weakly on one side of the issue can presumably be induced to express any of a variety of different positions.

Though widely believed, this hypothesis has rarely been tested. The most comprehensive test of it was reported by Krosnick and Schuman (1988), who explored the impact of attitude importance, intensity, and certainty on susceptibility to response effects. Surprisingly, they found that five such effects (response order, question order, tone of wording, balance, and acquiescence effects) were not smaller for important attitudes, intense attitudes, or attitudes held with great certainty. Only in the case of middle-alternative effects was the hypothesis confirmed. When asked questions for which a middle-alternative response is plausible (e.g., gun control laws should be kept as they are now, instead of being made stricter or less strict), offering the middle alternative explicitly in the question is most likely to attract respondents for whom the attitude is not important or intense (although see Stember and Hyman, 1949–1950).

Bishop (1990) conducted a similar set of analyses, and, like Krosnick and Schuman (1988), he found that attitude importance did not regulate the magnitude of question-order or response-order effects. And, like Krosnick and Schuman, Bishop found that attitude importance did moderate the magnitude of middle-alternative effects. But, in contrast to Krosnick and Schuman, Bishop found that attitude importance did seem to moderate the magnitude of balance effects—that is, including an argument against a particular policy in a question decreased expressed support for the policy, especially among people with unimportant attitudes. This finding is consistent with the speculation that balance effects occur through attitude change, and important attitudes are more resistant to change.

Krosnick (1991) reported an interesting reversal of the expected pattern. His focus was on the false-consensus effect—the tendency for people to overestimate the proportion of others who share their points of view on the issue. This tendency is generally stronger when respondents are asked first about others' attitudes and subsequently about their own, as compared to when respondents are asked first about their own views on an issue and then subsequently are asked how many others share this view (Baron and Roper, 1976; Krosnick, 1990b; McCauley, Kogan, and Teger, 1971; Mullen, Atkins, Champion, Edwards, Hardy, Story, and Vanderklok, 1985; Mullen, Driskell, and Smith, 1989; Mullen and Hu, 1988; though see Weinstein, 1984). Krosnick (1991) found that this effect of question order on the magnitude of the false-consensus effect was stronger among people who considered the issue to be highly personally important than among people who considered it to be unimportant.

Tourangeau, Rasinski, Bradburn, and D'Andrade (1989a, 1989b) reported even more complex results: an interaction between importance, ambivalence, and a question-order effect. Their interest was in the possibility that prior questions might prime beliefs that then influence answers to later target questions. Consistent with Krosnick and Schuman's (1988) and Bishop's (1990) conclusions, the priming effects Tourangeau et al. observed were no larger on average among respondents who considered the issue to be unimportant than among those who considered it highly important. However, Tourangeau et al. did observe a nonsignificant trend suggesting that the priming effects may have been slightly greater among respondents who said they had ambivalent feelings on the issue (Bishop, 1990, reported a similar finding). More important, though, Tourangeau et al. found that their priming effects were concentrated among respondents who both considered the issue important and were high in ambivalence.

In sum, it is currently unclear precisely what role attitude strength plays in regulating the occurrence of response effects. The relatively simple hypothesis that these effects are greater in the case of weaker attitudes has clearly been disconfirmed. It does seem that some attitude-strength dimensions may regulate some of these effects, although in rather complex fashions that depend upon the particular effect involved. It therefore appears that attitude strength is yet again worth taking into account when using attitude measures.

Conclusion

Whether one is interested in the impact of attitudes on behavior, on perceptions of others' attitudes, on interpersonal attraction, on superordinate attitudes, or on memory for attitude-relevant information, more informed predictions can be made with measures of attitude strength in hand than without them. The one exception to this rule is in the case of question-order and response-order effects in attitude measurement, which seem not to depend on attitude strength. But in general the weight of the evidence is strongly on the supporting side. It is therefore likely to prove rewarding to survey researchers to include one or more measures of attitude strength when assessing attitude direction. The pattern of relationships observed in respondents with strong attitudes will most likely be different from that observed among respondents with weak attitudes.

When it comes to giving advice on which measure of strength to use, the data base at hand is not sufficiently developed to make a clear recommendation. As we noted, the dimensions of attitude strength are only weakly correlated with one another, which means that one's choice among them may well be quite consequential. We therefore see two stances that one might take. As Abelson (1988) has done, one can measure all of the dimensions and aggregate them, on the theory that the small subset of individuals who score high on many measures is possessed of more of a general attitude-strength property (say, conviction) than the subset of uniformly low scorers. This strategy appears to produce coherent, albeit somewhat weak, relationships with other variables. The obvious disadvantage of this strategy is that a large number of attitude-strength questions must be asked for each attitude object.

An alternative tack is to make a theoretical and practical commitment to a particular strength measure, and work out its relationships to other variables in detail. Among the strength dimensions considered here, the two most promising would appear to be importance and extremity, because they appear to be the most well-researched of these variables. In our review 87 empirical results were cited. Importance was the applicable measure in 56 of these, extremity was mentioned 13 times, and the other strength variables together accounted for 18 references. We do not know, of course, with what frequency the various strength measures failed to show effects, since non-results are likely to find their ways into file drawers instead of journals and books (Rosenthal, 1979). And given our own areas of research emphasis, we are more likely to be informed about research on attitude importance that is in the publication pipeline than such work on other dimensions. Nonetheless, importance and extremity seem to be the most extensively documented dimensions to date, so it may prove most useful at this point in time to make use of these two factors.

———

Preparation of this chapter was supported in part by NSF Grant BNS-8920430 to Jon A. Krosnick. The authors wish to thank Roger Tourangeau and Robyn Dawes for their helpful comments.

References

ABELSON, R. P. (1987) The association of attitudinal conviction with attitude positions and issues. Unpublished data.

———— (1988) Conviction. *American Psychologist* 43, 267–275.

———— (1990) Psychological processes that make intergroup controversies worse. Paper delivered at the annual meeting of the International Society for Political Psychology, Washington, D.C.

ABELSON, R. P., and MILLER, J. C. (1967) Negative persuasion via personal insult. *Journal of Experimental Social Psychology* 3, 321–333.

AJZEN, I., and FISHBEIN, M. (1980) *Understanding Attitudes and Predicting Social Behavior.* Englewood Cliffs, NJ: Prentice-Hall.

ALDRICH, J. H., and McKELVEY, R. D. (1977) A method of scaling with applications to the 1968 and 1972 presidential elections. *American Political Science Review* 71, 111–130.

ALLISON, D. E., and MESSICK, D. M. (1988) The feature-positive effect, attitude strength, and the degree of perceived concensus. *Personality and Social Psychology Bulletin* 14, 236–241.

ALLPORT, F. H., and HARTMAN, D. A. (1925) The measurement and motivation of atypical opinion in a certain group. *American Political Science Review* 19, 735–760.

ASCH, S. E. (1946) Forming impressions of personality. *Journal of Abnormal and Social Psychology* 41, 258–290.

BARON, R. S., and ROPER, G. (1976) Reaffirmation of social comparison views of choice shifts: Averaging and extremity effects in an autokinetic situation. *Journal of Personality and Social Psychology* 33, 521–530.

BERENT, M. K. (1990) Attitude importance and the recall of attitude relevant information. Master's thesis. Columbus, OH: Department of Psychology, Ohio State University.

BISHOP, G. F. (1990) Issue involvement and response effects in public opinion surveys. *Public Opinion Quarterly* 54, 209–218.

BLANKENSHIP, A. B. (1940) The influence of the question form upon the response in a public opinion poll. *Psychological Record* 3, 345–422.

BONINGER, D. S., KROSNICK, J. A., and BERENT, M. K. (1990) The causes of attitude importance: Self-interest, social identification, and values. Manuscript. Columbus, OH: Department of Psychology, Ohio State University.

BORGIDA, E., and HOWARD-PITNEY, B. (1983) Personal involvement and the robustness of perceptual salience effects. *Journal of Personality and Social Psychology* 45, 560–570.

BRADBURN, N. M., and CAPLOVITZ, D. (1965) *Reports on Happiness: A Pilot Study of Behavior Related to Mental Health*. Chicago: Aldine.

BRENT, E., and GRANBERG, D. (1982) Subjective agreement and the presidential candidates of 1976 and 1980. *Journal of Personality and Social Psychology* 42, 393–403.

BUDD, R. J. (1986) Predicting cigarette use: The need to incorporate measures of salience in the Theory of Reasoned Action. *Journal of Applied Social Psychology* 16, 633–685.

BUDD, R. J., and SPENCER, C. (1984) Latitude of rejection, centrality, and certainty: Variables affecting the relationship between attitudes, norms, and behavioral intentions. *British Journal of Social Psychology* 23, 1–8.

BYRNE, D. (1961) Interpersonal attraction and attitude similarity. *Journal of Abnormal and Social Psychology* 62, 713–715.

———— (1971) *The Attraction Paradigm*. New York: Academic Press.

BYRNE, D., LONDON, O., and GRIFFITT, W. (1968) The effect of topic importance and attitude similarity-dissimilarity on attraction in an intrastranger design. *Psychonomic Science* 11, 303–304.

CANTRIL, H. (1944) *Gauging Public Opinion*. Princeton, NJ: Princeton University Press.

—————— (1946) The intensity of an attitude. *Journal of Abnormal and Social Psychology* 41, 1–12.

CHUANG, Y. C. (1988) The structure of attitude strength. Master's thesis. Columbus, OH: Department of Psychology, Ohio State University.

CIALDINI, R. B., LEVY, A., HERMAN, C. P., KOZLOWSKI, L., and PETTY, R. E. (1976) Elastic shifts of opinion: Determinants of direction and durability. *Journal of Personality and Social Psychology* 34, 663–672.

CLORE, G. L., and BALDRIDGE, B. (1968) Interpersonal attraction: The role of agreement and topic interest. *Journal of Personality and Social Psychology* 9, 340–346.

CONVERSE, J. M. (1987) *Survey Research in the United States: Roots and Emergence 1890–1960*. Berkeley, CA: University of California Press.

CONVERSE, P. E. (1964) The nature of belief systems in the mass public. In APTER, D. E. (ed.). *Ideology and Discontent*. New York: Free Press, pp. 206–261.

—————— (1970) Attitudes and nonattitudes: Continuation of a dialogue. In TUFTE, E. R. (ed.). *The Quantitative Analysis of Social Problems*. Reading, MA: Addison-Wesley, pp. 168–189.

—————— (1974) Comment: The status of nonattitudes. *American Political Science Review* 68, 650–660.

CONVERSE, P. E., and SCHUMAN, H. (1970) Silent majorities and the Vietnam war. *Scientific American*, 17–25.

CRANO, W. D., GORENFLO, D. W., and SHACKELFORD, S. L. (1988) Overjustification, assumed consensus, and attitude change: Further investigation of the incentive-aroused ambivalence hypothesis. *Journal of Personality and Social Psychology* 55, 12–22.

DAVIDSON, A. R., YANTIS, S., NORWOOD, M., and MONTANO, D. E. (1985) Amount of information about the attitude object and attitude-behavior consistency. *Journal of Personality and Social Psychology* 49, 1184–1198.

DAWES, R. M. (1989) Statistical criteria for establishing a truly false consensus effect. *Journal of Experimental Social Psychology* 25, 1–17.

DAWES, R. M., and SMITH, T. L. (1986) Attitude and opinion measurement. In LINDZEY, G., and ARONSON, E. (eds.). *Handbook of Social Psychology*, 3rd ed. New York: Random House, pp. 509–566.

ERIKSON, R. S., and LUTTBEG, N. R. (1973) *American Public Opinion: Its Origins, Content, and Impact*. New York: Wiley.

EWING, T. N. (1942) A study of certain factors involved in changes of opinion. *Journal of Social Psychology* 16, 63–88.

FAZIO, R. H. (1986) How do attitudes guide behavior? In SORRENTINO, R. M., and HIGGINS, E. T. (eds.). *The Handbook of Motivation and Cognition: Foundations of Social Behavior*. New York: Guilford Press, pp. 204–243.

Fazio, R. H., Chen, J., McDonel, E. C., and Sherman, S. J. (1982) Attitude accessibility, attitude-behavior consistency, and the strength of the object-evaluation association. *Journal of Experimental Social Psychology* 18, 339–357.

Fazio, R. H., and Zanna, M. P. (1978a) Attitudinal qualities relating to the strength of the attitude-behavior relationship. *Journal of Experimental Social Psychology* 14, 398–408.

_____ (1978b) On the predictive validity of attitudes: The role of direct experience and confidence. *Journal of Personality* 46, 228–243.

Festinger, L. (1957) *A Theory of Cognitive Dissonance*. Stanford, CA: Stanford University Press.

Fine, B. J. (1957) Conclusion-drawing, communicator credibility, and anxiety as factors in opinion change. *Journal of Abnormal and Social Psychology* 54, 369–374.

Fishbein, M., and Ajzen, I. (1975) *Belief, Attitude, Intention, and Behavior: An Introduction to Theory and Research*. Reading, MA: Addison-Wesley.

Gallup, G. (1941) Question wording in public opinion polls. *Sociometry* 4, 259–268.

Gorn, G. J. (1975) The effects of personal involvement, communication discrepancy, and source prestige on reactions to communications on separatism. *Canadian Journal of Behavioral Science* 7, 369–386.

Granberg, D., and Burlison, J. (1983) The abortion issue in the 1980 elections. *Family Planning Perspectives* 15, 231–238.

Granberg, D., and Holmberg, S. (1986) Political perception among voters in Sweden and the U.S.: Analyses of issues with explicit alternatives. *Western Political Quarterly* 39, 7–28.

Guttman, L., and Suchman, E. A. (1947) Intensity and a zero point for attitude analysis. *American Sociological Review* 12, 57–67.

Hahn, H. (1970) The political impact of shifting attitudes. *Social Science Quarterly* 51, 730–742.

Heider, F. (1958) *The Psychology of Interpersonal Relations*. New York: Wiley.

Hoelter, J. W. (1985) The structure of self-conception: Conceptualization and measurement. *Journal of Personality and Social Psychology* 49, 1392–1407.

Holtz, R., and Miller, N. (1985) Assumed similarity and opinion certainty. *Journal of Personality and Social Psychology* 48, 890–898.

Howard-Pitney, B., Borgida, E., and Omoto, A. M. (1985) Personal involvement: An examination of processing differences. Manuscript. Twin Cities, MN: Department of Psychology, University of Minnesota.

_____ (1986) Personal involvement: An examination of processing differences. *Social Cognition* 4, 39–57.

Hurwitz, J. (1986) Issue perception and legislative decision making: An application of social judgement theory. *American Politics Quarterly* 14, 150–185.

Hyman, H. H., and Sheatsley, P. B. (1947) Some reasons why information campaigns fail. *Public Opinion Quarterly* 11, 412–423.

Iyengar, S. (1990) Shortcuts to political knowledge: Selective attention and accessibility. In FEREJOHN, J., and KUKLINSKI, J. (eds.). *Information and the Democratic Process.* Urbana, IL: University of Illinois Press, pp. 160–185.

JACCARD, J., and BECKER, M. A. (1985) Attitudes and behavior: An information integration perspective. *Journal of Experimental Social Psychology* 21, 440–465.

JACKMAN, M. R. (1977) Prejudice, tolerance, and attitudes toward ethnic groups. *Social Science Research* 6, 145–169.

JOHNSON, B. T., and EAGLY, A. H. (1989) Effects of involvement on persuasion: A meta-analysis. *Psychological Bulletin* 106, 290–314.

JOHNSON, D. M. (1940) Confidence and the expression of opinion. *The Journal of Social Psychology, Society for the Psychological Study of Social Issues Bulletin* 12, 213–220.

JOHNSON, J. T., and JUDD, C. M. (1983) Overlooking the incongruent: Categorization biases in the identification of political statements. *Journal of Personality and Social Psychology* 45, 978–996.

JUDD, C. M., and JOHNSON, J. T. (1981) Attitudes, polarization, and diagnosticity: Exploring the effects of affect. *Journal of Personality and Social Psychology* 41, 25–36.

JUDD, C. M., and KROSNICK, J. A. (1982) Attitude centrality, organization, and measurement. *Journal of Personality and Social Psychology* 42, 436–447.

———— (1989) The structural bases of consistency among political attitudes: The effects of political expertise and attitude importance. In PRATKANIS, A. R., BRECKLER, S. J., and GREENWALD, A. G. (eds.). *Attitude Structure and Function.* Hillsdale, NJ: Erlbaum, pp. 99–128.

KAGAY, M. R. (1988) In judging polls, what counts is when and how who is asked what. *New York Times,* September 12, p. A16.

KALLGREN, C. A., and WOOD, W. (1986) Access to attitude-relevant information in memory as a determinant of attitude-behavior consistency. *Journal of Experimental Social Psychology* 22, 328–338.

KAPLAN, H. B. (1980) *Deviant Behavior in Defense of Self.* New York: Academic Press.

KATZ, D. (1940) Three criteria: Knowledge, conviction, and significance. *Public Opinion Quarterly* 4, 277–284.

KENDALL, P. (1954) *Conflict and Mood: Factors Affecting Stability of Response.* Glencoe, IL: Free Press.

KNOWER, F. H. (1936) Experimental studies of changes in attitude—III: Some incidence of attitude changes. *Journal of Applied Psychology* 20, 114–127.

KROSNICK, J. A. (1986) Policy voting in American Presidential elections: An application of psychological theory to American politics. Ph.D. dissertation. Ann Arbor, MI: University of Michigan.

———— (1988a) The role of attitude importance in social evaluation: A study of policy preferences, presidential candidate evaluations, and voting behavior. *Journal of Personality and Social Psychology* 55, 196–210.

———— (1988b) Attitude importance and attitude change. *Journal of Experimental Social Psychology* 24, 240–255.

_____ (1989) Attitude importance and attitude accessibility. *Personality and Social Psychology Bulletin* 15, 297–308.

_____ (1990a) Americans' perceptions of presidential candidates: A test of the projection hypothesis. *Journal of Social Issues* 46, 159–182.

_____ (1990b) Government policy and citizen passion: A study of issue publics in contemporary America. *Political Behavior* 12, 59–92.

_____ (1991) The impact of cognitive sophistication and attitude importance on response order effects and question order effects. In SCHWARZ, N., and SUDMAN, S. (eds.). *Order Effects in Social and Psychological Research.* New York: Springer-Verlag.

KROSNICK, J. A., and SCHUMAN, H. (1985) Exploratory studies of the relation between attitude importance and memory for attitude-relevant information. Manuscript. Columbus, OH: Ohio State University.

_____ (1988) Attitude intensity, importance, and certainty and susceptibility to response effects. *Journal of Personality and Social Psychology* 54, 940–952.

KROSNICK, J. A., and TELHAMI, S. (1990) Public attitudes and American policy toward the Arab-Israeli conflict. Manuscript. Columbus, OH: Department of Psychology, Ohio State University.

LAMM, H., and MYERS, D. G. (1978) Group-induced polarization of attitudes and behavior. In BERKOWITZ, L. (ed.). *Advances in Experimental Social Psychology*, vol. 11. New York: Academic Press.

LEMON, N. F. (1968) A model of the extremity, confidence and salience of an opinion. *British Journal of Social Clinical Psychology* 7, 106–114.

LEWIN, K. (1951) *Field Theory in Social Science.* New York: Harper & Row.

LORD, C., ROSS, L., and LEPPER, M. (1979) Biased assimilation and attitude polarization: The effects of prior theories on subsequently considered evidence. *Journal of Personality and Social Psychology* 37, 2098–2109.

MCCAULEY, C., KOGAN, N., and TEGER, A. I. (1971) Order effects in answering risk dilemmas for self and others. *Journal of Personality and Social Psychology* 20, 423–424.

MCCROSKEY, J. C., PRICHARD, S. V. O., and ARNOLD, W. E. (1967–1968) Attitude intensity and the neutral point on semantic differential scales. *Public Opinion Quarterly* 31, 642–645.

MCDILL, E. L. (1959) A comparison of three measures of attitude intensity. *Social Forces* 38, 95–99.

MCGRAW, K. M., LODGE, M., and STROH, P. (1990) On-line processing in candidate evaluation: The effects of issue order, issue importance, and sophistication. *Political Behavior* 12, 41–58.

MADSEN, D. B. (1978) Issue importance and group choice shifts: A persuasive arguments approach. *Journal of Personality and Social Psychology* 36, 1118–1127.

MARKS, G., and MILLER, N. (1982) The effect of certainty on consensus judgments. *Personality and Social Psychology Bulletin* 11, 165–177.

MARKS, L. J., and KAMINS, M. A. (1988) The use of product sampling and advertising:

Effects of sequence of exposure and degree of advertising claim exaggeration on consumers' belief strength, belief confidence, and attitudes. *Journal of Marketing Research* 25, 266–281.

MARSH, H. W. (1986) Global self-esteem: Its relation to specific facets of self-concept and their importance. *Journal of Personality and Social Psychology* 51, 1224–1236.

MEHLING, R. (1959) A simple test for measuring intensity of attitudes. *Public Opinion Quarterly* 23, 576–578.

MULLEN, B., ATKINS, J. L., CHAMPION, D. S., EDWARDS, C., HARDY, D., STORY, J. E., and VANDERKLOK, M. (1985) The false consensus effect: A meta-analysis of 115 hypothesis tests. *Journal of Experimental Social Psychology* 21, 162–283.

MULLEN, B., DRISKELL, J. E., and SMITH, C. (1989) Availability and social projection: The effects of sequence of measurement and wording of question on estimates of consensus. *Personality and Social Psychology Bulletin* 15, 84–90.

MULLEN, B., and HU, L. (1988) Social projection as a function of cognitive mechanisms: Two meta-analytic integrations. *British Journal of Social Psychology* 27, 333–356.

NEWCOMB, T. M. (1961) *The Acquaintance Process*. New York: Holt, Rinehart, and Winston.

OSGOOD, C. E., SUCI, G. J., and TANNENBAUM, P. H. (1957) *The Measurement of Meaning*. Urbana, IL: University of Illinois Press.

OSGOOD, C. E., and TANNENBAUM, P. H. (1955) The principles of congruity in the prediction of attitude change. *Psychological Review* 62, 42–55.

PAYNE, S. L. (1951) *The Art of Asking Questions*. Princeton, NJ: Princeton University Press.

PELHAM, B. W., and SWANN, W. B., JR. (1989) From self-conceptions to self-worth: On the sources and structure of global self-esteem. *Journal of Personality and Social Psychology* 57, 672–680.

PETERSEN, K., and DUTTON, J. E. (1975) Certainty, extremity, intensity: Neglected variables in research on attitude-behavior consistency. *Social Forces* 54, 393–414.

POWELL, J. L. (1977) Satirical persuasion and topic salience. *Southern Speech Communication Journal* 42, 151–162.

PRICE, V. (1989) Social identification and public opinion: Effects of communicating group conflict. *Public Opinion Quarterly* 53, 197–224.

RABINOWITZ, G., PROTHRO, J. W., and JACOBY, W. (1982) Salience as a factor in the impact of issues on candidate evaluation. *Journal of Politics* 42, 41–63.

RADEN, D. (1983) The interrelationships between the dimensions of social attitudes. Paper presented at the annual meeting of the Southern Sociological Association, Atlanta, GA.

———— (1985) Strength-related attitude dimensions. *Social Psychological Quarterly* 48, 312–330.

RHINE, R. J., and SEVERANCE, L. J. (1970) Ego-involvement, discrepancy, source credibility, and attitude change. *Journal of Personality and Social Psychology* 16, 175–190.

RHOLES, W. S., and BAILEY, S. (1983) The effects of level of moral reasoning on consistency between moral attitudes and related behaviors. *Social Cognition* 2, 32–48.

ROBERTS, J. V. (1985) The attitude-memory relationship after 40 years: A meta-analysis of the literature. *Basic and Applied Social Psychology* 6, 221–241.

ROKEACH, M., and KLIEJUNAS, P. (1972) Behavior as a function of attitude-toward-object and attitude-toward-situation. *Journal of Personality and Social Psychology* 22, 194–201.

ROSEN, G. M., and ROSS, A. O. (1968) Relationship of body image to self-concept. *Journal of Consulting and Clinical Psychology* 32, 100.

ROSENBERG, M. (1965) *Society and the Adolescent Self-Image*. Princeton, NJ: Princeton University Press.

ROSENBERG, M. J., VERBA, S., and CONVERSE, P. E. (1970) *Vietnam and the silent majority*. New York: Harper & Row.

ROSENTHAL, R. (1979) The "file drawer problem" and tolerance for null results. *Psychological Bulletin* 86, 638–641.

SAMPLE, J., and WARLAND, R. (1973) Attitudes and the prediction of behavior. *Social Forces* 51, 292–304.

SARAT, A., and VIDMAR, N. (1976) Public opinion, the death penalty, and the eighth amendment: Testing the Marshall hypothesis. *Wisconsin Law Review* 171, 171–206.

SCHUMAN, H., and PRESSER, S. (1981) *Questions and Answers in Attitude Surveys: Experiments on Question Form, Wording, and Context*. New York: Academic Press.

SCHWARTZ, S. H. (1978) Temporal instability as a moderator of the attitude-behavior relationship. *Journal of Personality and Social Psychology* 36, 715–724.

SCOTT, W. A. (1968) Attitude measurement. In LINDZEY, G., and ARONSON, E. (eds.). *Handbook of Social Psychology*, vol. 2. Reading, MA: Addison-Wesley, pp. 204–273.

SHAPIRO, M. J. (1969) Rational political man: A synthesis of economic and social-psychological perspectives. *American Political Science Review* 63, 1106–1119.

SHERIF, M., and HOVLAND, C. I. (1961) *Social Judgment: Assimilation and Contrast Effects in Communication and Attitude Change*. New Haven, CT: Yale University Press.

SMITH, T. W. (1982) Attitude constraint as a function of non-affective dimensions. General Social Survey Technical Report No. 39. Chicago, IL: National Opinion Research Center.

STEMBER, H., and HYMAN, H. (1949–1950) How interviewer effects operate through question form. *International Journal of Opinion and Attitude Research* 3, 493–512.

STOUFFER, S. A., GUTTMAN, L., SUCHMAN, E. A., LAZARSFELD, P. F., STAR, S. A., and CLAUSEN, J. A. (1950) *Measurement and Prediction*. Princeton, NJ: Princeton University Press.

SWANN, W. B., JR., and ELY, R. J. (1984) A battle of wills: Self-verification versus behavioral confirmation. *Journal of Personality and Social Psychology* 46, 1287–1302.

SWANN, W. B., PELHAM, B. W., and CHIDESTER, T. R. (1988) Change through paradox: Using self-verification to alter beliefs. *Journal of Personality and Social Psychology* 54, 268–273.

TANNENBAUM, P. H. (1956) Initial attitude toward source and concept as factors in attitude change through communication. *Public Opinion Quarterly* 20, 413–425.

TEDIN, K. L. (1974) The influence of parents on the political attitudes of adolescents. *American Political Science Review* 68, 1579–1592.

———— (1980) Assessing peer and parental influence on adolescent political attitudes. *American Journal of Political Science* 24, 136–154.

TESSER, A. (1978) Self-generated attitude change. In BERKOWITZ, L. (ed.). *Advances in Experimental Social Psychology* 11, New York: Academic Press.

TOURANGEAU, R., and RASINSKI, K. A. (1990) Conviction, conflict, and consistency of response. Manuscript. Silver Spring, MD: CODA.

TOURANGEAU, R., RASINSKI, K. A., BRADBURN, N., and D'ANDRADE, R. (1989a) Belief accessibility and context effects in attitude measurement. *Journal of Experimental Social Psychology* 25, 401–421.

———— (1989b) Carryover effects in attitude surveys. *Public Opinion Quarterly* 53, 495–524.

VALLONE, R. P., ROSS, L., and LEPPER, M. R. (1985) The hostile media phenomenon: Biased perception and perceptions of media bias in coverage of the Beirut massacre. *Journal of Personality and Social Psychology* 49, 577–585.

VAN DER PLIGT, J., ESTER, P., and VAN DER LINDEN, J. (1983) Attitude extremity, consensus, and diagnosticity. *European Journal of Social Psychology* 13, 437–439.

WATKINS, D., and PARK, J. (1972) The role of subjective importance in self-evaluation. *Australian Journal of Psychology* 24, 209–210.

WEINSTEIN, N. D. (1984) Why it won't happen to me: Perceptions of risk factors and susceptibility. *Health Psychology* 3, 431–457.

WILSON, T. D., DUNN, D. S., KRAFT, D., and LISLE, D. J. (1989) Introspection, attitude change, and attitude-behavior consistency: The disruptive effects of explaining why we feel the way we do. In BERKOWITZ, L. (ed.). *Advances in Experimental Social Psychology*, vol. 22. New York: Academic Press, pp. 287–343.

WILSON, T. D., KRAFT, D., and DUNN, D. S. (1989) The disruptive effects of explaining attitudes: The moderating effect of knowledge about the attitude object. *Journal of Experimental Social Psychology* 25, 379–400.

WILSON, T. D., HODGES, S.D., and POLLACK, S. E. (1990) Effects of explaining attitudes on survey responses. Manuscript. Charlottesville, VA: University of Virginia.

WOOD, W. (1982) Retrieval of attitude-relevant information from memory: Effects on susceptibility to persuasion and on intrinsic motivation. *Journal of Personality and Social Psychology* 42, 798–810.

WOOD, W., KALLGREN, C. A., and PREISLER, R. M. (1985) Access to attitude-relevant information in memory as a determinant of persuasion: The role of message attributes. *Journal of Experimental Social Psychology* 21, 73–85.

YOUNG, J., BORGIDA, E., SULLIVAN, J., and ALDRICH, J. (1987) Personal agendas and the relationship between self-interest and voting behavior. *Social Psychology Quarterly* 50, 64–71.

11

New Technologies for the Direct and Indirect Assessment of Attitudes

JOHN F. DOVIDIO
and RUSSELL H. FAZIO

Recent theoretical and empirical advances in the domain of attitudes and social cognition offer considerable food for thought for the survey researcher. Basic theory and research have provided new insights regarding such matters as the structure of attitudes, their activation from memory, and the processes by which they guide the individual's behavior. The theoretical distinctions that have been offered are ones that the survey researcher may find helpful when constructing a survey instrument. In addition, the methods by which these conceptual questions have been addressed are relatively novel to the field of social psychology, and these new "technologies" may themselves have direct applicability to the development of survey instruments. In this chapter we will review briefly some of the conceptual distinctions provided by recent theory and research, describe the methods that have been employed, and suggest how and when they might be of use to the survey researcher.

Overview
of Recent Theoretical Developments

As noted by Zanna and Fazio (1982), the focus of research concerning attitudes as predictors of behavior has been characterized by a shift from the general question, "Is there an attitude-behavior relation?" to a *when* question: "Under what conditions do what kinds of attitudes held by what kinds of individuals predict what kinds of behaviors?" Research on the *when* question has produced a lengthy catalog of situational variables (e.g., normative constraints) and individual differences (e.g., self-monitoring), as well as a set of qualities of the attitude itself (many of which are discussed in chapter 10 by Krosnick and Abelson as indicants of attitude strength), that moderate the attitude-behavior relation.

More recently, increased attention has been paid to what Zanna and Fazio referred to as a third-generational question—the issue of *how* attitudes guide behavior. This concern with underlying processes has led to the development of a model, the MODE model (Fazio, 1990a), that provides a general framework for much of this chapter. The recently proposed MODE model suggests that it is fruitful to view attitude-behavior processes as being of essentially two types. Although mixtures of the two types of processes are likely to occur, Fazio argues that two general classes of processes can be delineated—the basic difference between the two centers on the extent to which a behavioral decision involves conscious deliberation versus a spontaneous reaction to an attitude object or issue:

> An individual may analyze the costs and benefits of a particular behavior, and, in doing so, deliberately reflect upon the attitudes relevant to a behavioral decision. These attitudes may serve as one of the possibly many dimensions that are considered in arriving at a behavior plan, which may then be enacted. Alternatively, attitudes may guide an individual's behavior in a more spontaneous manner, without the individual's having actively considered the relevant attitudes and without the individual's necessary awareness of the influence of the attitude. Instead, the attitude may influence how the person interprets the event that is occurring and, in that way, affect the person's behavior (Fazio, 1990a, p. 78).

Obviously, the spontaneous processing mode begins with the presumption that not all social behavior is deliberative or reasoned. Instead, behavior may be more spontaneous in nature. Many daily social behaviors would appear to be of this sort (see Langer, 1978). For people to do otherwise—that is, for people to rely constantly on reflective reasoning processes in order to decide how to behave—would be enormously dysfunctional for daily living. The ease with which we all engage in normal social discourse alone suggests that much of our behavior is spontaneous rather than the planned outcome of some reflective process.

How might such spontaneous behaviors be influenced by one's attitude toward the object in question? To the extent that individuals engage in any construal, or interpretation, of the attitude object and the situation in which the attitude object is encountered, there exists the possibility of attitudes guiding behavior toward the object. By influencing such perceptions, attitudes may exert an impact upon the eventual behavior. Consistent with these notions, a rich and varied literature exists documenting that attitudes influence perceptions of the attitude object. Attitudes have been found to relate to what is perceived in an ambiguous scene (e.g., Hastorf and Cantril, 1954; Proshansky, 1943; Seeleman, 1940), to affect individuals' causal interpretations of a target person's behavior (e.g., Regan, Straus, and Fazio, 1974), and to affect individuals' evaluations of attitudinally relevant empirical evidence (e.g., Lord, Ross, and Lepper, 1979). In each of these cases, individuals with differing attitudes toward the target person, object, or issue have been shown to arrive at different perceptions and judgments of the same stimulus information.

Thus, when one encounters an attitude object, one's attitude can guide perceptions of the object in the immediate situation. These immediate perceptions, congruent as they are with one's attitude, can then prompt attitudinally consistent behavior. According to the model, it is through their mediating impact upon perceptions that attitudes guide behavior in a spontaneous fashion—that is, the individual need not consciously reflect upon feelings toward the attitude object for an attitudinally biased perception of the attitude object in the immediate situation to occur. Yet, such differential perceptions on the part of individuals with differing attitudes can lead them to respond very differently toward the attitude object.

According to the spontaneous processing model, whether such differential perceptions occur depends upon whether individuals' attitudes are activated from memory or not. In many instances the spontaneous attitude-behavior process simply may not be initiated. Although the model does not postulate that it is necessary for individuals to reflect upon their attitudes toward the object in question for selective perception to occur, it is necessary that individuals' evaluations of the attitude object be activated from memory upon encountering the attitude object. Unless the attitude is activated from memory, it cannot produce selective perception of the object in the immediate situation. Indeed, the individual may never view the object in evaluative terms; or if the person does consider the object evaluatively, this appraisal may be constructed on the spot on the basis of whatever information and features of the object happen to be salient at that moment. Thus, the key to the spontaneous processing model is attitude accessibility. The attitude must be activated from memory upon the individual's observation of the attitude object if the attitude is to guide subsequent behavior.

Beyond question, however, some social behavior is planned and deliberate. Indeed, we sometimes decide how we *intend* to behave and then follow through on that intention when we enter the situation. Deliberative processing is characterized by considerable cognitive work. It involves the scrutiny of available information and an analysis of positive and negative features, of costs and benefits. The specific attributes of the attitude object and the potential consequences of engaging in a particular course of action may be considered and weighed. Such reflection forms the basis for deciding upon a behavioral intention and, ultimately, behavior.

The name MODE model refers to *m*otivation and *o*pportunity as *de*terminants of the processing mode by which behavioral decisions are made. Deliberation is effortful and, in that sense, costly. In order to engage in deliberative processing, one must be both motivated to do so (e.g., out of concern about the costs of making a wrong decision) and have the opportunity to do so (e.g., the time and the cognitive resources).

The importance of motivation and opportunity in determining the nature of the attitude-to-behavior process is illustrated by a recent experiment conducted by Sanbonmatsu and Fazio (1990). While under instructions to form general evaluations of each of two stores, subjects were exposed to a series of statements describing a variety of departments (e.g., clothing, jewelry) of each of two fictitious department stores. One such store, Smith's, was described in generally favorable terms; two-thirds of the statements mentioned desirable attributes. The other store, Brown's, was described in predominantly unfavorable terms; two-thirds of the statements concerned undesirable attributes. Thus, overall evaluations would lead one to favor Smith's over Brown's.

However, the specific attributes ascribed to the camera departments of the two stores were designed to reverse the direction of this general preference. Brown's, the generally less favorable store, had the better camera department. The two statements describing Brown's camera department were both positive, whereas the two describing Smith's camera department were both unfavorable. The aim underlying the portrayal of the two stores was to create a situation in which subjects had constructed general attitudes toward each store, in addition to having the specific attributes of each store in memory.

At a later point in the experiment, the subjects were asked to imagine that they needed to buy a camera and to consider at which store they would do so. Choice of Brown's (the store with the better camera department) would be indicative of deliberative processing; subjects selecting Brown's would have undertaken the effort to retrieve from memory the specific attributes concerning the camera departments, and would have used that information to construct an attitude and a behavioral intention concerning the specific behavior of buying a camera at Brown's versus Smith's. Alternatively, choice of Smith's (the generally superior store with the inferior camera department) would be indicative of a relatively effortless strategy involving simple consideration of the previously formed attitudes toward each store.

The critical concern was with how decision strategy would be affected by the variables postulated to be important by the MODE model—motivation and opportunity. Prior to the introduction of the camera-buying scenario, both time pressure and motivation were manipulated. Subjects in the no-time-pressure condition were specifically instructed to take their time in answering the question that was to follow. Subjects in the time-pressure condition were warned that they would have only fifteen seconds in which to reach a decision about the question that was to follow. Motivation was crossed with time pressure and manipulated in a manner similar to that employed by Kruglanski and Freund (1983). In the high-motivation condition the subjects were informed that their decision would be compared to the decisions reached by the other subjects in the group, and that they would later have to explain their decision to the other subjects and the experimenter. This information was absent for subjects in the low-motivation condition.

The MODE model predicts that both motivation and opportunity are prerequisites for deliberative, attribute-based processing. Only then would subjects have the time and desire to retrieve specific bits of information from memory and realize that Brown's, although it might be generally inferior, was the better store at which to shop for a camera. This is precisely what the data revealed—a significant motivation × opportunity interaction that matched the predicted form. Subjects in the one cell of the design involving both motivation and opportunity displayed a significantly greater preference for buying a camera at Brown's than did subjects in any of the other three conditions. Thus, the findings corroborate the hypotheses of the MODE model with respect to motivation and opportunity. Both appear to be necessary conditions for a deliberative, reasoned process to operate.

Implications for Attitude Measurement

Target Attitudes as Function of Processing Mode

The theoretical distinction between spontaneous and deliberative processing has implications for attitude measurement and behavioral prediction. The findings from the Sanbonmatsu and Fazio (1990) experiment, for example, illustrate a point that we believe survey researchers might consider when constructing a survey instrument. Is the behavior that one is attempting to predict likely to provoke deliberative processing? Is it a behavior for which individuals would be highly concerned about the possibility of making a poor decision, and for which they have the opportunity to deliberate? The answer to this question has implications for the type of verbal items one might include in the survey.

Frequently, a global evaluation or attitude associated with an object is measured in order to predict behavior. This assessment is often achieved through the use of semantic differential or Likert scales. In other instances the specific beliefs about the attributes of an object and the evaluations of those attributes are measured in order to predict behavior (e.g., Ajzen and Fishbein, 1980). The MODE model suggests that to optimize the accuracy of predictions, the type of decision process that is expected to operate in the behavioral context should be considered. If behavior is expected to be guided by a particular global attitude, then broadly measuring that attitude will be the optimal means of predicting behavior. If, however, behavior is expected to be based on a deliberative analysis of a number of specific beliefs, then measuring those beliefs may be the more effective way of predicting behavior. Thus, the critical issue becomes how different aspects of attitudes relate to actions under different circumstances. The stimulus materials in the Sanbonmatsu and Fazio (1990) research were constructed so as to have global attitudes and specific attribute knowledge prompt differential decisions. Although this may have been a bit contrived relative to configurations that might exist in the real world, to the extent that any discrepancy exists between these two levels of specificity, awareness of and assessment directed at, the level at which individuals are likely to operate should optimize behavioral prediction.

Measurement Issues Within the Deliberative Mode

If motivation and opportunity are such that deliberative decision making is to be expected, traditional attitude-measurement techniques—as long as they are directed at the appropriate level—appear to provide satisfactory means of assessment. There is, however, one important caveat to this general conclusion. Individuals may express public attitudes that reflect more their impressions of socially desirable responses than their *true* private opinions. It is well documented in laboratory research that subjects are concerned about the evaluations of others and are motivated to behave in positive and appropriate ways (e.g., Weber and Cook, 1972). These evaluation concerns may moderate self-report responses and therefore are very likely to be present in the survey interview situation. In chapter 7 Abelson, Loftus, and Greenwald noted the prominent role of social desirability in vote overreporting. Here we analyze deliberative self-presentational biases in attitude reports, particularly in socially sensitive areas such as racial attitudes. For example, as a consequence of social-desirability influences, studies of interracial behavior that use overt and obtrusive measures (e.g., self-reports or public behaviors) generally produce more egalitarian and nonprejudiced responses among whites toward blacks than do investigations that use less reactive measures (e.g., private or nonverbal behaviors) (Crosby, Bromley, and Saxe, 1980).

The systematic consideration of social values in the expression of an attitude actually may occur at two levels. At one level, individuals may publicly express socially desirable attitudes even though they are aware that they privately hold other attitudes. At another level, individuals may express attitudes that reinforce a positive self-image and reflect an ideal rather than an actual self-concept. Individuals may be unwilling to admit to themselves that they can be characterized as possessing a particular kind of attitude (Gaertner and Dovidio, 1986). Whereas the first level involves a concern about others' evaluations, the second level focuses on the importance of self-evaluation. In either case, such considerations yield an attitudinal response that the survey researcher may have good reason to question.

The assessment of racial attitudes provides an excellent illustration. Several nationwide surveys indicate that the racial attitudes of white Americans toward black Americans are currently positive, accepting, and support-ive, and that these attitudes have consistently become more egalitarian across time (Schuman, Steeh, and Bobo, 1985). These survey procedures, however, involve obtrusive measures and public and deliberate responses, and thus may be influenced by social-desirability concerns. Because public norms of tolerance have changed for the better (which in itself represents progress), many social scientists have argued that surveys overestimate the amount of racial tolerance and underestimate the amount of covert prejudice in America today (Dovidio and Gaertner, 1986; Jackman and Muha, 1984).

Indeed, there is experimental evidence that survey respondents and research participants systematically alter their expressed racial attitudes and behaviors to appear in a more socially desirable light—unprejudiced and egalitarian—to others and to themselves. With respect to the anticipated evaluations of others, Sigall and Page (1971) found that white subjects who believed that their truthfulness was being monitored through their physiolog-ical responses (the "bogus pipeline" procedure) gave more negative evalua-tions of blacks and more positive evaluations of whites than did control subjects who did not believe that they were being physiologically monitored. McConahay, Hardee, and Batts (1981) found that subjects shifted their answers to appear more unprejudiced when a questionnaire was adminis-tered by a black experimenter than by a white experimenter, particularly for items that most obviously and directly addressed racial attitudes.

Recent studies of racial attitudes of white college students that have used traditional self-report methodologies reveal little prejudice. The results of a study that used an adjective-checklist procedure (see table 1) indicated that in 1990 whites' characterizations of blacks were substantially less negative than in the past and were no more negative than whites' characterizations of whites (Dovidio and Gaertner, 1991). In a survey conducted for this chapter that included questions on racial attitudes from the General Social Survey, white college students in 1989 showed unprecedented egalitarian attitudes (see table 2). In a third study in which subjects were asked to evaluate black and white people on several ubiquitous six-point bipolar scales (for example, *good* _ _ _ _ _ _ *bad*), no differences in evaluative ratings of blacks and whites were obtained (Dovidio, Mann, and Gaertner, 1989). Thus, in research using a variety of traditional self-report procedures, white college students generally avoided responses that could be interpreted, by others or by oneself, as being racially biased; instead, they consistently endorsed items indicating racial tolerance and acceptance.

Are such attitudinal self-reports—influenced as they are by social-desirability concerns—necessarily poor prognosticators of actual behavior? Under certain circumstances they may not be—namely, when the behavior itself is influenced by social norms in the same manner as the attitudinal self-reports are. For example, Gaertner and Dovidio (1986) demonstrated that in situations in which socially desirable and appropriate behavior is clearly defined, white subjects do not discriminate against blacks, a result that corresponds to subjects' generally nonprejudiced self-reports. Gaertner and Dovidio (1986), however, also report that white subjects do discriminate against blacks when they can justify or rationalize a negative response on the basis of an ostensibly non-race-related factor, producing less correspondence between self-reported attitude and actions. (See also Crosby, Bromley, and Saxe, 1980).

In a study by Gaertner and Dovidio (1977), for example, white subjects were led to believe that they were the only bystanders or were among three witnesses to an emergency involving a black or white victim. According to Darley and Latané (1968), the normatively appropriate behavior, helping, is clearly defined when a bystander is the only witness to an emergency. In contrast, the appropriate response when other bystanders are believed to be present is less clear and obvious: The presumed presence of other bystanders allows bystanders to diffuse responsibility (Darley and Latané, 1968), to relieve feelings of obligation to help by coming to the conclusion that someone else will act. Gaertner and Dovidio (1977) found that the white subjects who believed that they were the only witnesses to the emergency were as likely to help black victims as white victims. Thus, in the situation in which socially appropriate behavior was clearly defined, white subjects behaved in accordance with their generally nonprejudiced self-images and did not discriminate against the black victim. In addition, subjects' earlier self-reports of prejudice, based on their degree of agreement or disagreement with the statement, "I am prejudiced against blacks," significantly predicted their responses to the black victim. Subjects who reported greater prejudice intervened to help the black victim less quickly ($r = .42, p < .04$). When white bystanders believed that there were other capable witnesses and

Table 1a Percentage of Subjects Selecting a Trait to Describe Black Americans (formerly "Negroes") in 1933, 1951, 1967, 1982, 1988, and 1990.

	1933	1951	1967	1982	1988	1990
Superstitious	84	41	13	6	2	3
Lazy	75	31	26	13	6	4
Happy-Go-Lucky	38	17	27	15	4	1
Ignorant	38	24	11	10	6	5
Musical	26	33	47	29	13	27
Ostentatious	26	11	25	5	0	1
Very Religious	24	17	8	23	20	19
Stupid	22	10	4	1	1	3
Physically Dirty	17	—	3	0	1	0
Naive	14	—	4	4	2	3
Slovenly	13	—	5	2	1	1
Unreliable	12	—	6	2	1	4
Pleasure Loving	—	19	26	20	14	14
Sensitive	—	—	17	13	15	9
Gregarious	—	—	17	4	6	2
Talkative	—	—	14	5	5	8
Imitative	—	—	13	9	4	3
Aggressive	—	—	—	19	16	17
Materialistic	—	—	—	16	10	3
Loyal to Family	—	—	—	39	49	41
Arrogant	—	—	—	14	7	7
Ambitious	—	—	—	13	23	16
Tradition Loving	—	—	—	13	22	16
Individualistic	—	—	—	—	24	17
Passionate	—	—	—	—	14	17
Nationalistic	—	—	—	—	13	13
Straightforward	—	—	—	—	12	15
Intelligent	—	—	—	—	—	14
Sportsmanlike	—	—	—	—	—	13
Quick-Tempered	—	—	—	—	—	12
Artistic	—	—	—	—	—	12

Table 1b   Percentage of Subjects Selecting a Trait to Describe White Americans in 1933, 1951, 1967, 1982, 1988, and 1990.

	1933	1951	1967	1982	1988	1990
Industrious	48	30	23	21	13	10
Intelligent	47	32	20	10	6	15
Materialistic	33	37	67	65	41	46
Ambitious	33	21	42	35	35	33
Progressive	27	5	17	9	10	7
Pleasure Loving	26	27	28	45	32	23
Alert	23	7	7	2	1	4
Efficient	21	9	15	8	5	3
Aggressive	20	8	15	8	5	3
Straightforward	19	—	9	7	8	4
Practical	19	—	12	14	10	14
Sportsmanlike	19	—	9	6	4	3
Individualistic	—	26	15	14	24	19
Conventional	—	—	17	20	8	11
Scientific	—	—	15	4	3	3
Ostentatious	—	—	15	6	6	5
Conservative	—	—	—	15	22	26
Stubborn	—	—	—	20	8	10
Tradition Loving	—	—	—	19	22	13
Loyal to Family	—	—	—	—	20	19
Nationalistic	—	—	—	—	24	6
Boastful	—	—	—	—	13	10
Ignorant	—	—	—	—	10	12
Arrogant	—	—	—	—	—	26

213

Table 2   Trends Toward Acceptance and Tolerance in the Racial Attitudes of White Americans (National Opinion Research Center Surveys and College Student Survey).

	NORC 1972–1982	1985	NORC 1986	1987	Students 1989
How strongly would you object if a member of your family wanted to bring a black friend home to dinner? (Percent objecting strongly or mildly)	26%	20%	—	—	0%
Do you think there should be laws against marriages between blacks and whites? (Percent "yes")	34%	28%	—	24%	0%
If your party nominated a black for president, would you vote for him if he were qualified for the job? (Percent "no")	18%	15%	13%	—	1%
Do you think white students and black students should go to the same schools or separate schools? (Percent "separate schools")	12%	7%	—	—	0%
Some people think that blacks have been discriminated against for so long that the government has a special obligation to improve their living standards. Others believe that the government should not be giving special treatment to blacks. (Percent opposing "special treatment")	53%	—	52%	50%	26%

could rationalize their nonintervention with the belief that someone else would help, a different pattern emerged. Under these conditions subjects helped black victims less than white victims, and self-reported prejudice was a poor predictor of intervention. In fact, subjects who reported *lower* degrees of prejudice tended to help black victims *more slowly* ($r = -.26$). Thus, it is in cases in which behavior is not so clearly defined by norms of social appropriateness that one must question the predictive validity of traditional self-reports of attitude.

Measurement Issues Within the Spontaneous Mode

There is an additional complexity to the prediction of behaviors that are presumed to stem from a more spontaneous behavioral process. In addition to the issue raised above concerning the role of social desirability in attitude assessment and behavioral context, the likelihood that the attitude will be activated from memory is critically important. As noted earlier, for the attitude to guide spontaneous behavior, it must be activated from memory upon the individual's observation of the attitude object. Within this theoretical framework the likelihood of such activation is considered to be a function of the strength of the association in memory between the attitude object and one's evaluation of the object (see Fazio, 1986). It is this associative strength that is postulated to determine the accessibility of the attitude.

A number of empirical investigations—both field-based and laboratory-based, both correlational and experimental—have indicated that the impact that attitudes have upon judgments and behavior is a function of the strength of the object-evaluation association and, hence, the accessibility of the attitude (e.g., Fazio, Chen, McDonel, and Sherman, 1982; Fazio, Powell, and Williams, 1989; Fazio and Williams, 1986; Houston and Fazio, 1989). Essentially, variations in the strength of the object-evaluation association can be viewed as defining an attitude-to-nonattitude continuum reflecting the power of the attitude. At the attitude end of the continuum is the case of a strong association such that the attitude is capable of automatic activation upon mere observation of the attitude object. Automatic processes are effortless and are initiated spontaneously and inescapably upon the individual's encountering appropriate stimulus conditions (see Schneider and Shiffrin, 1977; Shiffrin and Schneider, 1977). Shiffrin and Dumais (1981) characterize as automatic any process that leads to the activation of some response "whenever a given set of external initiating stimuli are presented, regardless of a subject's attempt to ignore or bypass the distraction" (p. 117). Such automatic attitude activation produces appraisals of the object in the immediate situation that are congruent with the attitude and in that way guide behavior toward the object.

At the lower end of the continuum is the case of a nonattitude—an object for which no evaluative associate is available in the memory. The individual has no a priori attitude toward the object. At intermediate points of the continuum, the evaluation that is available in memory is not sufficiently associated with the attitude object to be capable of automatic activation. In these latter two cases, the individual is forced to construct an appraisal of the object in the immediate situation in which it is encountered. Because such immediate appraisals may be unduly influenced by momentarily salient features, they may not be representative of the individual's attitude, and thus behavior may not be attitudinally consistent. The implication is that one needs to know the position of an individual's attitude along this continuum (i.e., the strength of the object-evaluation association in memory) in order to make an assessment of whether the attitude is likely to be activated from memory and influence judgments and behavior in a spontaneous manner.

In summary we are focusing upon two potential difficulties in assessing an individual's attitude. The first is that there may be reason to question the individual's self-report when the issue involved is socially sensitive. People may, consciously or unconsciously, alter their expression of an attitude to conform to prevailing norms. Normative influences on attitudinal self-reports can yield poor predictors of behavior in situations that involve either deliberative or spontaneous behavioral decision making when social desirability concerns are not salient. This problem of poor prediction calls for some form of an indirect measure of attitude—ideally one that estimates the attitude without the individual's awareness that attitudes are even being assessed, or at least minimizes the concerns about responding in a socially desirable fashion. We shall discuss methodologies that have been employed to investigate the automatic activation of attitudes as one potential solution to this problem. The second issue is that the prediction of spontaneous behaviors can be improved by knowledge of the accessibility of the attitude from memory. In cases in which social-desirability concerns are not relevant, direct measures of attitude can be supplemented by an additional assessment of attitude accessibility. In cases in which one still has reason to mistrust a direct assessment, some of the indirect techniques that we shall discuss serve both to enhance the unobtrusiveness of the measurement procedure and to provide an indication of the likelihood that the attitude is capable of automatic activation from memory.

Minimizing Social-Desirability Concerns During Attitude Assessment

Traditional self-report measures of attitudes ask respondents to provide a rating on a bipolar scale (e.g., *good/bad*). In a case in which the social norm calls for positivity, the salient display of negative evaluative terms may make people very hesitant to employ the negative end of the scale. As mentioned earlier, Dovidio, Mann, and Gaertner (1989) obtained no differences in white subjects' evaluative ratings of blacks and whites when these ratings were made on a traditional six-point bipolar scale. Apparently, responses that could be interpreted as reflecting bias (e.g., *bad*) were obvious, and subjects consistently rated others, both blacks and whites, on the positive ends of the scales.

In contrast to these findings, the use of alternative self-report procedures that may be less familiar to respondents and may obscure socially desirable responses reveal greater racial bias in comparable college samples. On the assumption that respondents are particularly guarded about displaying *negative* bias, Dovidio, Mann, and Gaertner (1989) varied the rating-scale procedure slightly by placing positive and negative characteristics in separate scales (e.g., *good*: 1 = "not at all" to 7 = "extremely"; *bad*: 1 = "not at all" to 7 = "extremely"). When the ratings of blacks and whites on the negative scales were examined, no racial bias appeared: blacks were *not* rated more negatively than whites. The ratings on the positive scales, however, did reveal a significant difference. Whereas blacks were not rated more negatively than whites, whites *were* evaluated more positively than were blacks. Similarly, Gaertner and McLaughlin (1983, study 3) replaced the conventional positive and negative scales with moderately negative to very negative scales (e.g., *unambitious—lazy*) and moderately positive to very positive scales (e.g., *not lazy—ambitious*). Discrimination did not occur on the negative-negative scales but did appear on the positive-positive scales. Blacks were not rated as more lazy than whites, but whites were evaluated as more ambitious than blacks. Thus, perhaps because of the censoring related to concerns about one's self- and/or public image, white college students did not characterize blacks more negatively than whites—a response that could readily be interpreted as racial prejudice—but these respondents did systematically characterize whites more positively than blacks.

Recently, Pettigrew and Meertens (1989) have developed survey items that measure blatant and subtle prejudice toward out-groups. Responses to six different out-groups were obtained from seven independent probability samples in four West European nations. Blatant prejudice is direct and involves expressions of the inferiority of out-groups ("they come from less able races") and racial threat ("they have jobs we should have"). Subtle prejudice, in contrast, is indirect and less overtly negative. Specifically relevant to the findings for rating scales with our college student samples, subtle racism involves less positive feelings (e.g., sympathy) and orientations (e.g., admiration) toward out-groups, but *not* more negative feelings or beliefs. Pettigrew and Meertens's (1989) survey research demonstrated that whereas blatant prejudice predicted support for policies that would uncon- ditionally restrict the rights and opportunities of out-groups, subtle racism predicted support for the status quo or for restrictions when ostensibly non-race-related justifications (e.g., lack of credentials) were available.

Nontraditional measures of racial attitudes have also been developed particularly for attitudes toward black Americans. Because traditional racial-attitude measures were reactive, showed little correlation with racially relevant behaviors, and produced relatively high refusal rates that adversely affected telephone and face-to-face interviews, survey researchers developed more subtle and indirect items, which comprise the Symbolic Racism Scale (Kinder and Sears, 1981; Sears, 1988) and the Modern Racism Scale (McConahay, 1986). Symbolic (or modern) racism involves the "expression in terms of abstract ideological symbols and symbolic behaviors of the feelings that blacks are violating cherished values and making illegitimate demands for changes in the racial *status quo*" (McConahay and Hough, 1976, p. 38). An example of one of these items is, "Blacks are getting too demanding in their push for equal rights." The wordings of symbolic racism items "permit the expression of negative affect because giving the prejudiced response in each instance can be explained by racially neutral ideology or nonprejudiced race-relevant attributions" (McConahay, 1986, p. 100). In terms of validity, symbolic and modern racism scores have been demonstrated in survey research to be better predictors of voter antipathy to black candidates and opposition to school busing than were traditional measures of prejudice (McConahay, 1986; Sears and Allen, 1984; Sears and Kinder, 1985; Sears, Lau, Tyler, and Allen, 1980; see also Bobo, 1983, for a critique).

Such nontraditional self-report items and scales are obviously easy to employ in survey research and provide important information about aspects of an individual's attitude. These items apparently diminish the extent to which respondents' self-ratings are susceptible to social-desirability concerns and in that sense represent an important departure from traditional bipolar scales. Nevertheless, even such subtle measures provide no information regarding the likelihood that the attitude will be activated automatically from memory upon the individual's encountering the attitude object, and what the spontaneous aspects of the attitude are.

Measuring Automatic Attitude Activation: Indirect Attitude Assessment

In order to address the issue of automatic activation of attitudes, researchers (e.g., Fazio, Sanbonmatsu, Powell, and Kardes, 1986; Greenwald, Klinger, and Liu, 1989) have employed priming and latency procedures more typically associated with research efforts in cognitive psychology. For example, Fazio et al. (1986) employed a priming procedure that permitted the examination of the hypothesis that the mere presentation of an attitude object toward which an individual possesses a strong evaluative association in memory would automatically activate the evaluation. On each trial the prime that was presented was the name of an attitude object. Its presentation was followed by the display of a positive or a negative evaluative adjective. The subject's task was to press a key as quickly as possible to indicate whether the adjective had a positive or a negative connotation. The latency with which these judgments were made was examined.

To provide an example, assume that the attitude object "cockroach" is evaluated negatively by an individual and that this object-evaluation association is strong. Presentation of "cockroach" as the prime may automatically activate the negative evaluation. If the target adjective that is subsequently presented is also negative (e.g., disgusting), then the individual may be able to indicate relatively quickly that the target adjective has a negative connotation, that is, responding should be facilitated. Thus, the technique relies on the presence of facilitation as an indication that the evaluation associated with the primed attitude object has been activated upon its mere presentation.

Precisely such facilitation was observed on trials that involved evaluatively congruent primes (attitude objects) and target adjectives, provided that the attitude object was characterized by a strongly associated evaluation for the subject. In two of the experiments that Fazio et al. (1986) conducted, preexperimentally strong and weak associations were identified. In another experiment, the strength of the object-evaluation association was manipulated experimentally rather than measured. Regardless of whether strong associations were identified by measurement or created experimentally, such attitude objects yielded more facilitation on evaluatively congruent trials than did objects involving relatively weaker associations.

The presence of facilitation in this task suggests that the subject's attitude toward the object was activated automatically upon its mere presentation as the prime. It is important to keep in mind that the adjective connotation task did not require subjects to consider their attitudes toward the object. From the subject's perspective, the prime or attitude object was simply a *memory word* that the subject was asked to recite aloud at the end of the trial. The subject's primary task was to respond to the target adjective. Nevertheless, despite this irrelevance of attitudes to the immediate task concerns, exposure to objects for which subjects possessed strongly associated evaluations prompted activation of the evaluation.

Techniques such as this may provide a means of unobtrusively obtaining an estimate of an individual's spontaneous attitude. The potential exists for obtaining an indication of the extent to which the attitude object is associated in memory with positive versus negative evaluations. Both authors of this chapter have been pursuing such a strategy—Fazio and his colleagues with respect to the measurement of socially sensitive issues in general; and Dovidio, Gaertner, and their colleagues with respect to the assessment of racial attitudes in particular.

Fazio, Williams, and Sanbonmatsu (1990) have been working toward the development of a variant of the adjective connotation task described above as an unobtrusive measure of attitude. The specific task that these investigators have employed involves subjects' identification of an evaluative adjective as it gradually becomes legible on the computer screen. This target adjective is initially masked by a rectangle of dots. Gradually, and on a random basis, the dots are erased and the word becomes apparent. Thus, the word appears to emerge out of "noise." As soon as the subject can identify the word, the subject presses a key, which immediately erases the screen (so that the subject cannot "cheat") and announces the word aloud. How quickly the subject can identify the word is recorded. After the subject is trained on this task, the subject is informed that the task will now be made more difficult by preceding each target word with the presentation of a memory word. From the subject's point of view, the memory word is simply a word that needs to be remembered until the end of the trial and recited aloud immediately after identifying and announcing the target word. In actuality the memory word is the name of an attitude object. What is examined is the degree to which the subject's identification of the target word is facilitated by the presentation of the attitude object.

In the research by Fazio and his associates (1990), estimates of spontaneous attitudes were obtained by comparing the extent to which a given attitude object facilitated the identification of positive versus negative evaluative adjectives. The correspondence between these indirectly obtained estimates of spontaneously activated attitudes and traditional self-report measures then was examined. Two different sets of attitude objects were assessed in this way: a set involving socially sensitive issues, for which self-reports might be influenced by social desirability concerns, and a set of nonsensitive issues. The latter included such items as Russians, dentists, pizza, snakes, Snickers, and anchovies. For each object the mean rating on the self-report measure was computed as well as the mean estimate of attitude based upon the facilitation data. The sample's self-reported attitudes toward the nonsensitive issues were predicted fairly well by the indirect estimates. The rank-order correlation of these two sets of means was .63. Thus, even though subjects were never asked during the word identification task to consider or to report their attitudes toward the object that constituted the memory word, the pattern of facilitation provided a valid estimate of the sample's attitudes.

As alluded to earlier, Fazio, Williams, and Sanbonmatsu included a set of eight additional attitude objects in their study. What distinguished these eight from the other twelve was that they were attitude issues that can be characterized as socially sensitive. A sample of undergraduates had rated a large number of attitude issues with respect to the extent an individual might be reluctant to express publicly his or her true attitude toward the issue. It was on the basis of these ratings that these eight additional items were selected: pornography, contraceptives, Ku Klux Klan, abortion, blacks, premarital sex, Jews, and homosexuality. As we argued earlier, for socially sensitive issues there is reason to consider the role of social desirability in shaping subjects' self-reported attitudes. In this case the sample's self-reported attitudes and the estimates based upon the facilitation data did not correspond at all; the rank-order correlation for the two sets of means among these eight socially sensitive issues was −.11. Thus, for socially sensitive issues the unobtrusively obtained estimates of attitude provided a different portrayal of the sample's attitudes than did the direct self-reports.

Some of the disparities that were observed are worth noting. According to the self-report data, the sample viewed pornography very negatively; it ranked seventh among the eight issues and was rated far more negatively than, for example, premarital sex. Yet, according to the indirect assessment, pornography ranked second in positivity and was not discernably different from premarital sex, which ranked third. Jews and blacks were rated equivalently positive via the self-reports, but the indirect assessments revealed discriminability. Significantly more negativity toward blacks than toward Jews was apparent in the unobtrusive estimates of automatically activated attitudes. Any conclusions must be regarded as fairly tentative at this point, but it does appear that this unobtrusive technique can yield an assessment of individuals' evaluations regarding socially sensitive issues that is not captured by direct self-report measures.

Similar techniques have been employed in other recent research that has focused specifically on racial attitudes. As with the procedure described earlier, these techniques have the common feature of never directly asking a respondent for an evaluation of a racial group. In that way the biases associated with direct assessments are avoided. Yet, performance on the experimental task provides a measure of the nature of associations to the racial group in memory. In this research, as in the previous research on spontaneous attitudes in general, the focus is on evaluative associations rather than associations along potency or activity dimensions.

Two different types of paradigms have commonly been used. In one paradigm, a lexical decision task, the subject is presented simultaneously with two strings of letters and is asked to decide (yes or no) if both strings are words. On *word* trials faster responses are assumed to reflect greater association in memory between the two words. In classic work with this task, Meyer and Schvaneveldt (1971) demonstrated that highly associated words (e.g., doctor, nurse) produced faster responses than did unassociated words (nurse, apple). Using the lexical decision task to assess racial attitudes, Gaertner and McLaughlin (1983) paired the words *blacks* and *whites*, explicitly representing the racial categories, with positive and negative attributes. They found that subjects made their decisions about the letter strings faster when positive attributes were paired with whites than with blacks (see figure 1). Subjects, however, showed no difference in response latencies for negative attributes paired with whites and blacks.

In a second paradigm that has been employed, a priming task, the subject is presented with two words sequentially and is asked to decide if the second word, a characteristic, could *ever* describe the first (prime) word, a social category. In a study of racial attitudes by Dovidio and Gaertner (1991), on each trial the subject was first presented with a prime of *black* or *white* and asked to think about the racial groups. Each prime was then followed by a positive trait (e.g., *good*) or a negative characteristic (e.g., *bad*). Note that subjects were *not* directly asked to make personal judgments concerning the appropriateness of characteristics to racial groups; the stimuli on the trials of interest were constructed such that the response would always be yes, the characteristic could *potentially* describe a member of the primed racial group.

The latency results paralleled those of Gaertner and McLaughlin (1983) (see figure 1). Differences in response latencies between black and white primes occurred for positive but not for negative attributes. As illustrated in figure 1, in both racial attitude studies, negative characteristics were not more associated with blacks than with whites; in both experiments, however, positive characteristics were more associated with whites than with blacks. The magnitudes of the effects for positive characteristics in the Gaertner and McLaughlin (1983) and the Dovidio and Gaertner (1991) experiments were comparable in terms of effect-size and raw-score differences (100 to 200 msec) with latency effects for prototypic and nonprototypic members of natural object categories (Rosch, 1975) and relevant and irrelevant self-constructs (Bargh and Tota, 1988).

Additional priming studies have demonstrated that despite the apparent rejection of traditional racial stereotypes that currently occurs in adjective checklist studies (see table 1), white subjects continue to respond faster to traditional white stereotypic words (e.g., *ambitious, conventional*) following a white prime than following a black prime, and faster to black stereotypic words (e.g., *musical, lazy*) following a black prime than following a white prime (Allen, 1990; Dovidio, Evans, and Tyler, 1986). The generalizability of the effects of semantically primed racial categories is also demonstrated by experiments using photographs as primes. Baker and Devine (1988) extended the semantic priming study of Dovidio et al. (1986) with faces as primes and replicated their results: Subjects responded faster to black stereotypic words following faces of blacks than of whites; they also responded faster to white stereotypic words following photographs of whites than of blacks. In another study Zárate and Smith (1990) demonstrated that individuals who categorize

Figure 1.   Results of lexical decision task and priming response latency studies: Positive traits are associated more with whites than with blacks, but negative traits are *not* associated more with blacks than with whites.

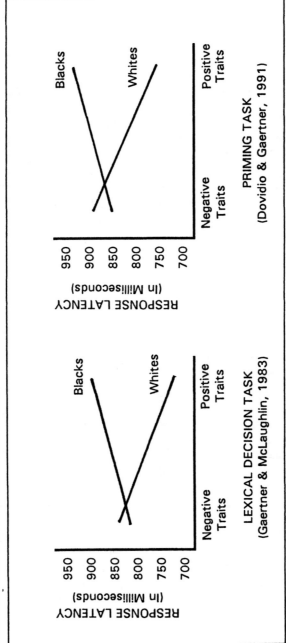

photographs on the basis of race hold stronger stereotypic associations. Taken together, these results suggest that response-latency methodologies provide measures that are freer from social-desirability influences than are many traditional survey procedures.

Although the latency methods involved in these particular priming studies help to avoid contamination from the gross impression management strategies commonly associated with self-report measures, the procedure involving the task of whether a given characteristic could *ever* be descriptive of a member of a particular race does not preclude the influence of some fundamental, controlled processes (see Messick and Mackie, 1989). Because the task involves subjects actively considering their representation of blacks, it does not necessarily capture only the elements of the representation and aspects of the attitude that are capable of automatic activation. Furthermore, the mere knowledge that these studies involve judgments of blacks may prime the conscious, egalitarian aspects of subjects' self-images and reduce racial bias, particularly for negative attributes. Given these concerns, additional research by Dovidio and Gaertner (1991) employed a method used by Bargh and Pietromonaco (1982) for studying *nonconscious* processes.

Briefly, subjects were presented with instructions similar to the instructions used in the previous priming study. They were told that they would see a string of letters, *P*'s or *H*'s, on the left or right side of a computer screen. When they saw *P*'s, they were asked to think of a typical person; when they saw *H*'s, they were instructed to think of a typical house. Subjects were then presented with various characteristics, including the positive and negative traits used in the earlier priming study, and asked to decide if each trait could ever describe the designated category (i.e., person or house). What subjects were not informed about was that either the word *black* or *white* was presented subliminally for a fraction (less than a tenth) of a second before the *P*'s (representing the person category). Thus, the purpose of this study was to determine how the nonconscious associations with black and white persons corresponded to conscious associations and attributions.

The results for positive characteristics were similar to the results for the priming study that involved conscious, controlled processes. Subjects responded to positive characteristics more quickly following the white subliminal prime than following the black subliminal prime. Even nonconsciously, then, positive characteristics are associated more with whites than with blacks. For the negative traits, however, there was a discrepancy between nonconscious and conscious responding. Specifically, negative characteristics were responded to significantly faster following a black prime than following a white prime. Thus, even though at a conscious level whites reject negative attributions of blacks, at a *non*conscious level they do have negative associations reflecting automatic and spontaneous reactions. This study therefore suggests that at least some people who consciously and genuinely embrace egalitarian personal ideals may, *outside of their awareness*, still harbor negative feelings toward blacks that may be spontaneously available. Additional research supports this conclusion and indicates that these effects are due to racial categorization and not simply based on spontaneous associations with the colors black and white. Devine (1989), without using the specific label *black*, found automatic activation of negative racial stereotypes of blacks, regardless of whether white subjects scored high or low in prejudice on a self-report measure (McConahay's [1986] Modern Racism Scale). Given the opportunity for deliberation, however, low-prejudice-scoring subjects inhibited these spontaneous reactions and replaced them with more egalitarian thoughts.

The applicability of masking procedures has also been demonstrated to extend to social categories other than race. In a study of ageism, Perdue and Gurtman (1990) presented the words *young* and *old* very briefly and masked these primes immediately with positive and negative adjectives. The subject's task was to decide if the adjective had a positive or negative connotation. These researchers found that college students made faster decisions about positive traits after subliminal exposure to the prime *young* than to the prime *old*, and displayed faster responses to negative traits after being subliminally primed by the word *old*. Consistent with the well-documented in-group favoritism effect (Brewer, 1979; Messick and Mackie, 1989), Perdue, Dovidio, Gurtman, and Tyler (1990) found, across the two masked-prime procedures just discussed, that subjects had significantly faster responses to positive traits following subliminal in-group designators (*we, us, ours*) than out-group designators (*they, them, theirs*). Subjects also tended to respond more quickly to negative traits following out-group, relative to in-group, designators. In addition, their experiment, which included a control priming condition (i.e., XXX versus we or they), demonstrated that whereas in-group pronouns activated more positive and less negative associates in relation to a neutral prime, out-group pronouns did not (Perdue et al., 1990, experiment 3). Thus, as Brewer (1979) proposed, intergroup bias, at least in a minimal intergroup situation, is predominantly the result of in-group enhancement rather than out-group derogation. Because subjects in each of these studies were not aware of the purposes of the experiments or conscious of the masked primes, these procedures offer the promise of truly nonreactive measures of automatic processes and spontaneous attitudes.

Evidence Regarding Predictive Validity

As discussed earlier, whether an indirect assessment of attitudes based upon their automatic activation from memory yields superior predictive power will depend upon the extent to which the behavior that is to be predicted is deliberative in nature and governed by social norms. We would expect traditional self-report measures to exhibit some predictive validity in cases in which social norms influence deliberative behavior. Because both the attitudinal self-report and the behavior reflect individuals' responsiveness to the social norm, reasonable correspondence between the attitude and the behavior is to be expected (as illustrated by Gaertner and Dovidio, 1977). The problem for prediction arises when the attitudinal measure reflects individuals' concern with social desirability, but the behavior of interest is spontaneous in nature and is not constrained by social norms.

Traditional measures of assessing prejudice, such as Woodmansee and Cook's (1967) Multifactor Racial Attitude Inventory (MRAI), are generally reactive and obtrusive and do raise social desirability concerns. Our framework would thus suggest that these measures would correlate more highly with deliberate, and similarly normatively controlled, behaviors than with more spontaneous, and less normatively influenced, behaviors. Consistent with this expectation, shortened versions of the MRAI correlate significantly with highly deliberated actions, such as self-reports of racially oriented voting behavior (Weigel and Howes, 1985), but not with spontaneous reactions, such as incidental helping (Dovidio and Gaertner, 1981).

More spontaneous behaviors that are not influenced by social norms should be better predicted by the sort of indirect assessment techniques that we have been discussing. To evaluate this possibility, a study was conducted for this chapter (Dorta and Dovidio, 1991). Racial attitudes of white college men were assessed using the Modern Racism Scale and the Traditional Racism Scale (McConahay, 1986), and using latencies to positive and negative characteristics following masked black and white primes (see Dovidio and Gaertner, 1991). The scales are direct assessments of deliberate racial attitudes; the latencies permit an indirect estimate of spontaneous attitudes based upon the automatic activation of evaluative associations. The measure of racial attitude stemming from the latency task was the sum of two difference scores: the extent to which subjects responded faster to positive characteristics (e.g., *good*) following the subliminal white prime than following the subliminal black prime (a positivity toward whites measure) plus the extent to which subjects responded faster to negative traits (e.g., *bad*) following the masked black prime than following the masked white prime (a negativity toward blacks measure).

In the experiment, subjects interacted over "closed-circuit television" with two other college students (actually prerecorded confederates) on self-disclosure tasks. Each participant took turns listening to the partner and speaking; one of the partners was white and the other was black. At the end of each interaction, subjects completed seven-point ("not at all" to "very much") rating scales reflecting impressions of their partners. For this chapter the dimension of primary concern is the evaluative factor that emerged from factor analysis. This dimension involved the items *likable, sincere, responsible*, and *admirable*, as well as the reverse-scored items *annoying, dishonest*, and *disreputable*. One measure of bias was the *relative* evaluation of the confederates, that is, the difference in ratings of the white and black confederates (whose behaviors were standardized and counterbalanced across subjects). The components of this relative evaluation measure, evaluative ratings of black and white confederates, were also separately examined.

The latency racial attitude measure was predictive of the relative evaluations, $r = .36$, $p < .07$. Subjects whose spontaneous attitudes reflected relatively positive associations with whites and negative associations with blacks formed more favorable impressions of white, relative to black, confederates. The two components of the overall latency measure individually showed similar effects. The measure of positivity toward whites was significantly correlated with relative evaluative ratings, $r = .42$; the measure of negativity toward blacks was directly, but not significantly, correlated with these ratings, $r = .26$. In contrast the correlations of traditional and modern racism scores with relative evaluative ratings were *negative* ($r = -.29$; $r = -.22$); unexpectedly, subjects higher on these measures tended to evaluate black confederates more favorably than white confederates.

Considering the components of the relative *evaluative* measure, evaluations of black confederates were significantly negatively correlated with the overall latency measure ($r = -.43$) and with the negativity toward blacks measure ($r = -.43$). Subjects who displayed evidence of relatively strong negative associations with blacks in the latency task evaluated black confederates less favorably. Traditional and modern racism scores were not related to evaluations of black confederates (r's of $-.02$ and $-.05$, respectively). Only the positivity toward whites measure tended ($p < .07$) to correlate with positive evaluations of white confederates, $r = .38$. Subjects who had relatively strong positive associations with whites in the masked-prime study tended to form more positive impressions of white confederates. These results therefore support the hypothesis that impressions that are probably formed spontaneously in social interactions may be better predicted by the strength of automatic evaluative activation than by more traditional attitude measures that are much more susceptible to concerns with social desirability.

THE QUESTION OF PRAGMATICS.   Obviously, any survey researcher is concerned with the pragmatics of conducting a survey. The indirect attitude-assessment techniques that we have described are not easy to employ and, relative to brief telephone interviews, are likely to be costly. In some cases, particularly when the issues are not socially sensitive, it may be possible to use alternative procedures, such as free recall, that do not require sophisticated technology but correlate with response latency (Fazio, Powell, and Williams, 1989). Latency measures, however, have broad applicability to issues and appear to provide reliable and valid indications of associative strength in memory.

We will be the first to admit that there are practical difficulties in implementing indirect attitude-assessment techniques of this type. Yet, at the same time, it seems important to emphasize that the available evidence indicates that such indirect techniques produce more valid attitudinal estimates for issues that are socially sensitive in nature. Modern technology has progressed to the point that it is easy to imagine that face-to-face interviews might be conducted with the aid of highly portable laptop computers, which permit the use of the indirect techniques that we have discussed. In fact, some of our research (Fazio and Williams, 1986) already has successfully used portable computers for recording latencies in field settings.

There are also difficulties in communicating the results of studies that measure response latencies in ways that are meaningful to a broad and diverse audience. Whereas the report of the percentage for and against a particular statement is immediately intelligible, the presentation of average latencies to characteristics and questions is much less comprehensible to the general public. It is possible, however, to rescale latency data in ways that have intuitive appeal for most audiences, for example, as proportions of a sample that exhibit effects of different magnitudes.

Enhancing the Predictive Utility of Direct Attitudinal Assessments

Thus far we have discussed cases in which the survey researcher has reason to mistrust respondents' verbal self-reports of their attitudes. What about attitude issues that are not characterized by such social sensitivity? The indirect assessment techniques that we have presented might still be employed. They have the advantage of providing an indication as to whether the individual's attitude is likely to be activated from memory when he or she encounters the attitude object. According to the MODE model, this issue of attitude accessibility is particularly central to the prediction of spontaneous behaviors—ones for which the individual lacks the motivation to deliberate carefully regarding the value of the decision alternatives.

As mentioned earlier, however, these indirect techniques are not simple to employ. Fortunately, direct measures of attitude can be supplemented in such a manner as to easily assess the accessibility of the attitude from memory. Recall the earlier summary of the research on automatic attitude activation conducted by Fazio et al. (1986). The strength of the object-evaluation association was found to determine the likelihood that the attitude would be activated automatically from memory upon the presentation of the attitude object. It was mentioned that two of these experiments involved the identification of preexperimentally strong and weak associations via a measurement procedure. That measurement procedure was latency of response to a direct attitudinal inquiry. Subjects were presented with the name of an attitude object and asked to indicate their evaluation of the object as quickly as possible by pressing either a *good* or a *bad* key. Relatively fast responses were presumed to be indicative of strong, highly accessible associations and relatively slow responses to be indicative of weak associations (see Fazio et al., 1982; Powell and Fazio, 1984). Attitude objects for which the subject was able to respond relatively rapidly when faced with an attitudinal inquiry produced more facilitation in the subsequent adjective connotation task than did attitude objects for which the subject responded relatively slowly when faced with a direct attitudinal inquiry. Thus, latencies of response to a direct query are related to the likelihood that an attitude will be activated from memory.

The implication of this finding is that direct measures of attitude can be supplemented by an assessment of the latency with which the attitudinal response is made. Such latency data provide an indication of the accessibility of the attitude from memory. This strategy has been followed in a number of studies concerned with the utility of attitudes as predictors of judgments of new information regarding the attitude object and of behavior toward the attitude object. The studies were conducted as tests of the propositions that attitude accessibility serves as a moderator of the relation between attitudes and subsequent perceptions of the attitude object and of the relation between attitudes and subsequent behavior toward the object.

During the summer preceding the 1984 presidential election, Fazio and Williams (1986) measured attitudes toward Reagan and the accessibility of those attitudes, as indicated by latency of response to the attitudinal inquiry, within a large sample of townspeople. Judgments of the performance of the candidates during the televised debates held later in the fall served as the measure of subsequent perceptions. Just as postulated by the model, correlations between attitudes and perceptions were higher among those individuals who were able to respond relatively quickly to the attitudinal inquiry (the high-accessibility group) than among those who responded relatively slowly (the low-accessibility group).

A similar finding was observed by Houston and Fazio (1989) in a study involving judgments of research evidence concerning the efficacy of capital punishment. This investigation was modeled after work done by Lord, Ross, and Lepper (1979). Their research indicated that people's attitudes toward the death penalty were predictive of their judgments in regard to the quality of two ostensibly empirical investigations—one of which purported to support the deterrent efficacy of capital punishment and one of which did not. Individuals with attitudes favorable to the death penalty viewed the pro-capital punishment study as better conducted and more convincing (and the anti-capital punishment study as more poorly conducted and less convincing) than did individuals with negative attitudes. Houston and Fazio (1989, experiment 1) found this effect to be moderated by the accessibility of subjects' attitudes toward the death penalty. The relation between attitudes and judgments about the studies was stronger among individuals whose latencies of response to an attitudinal inquiry regarding the death penalty were indicative of a relatively accessible attitude than it was among individuals whose attitudes were less accessible.

The postulated role of attitude accessibility as a moderator of the attitude-behavior relation also has received support. Fazio and Williams's (1986) investigation of the 1984 presidential election also examined attitude-behavior consistency. Immediately following election day, and three months after their participation in the initial survey, in which their attitudes toward Reagan and the accessibility of those attitudes had been assessed, the participants were telephoned and asked to reveal how they had voted. Attitudes were much more predictive of voting behavior among those individuals who had responded relatively quickly to the attitudinal inquiry concerning Reagan. Indeed, within the high-accessibility group, attitudes toward Reagan accounted for nearly 80% of the variance in voting behavior, compared to 44% within the low-accessibility group.

A recent study by Fazio, Powell, and Williams (1989) indicates that this moderating role of attitude accessibility is evident in situations involving actual behavior, as opposed to a self-report of behavior as in the voting study. The study involved attitudes and behavior toward a set of ten products (e.g., Sun-Maid raisins, Dentyne gum, and Mounds candy bar). In the preliminary phase of the experiment, subjects responded to the names of a large number of products, including the ten target items, by pressing either a *like* or a *dislike* button. The latency of the responses was recorded and served as the basis for indexing the accessibility of subjects' attitudes toward each of the ten products. Following this task, subjects rated the extent of their liking along a typical seven-point scale, which constituted the attitude measure. In order to obtain behavioral data, subjects were shown a table, on which the ten target products had been arranged, and informed that they could select five to take as "reimbursement" for having participated in the experiment.

The major concern was the extent to which the subjects' selections were related to their attitudes. For each product subjects were classified into high-, moderate-, and low-attitude accessibility groups, and the correlation between attitudes and having selected the product or not was examined within each group. Averaged across the ten products, the correlations displayed a significant linear trend as a function of the level of attitude accessibility. The more accessible a subject's attitude toward a given product was, the more likely it was that product selection behavior was consistent with that attitude.

Together, the various investigations that have been summarized indicate the importance of the attitude-activation component of the model (see Fazio, 1989, for a fuller review of such work). Both the degree to which selective processing of subsequently presented information about the attitude object occurs and the degree to which attitude-behavior consistency occurs depend upon the accessibility of the attitude from memory, just as suggested by the model. Such attitude accessibility can be indexed reasonably well by noting the latency of individuals' responses to a direct attitudinal inquiry.

Pragmatics

In the present context the success of the above investigations implies that the predictive utility of direct assessments of attitude can be enhanced by supplementally measuring the latency of the attitudinal response. Again, in door-to-door interviews, this can be readily accomplished with a computer-assisted personal interview (CAPI). Furthermore, because computers are currently commonly used on-line with telephone interviews, this technology also has potential for application in telephone surveys. As the prevalence of touch-tone phones increases, it will become more and more practical to have respondents simply press a particular button on their phones to indicate a given evaluative rating. The latency of these button-presses can be measured by an appropriately programmed microcomputer. Alternatively, the use of a voice-activated switch has the potential for permitting the subject's verbal enunciation of a response to serve as the terminator of the timing sequence (although account has to be taken of possible extraneous sounds over the phone).

Latency of response to a direct query, then, can be fairly easy data to collect. This is not meant, however, to imply that such data need not be collected with considerable caution and forethought. Latency data are remarkably "noisy." The noise emanates from a variety of sources. Individuals themselves respond at very different rates. On any given trial, an individual's attention can wander. An individual can exhibit confusion regarding the matching of his or her implicit response to the response options that are available. Every effort should be undertaken to do whatever is possible to reduce this noise level.

Fazio (1990b) has provided a discussion of a number of practical guidelines regarding the administration of response-latency measures and analysis of the resulting data. These include such matters as instructions to be given to the respondent, the inclusion of practice trials to familiarize respondents with the nature of the task, and the use of filler trials to provide an index of a given subject's baseline speed of responding. The interested reader is referred to Fazio (1990b) for details. The point that we wish to emphasize here is that despite their apparent simplicity, response latency measures need to be employed carefully if they are to yield useful data. Nevertheless, the available evidence indicates that if they are used appropriately, latency measures can be very informative.

Conclusion

As Abelson notes in chapter 9, the complexity of social attitudes cannot be adequately captured by a single, direct, verbal measure. Associations in memory between an object and an evaluation can vary markedly in strength. Some are sufficiently strong that they are capable of automatic activation upon mention or observation of the attitude object; others are not. A consideration of actual behavior introduces additional complexity. Behavior itself, including verbal reports of one's attitudes, can stem from a spontaneous process or, given that the individual has sufficient motivation and opportunity, from a deliberative process. In any case, publicly expressed attitudes and behavior can be influenced by social norms. It is these complexities that make attitude assessment, and the prediction of behavior from such assessments, so difficult.

We fully realize that some of the assessment procedures that we have advocated in this chapter are not yet sufficiently well specified for a survey researcher to employ them immediately and easily in survey research. We doubt that the state of the field's knowledge at this point in time permits such detailed specification. Nonetheless, it seems apparent to us that recent theoretical and measurement advances clearly point to issues of which survey researchers should be aware and to alternative assessment procedures that represent *potential* solutions to the difficulties inherent in traditional direct measures of attitude. As further research is conducted and as computer technology advances, the practical utility of these alternative "technologies" also will increase.

Preparation of this chapter was supported by Grant MH38832 and by Research Science Development Award MH00452 from the National Institute of Mental Health to Russell H. Fazio and by funds from the

Colgate University Research Council to John F. Dovidio. We express our
gratitude to Robert Abelson, Robyn Dawes, Samuel Gaertner, James
Sherman, and Judith Tanur for their helpful suggestions on earlier drafts.

References

AJZEN, I., and FISHBEIN, M. (1980) *Understanding Attitudes and Predicting Social Behavior*. Englewood Cliffs, NJ: Prentice-Hall.

ALLEN, J. L. (1990) Influence of affective states on cognitive representations of racial stereotypes. Paper presented at the annual meeting of the Eastern Psychological Association, Philadelphia, PA, March.

BAKER, S. M., and DEVINE, P. G. (1988) Faces as primes for stereotype activation. Paper presented at the sixtieth annual meeting of the Midwestern Psychological Association, Chicago, IL, April.

BARGH, J. A., and PIETROMONACO, P. (1982) Automatic information processing and social perception: The influence of trait information presented outside of conscious awareness on impression formation. *Journal of Personality and Social Psychology* 43, 437–449.

BARGH, J. A., and TOTA, M. E. (1988) Context-dependent automatic processing in depression: Accessibility of negative constructs with regard to self but not others. *Journal of Personality and Social Psychology* 54, 925–939.

BOBO, L. (1983) Whites' opposition to busing: Symbolic racism or realistic group conflict? *Journal of Personality and Social Psychology* 45, 1196–1210.

BREWER, M. B. (1979) In-group bias in the minimal intergroup situation: A cognitive-motivational analysis. *Psychological Bulletin* 86, 307–324.

CROSBY, F., BROMLEY, S., and SAXE, L. (1980) Recent unobtrusive studies of black and white discrimination and prejudice: A literature review. *Psychological Bulletin* 87, 546–563.

DARLEY, J. M., and LATANÉ, B. (1968) Bystander intervention in emergencies: Diffusion of responsibility. *Journal of Personality and Social Psychology* 8, 377–383.

DEVINE, P. G. (1989) Stereotypes and prejudice: Their automatic and controlled components. *Journal of Personality and Social Psychology* 56, 5–18.

DORTA, N. J., and DOVIDIO, J. F. (1991) Racial prejudice and discrimination: An examination of the relationship between attitudes and impressions. Paper presented at the annual meeting of the Eastern Psychological Association, New York, April.

DOVIDIO, J. F., EVANS, N., and TYLER, R. B. (1986) Racial stereotypes: The contents of their cognitive representations. *Journal of Experimental Social Psychology* 22, 22–37.

DOVIDIO, J. F., and GAERTNER, S. L. (1981) The effects of race, status, and ability on helping behavior. *Social Psychology Quarterly* 44, 192–203.

_____ (1986) Prejudice, discrimination, and racism: Historical trends and contemporary approaches. In DOVIDIO, J. F., and GAERTNER, S. L. (eds.). *Prejudice, Discrimination, and Racism*. Orlando, FL: Academic Press, pp. 1–34.

_____ (1991) Changes in the nature and expression of racial prejudice. In KNOPKE, H., NORRELL, J., and ROGERS, R. (eds.). *Opening Doors: An Appraisal of Race Relations in Contemporary America*. Tuscaloosa, AL: University of Alabama Press, pp. 201–241.

DOVIDIO, J. F., MANN, J., and GAERTNER, S. L. (1989) Resistance to affirmative action: The implications of aversive racism. In BLANCHARD, F., and CROSBY, F. (eds.). *Affirmative Action in Perspective*. New York: Springer-Verlag, pp. 81–102.

FAZIO, R. H. (1986) How do attitudes guide behavior? In SORRENTINO, R. M., and HIGGINS, E. T. (eds.). *The Handbook of Motivation and Cognition: Foundations of Social Behavior*. New York: Guilford Press, pp. 204–243.

_____ (1989) On the power and functionality of attitudes: The role of attitude accessibility. In PRATKANIS, A. R., BRECKLER, S. J., and GREENWALD, A. G. (eds.). *Attitude Structure and Function*. Hillsdale, NJ: Erlbaum, pp. 153–179.

_____ (1990a) Multiple processes by which attitudes guide behavior: The MODE Model as an integrative framework. In ZANNA, M. P. (ed.). *Advances in Experimental Social Psychology*, vol. 23. Orlando, FL: Academic Press, pp. 75–109.

_____ (1990b) A practical guide to the use of response latency in social psychological research. In HENDRICK, C., and CLARK, M. S. (eds.). *Review of Personality and Social Psychology*, vol. 11. Newbury Park, CA: Sage, pp. 74–97.

FAZIO, R. H., CHEN, J., McDONEL, E. C., and SHERMAN, S. J. (1982) Attitude accessibility, attitude-behavior consistency, and the strength of the object-evaluation association. *Journal of Experimental Social Psychology* 18, 339–357.

FAZIO, R. H., POWELL, M. C., and WILLIAMS, C. J. (1989) The role of attitude accessibility in the attitude-to-behavior process. *Journal of Consumer Research* 16, 280–288.

FAZIO, R. H., SANBONMATSU, D. M., POWELL, M. C., and KARDES, F. R. (1986) On the automatic activation of attitudes. *Journal of Personality and Social Psychology* 50, 229–238.

FAZIO, R. H., and WILLIAMS, C. J. (1986) Attitude accessibility as a moderator of the attitude-perception and attitude-behavior relations: An investigation of the 1984 presidential election. *Journal of Personality and Social Psychology* 51, 505–514.

FAZIO, R. H., WILLIAMS, C. J., and SANBONMATSU, D. M. (1990) Toward an unobtrusive measure of attitude. Manuscript. Bloomington, IN: Indiana University.

GAERTNER, S. L., and DOVIDIO, J. F. (1977) The subtlety of white racism, arousal, and helping behavior. *Journal of Personality and Social Psychology* 35, 691–707.

_____ (1986) The aversive form of racism. In DOVIDIO, J. F., and GAERTNER, S. L. (eds.). *Prejudice, Discrimination, and Racism*. Orlando, FL: Academic Press, pp. 61–89.

GAERTNER, S. L., and McLAUGHLIN, J. P. (1983) Racial stereotypes: Associations and ascriptions of positive and negative characteristics. *Social Psychology Quarterly* 46, 23–30.

GREENWALD, A. G., KLINGER, M. R., and LIU, T. J. (1989) Unconscious processing of dichoptically masked words. *Memory and Cognition* 17, 35–47.

HASTORF, A. H., and CANTRIL, H. (1954) They saw a game: A case study. *Journal of Abnormal and Social Psychology* 49, 129–134.

HOUSTON, D. A., and FAZIO, R. H. (1989) Biased processing as a function of attitude accessibility: Making objective judgments subjectively. *Social Cognition* 7, 51–66.

JACKMAN, M. R., and MUHA, M. J. (1984) Education and intergroup attitudes: Moral enlightenment, superficial democratic commitment, or ideological refinement? *American Sociological Review* 49, 751–769.

KINDER, D. R., and SEARS, D. O. (1981) Prejudice and politics: Symbolic racism versus threats to "the good life." *Journal of Personality and Social Psychology* 40, 414–431.

KRUGLANSKI, A. W., and FREUND, T. (1983) The freezing and unfreezing of lay-inferences: Effects of impressional primacy, ethnic stereotyping, and numerical anchoring. *Journal of Experimental Social Psychology* 19, 448–468.

LANGER, E. J. (1978) Rethinking the role of thought in social interaction. In HARVEY, J. H., ICKES, W., and KIDD, R. F. (eds.). *New Directions in Attribution Research*, vol. 2. Hillsdale, NJ: Erlbaum, pp. 35–58.

LORD, C. G., ROSS, L., and LEPPER, M. R. (1979) Biased assimilation and attitude polarization: The effects of prior theories on subsequently considered evidence. *Journal of Personality and Social Psychology* 37, 2098–2109.

McCONAHAY, J. B. (1986) Modern racism, ambivalence, and the modern racism scale. In DOVIDIO, J. F., and GAERTNER, S. L. (eds.). *Prejudice, Discrimination, and Racism*. Orlando, FL: Academic Press, pp. 91–125.

McCONAHAY, J. B., HARDEE, B. B., and BATTS, V. (1981) Has racism declined in America? It depends upon who is asking and what is asked. *Journal of Conflict Resolution* 25, 563–579.

McCONAHAY, J. B., and HOUGH, J. C. (1976). Symbolic racism. *Journal of Social Issues* 32, 23–45.

MESSICK, D. M., and MACKIE, D. M. (1989) Intergroup relations. In ROSENWEIG, M. R., and PORTER, L. W. (eds.). *Annual Review of Psychology* 40, 45–82.

MEYER, D. E., and SCHVANEVELDT, R. W. (1971) Facilitation in recognizing pairs of words: Evidence of dependence between retrieval operations. *Journal of Experimental Psychology* 90, 227–234.

PERDUE, C. W., DOVIDIO, J. F., GURTMAN, M. B., and TYLER, R. B. (1990) "Us" and "Them": Social categorization and the process of intergroup bias. *Journal of Personality and Social Psychology* 59, 475–486.

PERDUE, C. W., and GURTMAN, M. B. (1990) Evidence for the automaticity of ageism. *Journal of Experimental Social Psychology* 26, 199–216.

PETTIGREW, T. F., and MEERTENS, R. W. (1989) Responses toward outgroups in the Netherlands. Paper presented at the First European Congress of Psychology, Amsterdam, Netherlands, July.

POWELL, M. C., and FAZIO, R. H. (1984) Attitude accessibility as a function of repeated attitudinal expression. *Personality and Social Psychology Bulletin* 10, 139–148.

PROSHANSKY, H. M. (1943) A projective method for the study of attitudes. *Journal of Abnormal and Social Psychology* 38, 393–395.

REGAN, D. T., STRAUS, E., and FAZIO, R. H. (1974) Liking and the attribution process. *Journal of Experimental Social Psychology* 10, 385–397.

ROSCH, E. (1975) Cognitive representations of semantic categories. *Journal of Experimental Psychology: General* 104, 192–233.

SANBONMATSU, D. M., and FAZIO, R. H. (1990) The role of attitudes in memory-based decision making. *Journal of Personality and Social Psychology* 59, 614–622.

SCHNEIDER, W., and SHIFFRIN, R. M. (1977) Controlled and automatic human information processing: I. Detection, search, and attention. *Psychological Review* 84, 1–66.

SCHUMAN, H., STEEH, C., and BOBO, L. (1985) *Racial attitudes in America: Trends and interpretations*. Cambridge, MA: Harvard University Press.

SEARS, D. O. (1988) Symbolic racism. In KATZ, P., and TAYLOR, D. (eds.). *Towards the Elimination of Racism: Profiles in Controversy*. New York: Plenum, pp. 53–84.

SEARS, D. O., and ALLEN, H. M., JR. (1984) The trajectory of local desegregation controversies and whites' opposition to busing. In BREWER, M. B., and MILLER, N. (eds.). *Groups in Contact: The Psychology of Desegregation*. New York: Academic Press, pp. 123–151.

SEARS, D. O., and KINDER, D. R. (1985) Whites' opposition to busing: On conceptualizing and operationalizing group conflict. *Journal of Personality and Social Psychology* 48, 1141–1147.

SEARS, D. O., LAU, R. R., TYLER, T. R., and ALLEN, H. M., JR. (1980) Self-interest vs. symbolic politics in policy attitudes and presidential voting. *American Political Science Review* 74, 670–684.

SEELEMAN, V. (1940) The influence of attitudes upon the remembering of pictorial material. *Archives of Psychology* No. 258.

SHIFFRIN, R. M., and DUMAIS, S. T. (1981) The development of automatism. In ANDERSON, J. R. (ed.). *Cognitive Skills and Their Acquisition*. Hillsdale, NJ: Erlbaum, pp. 111–140.

SHIFFRIN, R. M., and SCHNEIDER, W. (1977) Controlled and automatic human information processing: II. Perceptual learning, automatic attending, and a general theory. *Psychological Review* 84, 127–190.

SIGALL, H., and PAGE, R. (1971) Current stereotypes: A little fading, a little faking. *Journal of Personality and Social Psychology* 18, 247–255.

WEBER, S. J., and COOK, T. D. (1972) Subject effects in laboratory research: An examination of subject roles, demand characteristics, and valid inferences. *Psychological Bulletin* 77, 273–295.

WEIGEL, R. H., and HOWES, P. W. (1985) Conceptions of racial prejudice: Symbolic racism revisited. *Journal of Social Issues* 41, 117–138.

WOODMANSEE, J. J., and COOK, S. W. (1967) Dimensions of verbal racial attitudes: Their identification and measurement. *Journal of Personality and Social Psychology* 7, 240–250.

ZANNA, M. P., and FAZIO, R. H. (1982) The attitude-behavior relation: Moving toward a third generation of research. In ZANNA, M. P., HIGGINS, E. T., and HERMAN, C. P. (eds.). *Consistency in Social Behavior: The Ontario Symposium,* vol. 2. Hillsdale, NJ: Erlbaum, pp. 283–301.

ZARATE, M. A., and SMITH, E. R. (1990) Person categorization and stereotyping. *Social Cognition* 8, 161–185.

PART

V

SOCIAL INTERACTION

12

Validity and the Collaborative Construction of Meaning in Face-to-Face Surveys

LUCY SUCHMAN
and BRIGITTE JORDAN

Interviews as Interaction

For statistically based social science, survey research is the principal means of obtaining data about the social world. The interview from this point of view is a standardized data collection procedure that uses a questionnaire as its instrument of measurement. The interview is also, however, an essentially interactional event. From the moment that the interviewer sits down across from the respondent and begins to talk, the survey interview assumes and relies upon a wealth of conventions and resources from ordinary conversation. At the same time, the concern with standardized procedures and the statistical notion of error that standardization is intended to address impose constraints on the survey interview that make it significantly different from ordinary conversation. Those constraints have consequences both for the way the interview proceeds and the data that it produces.

In this paper we look at the survey interview as a standardized procedure that relies upon, but also suppresses, crucial elements of ordinary conversation. Our analysis is based on videotapes of five special interviews: three using the General Social Survey and two using the National Health Interview Survey.[1]

1. The videotapes were made for research purposes in conjunction with the Seminar on Cognitive Aspects of Survey Methodology sponsored by the Committee on National Statistics of the Commission on Behavioral and Social Sciences and Education of the National Research Council. (For a report on that seminar see Jabine, Straf, Tanur, and Tourangeau, 1984.) They show interviews with volunteer respondents. Trained Census Bureau interviewers were hired by

241

Our argument, in brief, is the following:

1. There is an unresolved tension between the survey interview as an interactional event and as a neutral measurement instrument. On the one hand, the interview is commonly acknowledged to be fundamentally an interaction. On the other hand, in the interest of turning the interview into an instrument, many of the interactional resources of ordinary conversation are disallowed.

2. The success of the interview as an instrument turns on the premise that (a) relevant questions can be decided in advance of the interaction, and (b) questions can be phrased in such a way that, as long as they are read without variation, they will be heard in the intended way and will stimulate a valid response.

3. The premises of item 2 fail insofar as (a) topics that come from outside a conversation run the risk of irrelevance, and (b) as an ordinary language procedure, the survey interview is inherently available for multiple interpretations of the meaning of both questions and answers.

4. Compared with ordinary conversation, the survey interview suppresses those interactional resources that routinely mediate uncertainties of relevance and interpretation.

Our summary finding is that the validity of survey data is potentially undermined by the same prohibition against interaction that is intended to ensure reliability. As a remedy, we recommend a collaborative approach that would allow the kinds of interactional exchanges between interviewer and respondent necessary to ensure standardized interpretations, without introducing interviewer bias. This idea has also recently been advanced by Briggs (1986) and Mishler (1986), but it has yet to receive the exploration that it deserves and the development that would enable its serious incorporation into survey research practice.

The analysis is organized in the following manner. In section 2 we look at

---

the committee to administer the NHIS questionnaire as they would for the survey; similarly, trained interviewers administered the GSS questionnaires. These particular interviews, however, were not part of the respective surveys. Our analysis of the videotapes was carried out during the summer of 1986, funded by the Committee on Cognition and Survey Research of the Social Science Research Council and by Xerox Palo Alto Research Center. We take the five interviews as case studies that reveal classes of trouble of a potentially more widespread nature. Whereas we cannot know the precise distribution of such troubles across survey interviews, their presence in these five at least raises the possibility of a more general problem. Our discussions of the data with veteran survey researchers lead us to believe that in fact the troubles identified are not totally idiosyncratic.

the differences between the survey interview and ordinary conversation, focusing on the survey instrument's external control over who speaks and on what topic, prohibitions against any redesign of questions by the interviewer and special requirements placed on the form of answers, problems of question relevance and meaning, and failures in the detection and repair of misunderstanding. Section 3 puts forward recommendations for a research program to explore a more collaborative, interactional approach to achieving survey reliability and validity.

Differences Between the Interview and Conversation

> The interviewer is charged with the responsibility of conducting *inquiry* in something of the manner of a *conversation*. The product of the encounter is supposed to be good "hard" data—the stuff of codes and numbers and computer analysis. The process is supposed to be at least somewhat "soft"—the stuff of pleasant acquaintance. (Converse and Schuman, 1974, p. 22)

In what follows we look closely at just how the survey interview is in the "manner of a conversation" and, more importantly, how it is not. The constraints on the interview that we observe, which distinguish it from ordinary conversation, are all imposed in the interest of *standardization*: standardization is what identifies the interview process as a scientific procedure. To ensure the standardization of the procedure, the interactivity of ordinary conversational processes is suppressed. We will argue, however, that this strategy mistakes sameness of words for stability of meanings. Stability of meaning, the real basis for standardization and ultimately for validity, in fact requires the full resources of conversational interaction.

Local Versus External Control

Researchers interested in face-to-face communication have taken ordinary, naturally occurring conversation as the primary form of interaction and as the baseline for their analyses.[2] The organizational properties of ordinary conversation represent the minimal constraints required for orderly, mutually intelligible talk. The central organizational feature of ordinary conversation is that who talks, and about what, is controlled from within the conversation by the participants themselves.

2. See Sacks, Schegloff, and Jefferson (1974). For useful surveys of recent work in conversation analysis, see Levinson (1983), chapter 6, and Goodwin and Heritage (1990).

In an important sense local control over the conversation is what sustains participants' interest in talking to each other. The basic assumption in ordinary conversation is that the participants will together find a topic that is of mutual interest, and will explore it to whatever depth they choose. In contrast to this local control from within the conversation, the survey instrument is constructed ahead of time and is imposed on the participants from the outside. The interviewer is the administrator of the survey research-er's agenda, the respondent is a data point in the sample. Turns at talk are preallocated such that invariably the interviewer asks the questions, the respondent answers them. The choice and order of topics—what will get talked about and when—is established by an absent third party, and is not subject to alteration according to any local interests of either interviewer or respondent.

The questionnaire designer attempts to control not only *what* gets talked about in the interview, but precisely *how* topics get talked about as well. In particular the standardized procedural model of the interview is enforced through the mandate that the interviewer effectively *not* be available for interaction. Interviewers are enjoined (though perhaps with only limited success) against any variation from the question as written. This injunction against interaction reflects the idea that the survey interview has been successfully standardized only to the extent that there is no variation in the words that the interviewer speaks. We will return to the problems in this notion of standardization below and suggest an alternative. For the moment the observation is simply that one result of the invariance approach to standardization is that while the interview has the superficial appearance of interaction (two or more people sit down facing one another to talk), that appearance is misleading. As respondents realize that their expectations for ordinary conversation are violated, and violated without recourse, they may react with boredom (with consequent intellectual if not physical withdrawal) and impatience (resulting in answers designed to "get it over with.") More fundamentally, the injunction against interaction means that certain basic resources for establishing shared understanding, essential to successful communication, are effectively prohibited.

Recipient Design of Questions

To the extent that ordinary conversation is locally controlled, speakers can be sensitive to the history of the current talk and can accommodate specific listeners. Interviewers, in contrast, are trained not to redesign questions based either on information acquired in previous responses or on the observable circumstances of a particular respondent. Questions cannot be modified on the spot as they would be in ordinary conversation, but rather must be designed for anyone and must exhaust the range of possible circumstances. The use of an exhaustive specification of conditions, in advance of a response, is intended to obviate the need for negotiation between interviewer and respondent. This strategy, however, results in questions that are awkward and whose construction is difficult to parse. Typically we get a string of "or's" or modifying clauses incorporated into the question itself.[3]

> → I: During those two weeks, did anyone in the family receive healthcare at home or go to a doctor's office, clinic, hospital, or some other place? Include care from a nurse or anyone working with or for a medical doctor. Do not count times while an overnight patient in a hospital.
>
> Mrs: (pause) No::
>
> (NHIS, E family)

In the case of a negative answer to an initial inquiry, the concern that some condition might be missed that in fact falls within the criteria of the question is legitimate; for example, respondents might say they had not received care in response to the first sentence in the question above if they had only spoken to a nurse. But in the case of an affirmative to the initial clause, the continuation of the question becomes not only awkward but also inappropriate:

> I: Was the total combined family income during the past twelve months, that is, yours, your wife's, Judith's, and Jerry's, more or less than twenty thousand dollars.
>
> Mrs: More.
>
> → I: Include money from jobs, social security, retirement income, unemployment payments, public assistance, and so forth. Also include income from interest, dividends, net income from business, farm, or rent, and any other money income received.
>
> Mrs: More. It was more income.
>
> (NHIS, E family)

---

3. The examples offered here are meant to be illustrative of a class of interactional troubles. Simplified transcript notation is as follows:
    → item of analytic interest
    :: prolongation of the preceding word
    [point of onset of overlapping talk
    · falling intonation
    ? rising intonation
    — abrupt shift or break in ongoing utterance
Speakers are designated as I (interviewer), R (single respondent), Mrs. (wife in family interviews), Mr. (husband in family interviews), or the first initial of an additional family member.

Ordinarily the completion of a question effects a turn transition to the addressee, who is obligated to respond. In this case Mrs. E provides a response at the first appropriate place, rendering the additional instructions irrelevant. The continuation by the interviewer effectively ignores that response and requires that Mrs. E reiterate an answer she has already provided.

A second aspect of the prohibition against redesign is that the interviewer is not allowed to make inferences based on information she has heard before. Questions designed in anticipation of a particular answer cannot be redesigned in light of some other kind, with the result that potentially inappropriate or nonsensical questions must get asked:

I: When did you last see or talk to a doctor or assistant about the derma-
        titis under the neck.

Mrs: I didn't.

I: The doctor was never seen?

Mrs: No.

I: What was the cause of the dermatitis under the neck.
        [

Mrs.   My violin. (laughs)   The chin rest of my violin.

→ I: The chin rest of your violin. (long pause while interviewer writes) Did,
        uhm, the dermatitis under your neck result from an accident or an in-
        jury.

Mrs: No, it wasn't an injury. It was a contact dermatitis. So:: (pause)

I: Under:: Is that the entire neck? Or::

Mrs: No, (showing with hand) the, the, where my chin, where my, uh,
        the, my neck, the uh, sort of under part of my chin
        contacted the chin rest on my violin.
        [

I: That's the, left side.

Mrs: Yes.

I: Left side. (pause while writes) When was, uh, the dermatitis under
        your neck first noticed.

Mrs: I, uh, ha—about two years ago, I, uh, bought a new violin. And it had a
        new chin rest.

→ I: About how many days since (pause) May twenty-ninth a year ago has
        this condition kept you in bed more than half of the day.

Mrs: Never. (smiles)

→ I: Were you ever hospitalized::for
                            [

Mrs: No.

I: Do you still have this condition.

Mrs: If::I forget to put a handkerchief or something over my, the chin rest
         of my violin it comes back. So I'm very careful to use::a covering. Over
         my chin rest.

(NHIS, E family)

A danger of training interviewers not to redesign questions, particularly
insofar as that requires suppression of basic interactional skills and sensitivi-
ties, is that the interviewer *disattends* the circumstances of the respondent
and of the interview. A graphic demonstration of this occurs in the interview
with the U family, when the phone rings loudly and the interviewer in no way
orients to the fact that someone might have to pick it up. Another occurs in
one of the General Social Survey interviews, where the interviewer asks a
respondent with her child beside her on the couch to say whether she more or
less agrees, or more or less disagrees, with the statement:

I: It's hardly fair to bring a child into the world with the way things look for the
         future.

R: Ah::ha, obviously I::disagree with that.

(GSS FW30)

Converse and Schuman (1974) point to the "cross pressures between the
social demands for conversations and the scientific demands for inquiry," and
recommend that:

> When questions prove peculiarly inappropriate to a given respondent's situa-
> tion, there is probably no remedy better than bearing the incongruity with
> humor—with the respondent if need be (p. 60).

Despite this recommendation, however, the proscription against redesigning
questions is likely to extend to a prohibition against breaking the frame of the
interview script at all.[4] One consequence is to inhibit whatever natural
inclination the interviewer might have to shift her perspective to that of the

---

4. The objection may be raised that while the interviewers behave here as they do because they
are under the scrutiny of a video camera, they should be expected to act quite differently in the
field, in particular taking on much more of the interactive role that we recommend. The point is
that precisely because they were under scrutiny, we can assume that these interviewers behaved
according to what they took to be the normative prescriptions of their training. Our recommendation, then, should be taken as relevant to the question of what, in fact, we want those normative
prescripts to be.

respondent in advance of asking a question and to modify the question accordingly, or even to commiserate with the respondent about the troubles that the question as written poses for her particular situation. As well as setting up an interactional strangeness through inappropriate questions, or more importantly, through the interviewer's failure to acknowledge inappropriate questions, this stand effectively denies the respondent's experience of the interview.

In addition to the redesign that speakers routinely provide based on their ability to take the role of the hearer and to recognize an inappropriate question before they ask it, the organization of conversation provides that instead of responding, the recipient of a question may decline to answer or may ask for some modification of the question's underlying premises. Addressees in ordinary conversation have the option of telling a speaker that he or she is asking the wrong question, or that in asking the question he or she is assuming something about the addressee that is not the case. The interview, in contrast, does not provide an opportunity for the respondent to make a correction to the question's premises. An answer to the question as written and in the terms prescribed is a nonnegotiable requirement for what constitutes an acceptable response.

This violation of the norms of ordinary conversation is exemplified in the following respondent's protest regarding a question on "the problems of the big cities":

> I: . . .   solving the problems of the big cities
>
> → R: Ahm:: (long pause) Some questions seem to be (little laugh) hard to answer because it's not a matter of how much money, it's—
>
> I: Alright, you can just say whether you think it's too much, too little, or about the right amount, or if you feel that you don't know you can::say that of course.
>
> R: Ah, from the various talk shows and programs on TV and in the newspapers, ah, it could be viewed that they're spending maybe the right amount of money, but it isn't so much the *money* that they're spending, it's other things that—
>
> I: Well, do you think we're spending too much, too little, or about the right amount.
>
> R: Ahm, I'll answer I don't know on that one.
>
> (GSS FB30)

The respondent here expresses her trouble with the question, namely, that solving the problems of the big cities is not for her a question of money. In response she's asked to say whether she thinks, "we're spending too much, too little," and so on. The problem with this response is that the respondent is neither being allowed to say what she thinks (the interviewer's apparent invitation notwithstanding), nor are the real constraints on what she can say, imposed by the interview schedule, acknowledged to be potentially troublesome. The solution the respondent adopts, to defer to a "don't know" answer, is interactionally graceful and expedites the business of getting on with the interview (which the interviewer's interruptions clearly demonstrate to be the business at hand), but loses for the record the respondent's opinion on this issue.

Finally, the prohibition against redesign leads to a depersonalization of the interview in ways that we believe detract from respondents' sense of involvement with or responsibility for the interview responses. In ordinary conversation speakers demonstrate their involvement through the ways that their utterances are fit to the hearer's particular situation. In the interview, in contrast, variation occurs only as the substitution of items within a standardized format. In the cases analyzed here, the interview, rigidly constrained by an externally imposed, often repetitious script, becomes observably boring to respondents. So, for example, a series of questions in the NHIS is repeated with different names in the names slot, or different conditions in the health-problem slot. Respondents are quick to discern this pattern, with the result that the interaction becomes pro forma and predictable:

I: During those two weeks, did you work at any time at a job or business, not counting work around the house.

Mr: Yes.

I: During those two weeks, did you miss any time from a job or business because of illness or injury.

Mr: No.

I: During those two weeks, did you stay in bed because of illness or injury.

Mr: No

I: Was there any time during those two weeks that you cut down on the things you usually do because of illness or injury.

Mr: No.

I: Okay, now we might show the calendar to *Mrs*. U.

→ Mrs: I had a feeling that was coming.

I: (little laugh) During those two weeks did you work at any time at a job or business, not counting work around the house.

Mrs: Yes.

(NHIS, U family)

With a single respondent, a deliberate act of noncooperation would be required to terminate an interview before its official end. In the family interviews, however, members of the U family quietly leave the room until only Mrs. U remains to carry through the interview. In another case Mr. E remains present throughout, but with a magazine on his lap to which he turns, leaving Mrs. E as the default respondent for questions about both herself and the children. In ordinary conversation it is in part participants' local control over who will speak next and what will be said that maintains the unpredictability of the interaction, which in turn sustains its interest.

Requirements on the Answer

In addition to displacing control of questions from the participants to a third party, the interview schedule imposes external constraints on what form answers should take. These constraints result in two somewhat contradictory problems:

—In some cases, responses that require elaboration are disallowed.

—In other cases, responses that in ordinary conversation are "good enough" in survey interviews require unreasonable elaboration.

ELABORATION DISALLOWED.   The interviewer completing a schedule of pre-coded questions is required to elicit a response that corresponds to one of the available response options. This often requires pursuing an answer until it reduces to an acceptable response:

I: First I would like to talk to you, Mrs. T, about some things people think about today. We are faced with many problems in this country, none of which can be solved easily or inexpensively. I'm going to name some of these problems, and for each one I'd like you to tell me whether you think we're spending too much money on it, too little money, or about the right amount. First, the space exploration program. Are we spending too much, too little, or about the right amount.

R: We live in a society of persons and they feel that progress has to be made. And due to the, ah, the values of, you know, going into other territories, ah, those who are in authority feel that they're doing fine but the average person no doubt probably has some thought about it because they know that people are still starving to death.

I: Well, first do, do you think we're spending too much, too little or about the right amount on the space exploration program.

R: Based upon general conversations from persons, ah, it's ah, the common view is that they're spending maybe too much money.

I: Is that what you think?

R: Well, yes, they're spending too much.

I: Too much.

R: Yes.

(GSS FB30)

Although we can assume that there is something in the common culture that we might call "interview mode," and that people have some idea of what it means to operate in that mode, it is not clear how widespread this notion is and what exactly are respondents' expectations about the survey interview. In this regard the respondent above is instructive insofar as we can see the process of her socialization over the course of the interview. Our hunch is that she initially takes the interview to have a kind of talk show format, wherein she is to provide her opinions in the form of a commentary on topics raised by the interviewer. The extensive and elaborate opening remarks by the interviewer contribute to this expectation and appear to be heard as an invitation to produce a response in kind. But what this respondent hears in the first question as an invitation to talk, to give her opinion, she discovers to be a fixed choice between items, where the possible terms of her answer are already decided and are nonnegotiable. The interview comes to be transformed from an interactive "talking with" someone, to the solitary production of acceptable answers to questions: answers whose adequacy for the purposes of the interview respondents come to be able to evaluate, but in which they may have little personal investment.

Failure to allow stories and elaborations can create not only interactionally awkward situations, but problems of validity as well insofar as the story or elaboration may contradict the initial response. As long as interviewers stop at the first acceptable response, the validity problem will never become apparent. Coincidentally, we came across an example of this complication in an interview with a physician in connection with another research project:[5]

I: When you think about other doctors in general, how would you
      compare yourself to them. Are you very similar or different?

R: I think I'm pretty similar to most doctors.

→   Except that a lot of doctors try to stay right in the mainstream of
      medicine. They don't like to be out, away from the drug-oriented
      type of medical treatment. In other words, you have a problem, you
      have a drug for it, and that'll take care of it. Or surgery or some-

5. Interview with Dr. P, 7/24/85, reported in Hunt, Jordan, Irwin, and Browner (1989) and in Hunt, Browner, and Jordan (1990).

thing. Cut it off, and you'll be fine. (laughs) And most doctors have that attitude. Then there's a small group that believe in the reason that you have doctors in the first place. And that is that we're more holistic. So we can use a more natural approach. The hippocratic approach. So I think I'm more like that group.

I: You think that's a smaller group.

R: Yes, that's a smaller group now.

In this case a response that starts out asserting R's likeness to the mainstream is transformed by the elaboration into an identification with a minority group. The more common form of this "yes, but" phenomenon results from a general bias of participants in conversation toward agreement, where the initial yes is subsequently modified to anything but yes (see Pomerantz, 1984). Not pursued, however, such a misleading first response will be coded at face value, and the qualifications or contradiction it masks may never be detected.

ELABORATION INAPPROPRIATELY PURSUED.   Another order of interactional trouble arises from the fact that ordinary conversation is replete with statements offered as adequate for the participant's practical purposes at hand, but with the implicit understanding that no claims are made as to their certainty or accuracy. Offered as casual talk, such statements are taken in a survey like the NHIS as facts that can be subjected to detailed examination:

    I: During those two weeks did she [daughter] miss any time from a job or business because of illness or injury.

→ Mrs: (pause, looking at Mr. E) I don't know, I don't know if she did have one day when she didn't go to work, when she didn't feel too well, I think one day, she didn't.

    I: One day.

    Mrs: Mm hm.

    I: And you, uh, during that two-week period she missed, uh,

    Mrs: One day.

    I: one day. During those two weeks, did she stay in bed because of illness or injury.

    Mrs: I think she was in bed one—that one day. She didn't feel well.

    I: And you mentioned one day she stayed in bed::

    Mrs: Mm hm, yes.

→ I: Because of illness. (pause, interviewer writing) On how many of the days missed from work did she stay in bed more than half of the day, because of illness or injury.

Mrs: Well, I'm not sure she was in bed all—I don't know. She was in, she was in her room and, and she came dow— she didn't get up in the morning, but she came down fo— to eat, you know, I didn't follow her because I went to work.

Mr: She came down for dinner.

Mrs: She came down for dinner, so::

→ I: So she was in bed?

Mrs: She was in her room, yes, she was in bed. She didn't feel well.

I: Not counting the day missed from work, and in bed, was there any other time during those two weeks that she cut down on the things she usually does because of illness or injury.

Mrs: (pause) I don't think so.

→ I: What condition caused her to miss work, and stay, or stay in bed during those two weeks.

Mrs: (smiles, looks to Mr. E)

Mr: I think she had a cold, didn't she?

Mrs: Yes, she had:: She had a sore throat.

I: Sore::

Mrs: Sore throat or cold.

Mr: Sore throat or cold, yes.

→ I: Did any other condition cause her to miss work, or stay in bed during that period.

Mrs: Not that I know of.

And later in the interview:

→ I: When did [your daughter] last see or talk to a doctor or assistant about her sore throat.

Mrs: Well, she didn't talk to one, to a doctor about the sore throat this time, but in the fall, I believe it was in October (looks to Mr. E), she had a flu. She was run down. And she was, I believe she was ill for about a week. She had a flu, and she had a fever. And she went to Dr. C, twice she went to Dr. C.

I: This was, uh, you stated in the fall::

Mrs: In the fall of the year.

I: Has she seen a doctor about, uh, her sore throat::

Mrs: No, not this week, no. Not this last time.

→ I: What was the cause of, uh, her sore throat.

Mrs: (shrugs) She had a cold. I don't know::

→ I: Did the sore throat result from an accident or an injury?
  Mrs: No.
  (NHIS, E family)

In spite of the fact that Mrs. E at first expresses some uncertainty about whether or not her daughter even stayed home from work, and is clearly uncertain about her daughter's activities or condition on that day, she does her best here to cooperate with the interviewer in the production of facts about the case. The sore throat, offered as an acceptable reason to miss a day of work, is subsequently treated as a medical condition and pursued as such. Mrs. E's attempt to make sense out of the question, "When did [your daughter] last see or talk to a doctor or assistant about her sore throat," which of course presupposes that she did have a sore throat, and that it was severe enough to warrant talking to a doctor, or an assistant, leads to a diversion off into another incident where her daughter did talk to a doctor, but which is unrelated to this condition.

Establishing Relevance

In any interaction, questions are heard and responses are produced against a background of unspecified assumptions about the world. Ordinary conversation affords sufficient occasion to discover differences in world-view and sufficient leeway to accommodate differences, that explicit discussion of assumptions rarely takes place. In ethnographic field interviews, which are specifically concerned with such differences, background assumptions are frequently discussed and compared explicitly. In survey interviews, however, apparent mismatches in world-view are neither negotiated through interaction nor acknowledged, and are masked in precoded responses.

For example, questions about family health in the NHIS produce accounts of incidents that family members judge relevant to the topic. In follow-up questions, however, it becomes evident that the issues with which the NHIS is concerned are not health problems in whatever way the family would define them, but only insofar as a given trouble limits activities, particularly work and school activities, during a specific period of time. By the same token, interest in how the family deals with their health problems is confined to the extent to which they seek professional medical care of specified kinds. Over the course of the questions, it becomes apparent that the questionnaire defines health and illness as having to do with loss of work time and utilization of medical facilities and staff. What family health and illness might comprise for the family is unclear and not relevant.

One result of the effort to fit a family's problems into the criteria that the questionnaire provides is an escalation of routine troubles into medical conditions. Mrs. E, as we saw above, has a contact dermatitis where the skin under her chin breaks out when she plays her violin. She knows how to take care of it (by placing a handkerchief over the chin rest) and in no way treats it as a medical problem. Nevertheless, she is asked to recast her experience in medical terms. This insistence on the medicalization of mundane troubles is the direct outcome of differences in the ways in which the question's designer sees the world and the respondent experiences it. From the point of view of the intent of the question, mundane troubles have been successfully transformed into data about medical conditions. From the point of view of the respondents, this may or may not constitute a valid characterization.

A set of different but comparably stringent preconceptions inform the GSS. For example, the questions assume that people view themselves in terms of their relationship to a series of independent institutions, such as religion, politics, education, and the like. This assumption runs into trouble when one respondent is asked:

I: Generally speaking, do you usually think of yourself as a Republican, Democrat, Independent, or what.

R: As a person.

I: As a Republican::

R: No.

I: Democrat::

R: No.

I: Independent or what.

R: Uhm:: I think of myself as a (pause) Christian.

I: OK. (writing) But politically, would you have any particular::(inaudible)

R: I am one of Jehovah's Witnesses so, you know, when it comes to::

I: I see.

R: So I'm, I am acclimated toward government, but it is that of Jehovah God's kingdom.

I: Yes.

(GSS FB30)

What we see here are two different views of the world, where the respondent's category system does not separate the religious from the political (or, if one takes the intended narrow meaning of the question, does not include a political domain at all). In the face of such evidence for discrepant worldviews between researchers and respondents, it falls to researchers to establish that such different relevancies do not undermine the validity of survey responses.

Clarification of Meaning

In the survey interview neither the respondent nor the interviewer has access to what is perhaps the most basic resource for shared understanding in conversation; namely, interactional procedures for identifying and repairing routine uncertainties of meaning, or troubles in understanding. The most ubiquitous of these procedures in normal conversation is a side sequence to the main line of talk, initiated by the recipient of a troublesome utterance, requesting clarification or elaboration. Because standardization is identified with not varying the wording of questions, however, the interviewer is not generally available for such clarifications.

The meaning of an utterance does not inhere in the language, but is a product of interaction between speakers and hearers. In ordinary conversation, utterances can be elaborated to whatever level of detail participants require. So if the response to a question is cursory, vague, ambiguous, or the questioner simply wants to hear more, he or she can ask the respondent to say more. The producer of a question is taken to have the license and authority to clarify what it is that the question is designed to discover. In the interview, however, the person who asks the question is simply its administrator, trained to resist the respondent's appeals to him or her to elaborate on its intent:

I: Alright, let me just ask the question again so I'm sure I have it correct. We have one day that he missed from school. Uh, not counting that day missed from school, during that period how many *other* days did he cut down for *more* than half the day, because of illness or injury. You would say no then, is that correct.

Mrs: To the best of my knowledge, it's no.

Son: (protests visibly but inaudibly)

I: Okay, yea. Now::

Son: (protesting more loudly)

Mrs: (puts hand on son's head, laughing) But he obviously was at school, so I cou, I couldn't know::

I: Right. Well this would be cutting down on all, on the things that he *usually* does during the day.

Son: Yea.

I: For more than half the day.

Mr: For more than half the day.

Son: Yes.

Mrs: Well that's true, you usually write. Because he hurt his thumb he couldn't write.

→ I: Oh, alright. Now whatever you think is most correct then. Uh, we would go back to, we have one day, we're attempting to discover the days that he cut down or, during that period. And we know that he missed one day from school. Now in addition to that one day missed from school, how many other days did he cut down more than half the day, because of illness or injury.

→ Mrs: Uh huh. I guess the problem I'm having with the question is, when you say cut down his activities, does that mean that, that he really, you know, wasn't:: doing things actively or that he wasn't doing what he would normally do::

→ I: Well we, uh, we take the thing that the person would normally do. And this would mean that he would cut down on those activities that he would normally do during the day. He would cut down for, whatever activity he might be doing, for that portion of the day. That he would cut down more than half the day on his usual activities.

Mrs: Mm hm, well I'm inclined to say yes I guess that, for about five days.

I: Five days in addition to the one::

Mrs: Yes, in addition to the one day.

Mr: That's stretching it.

Mrs: You think so? We don't know, (laughing) there's a difference of opinion, so::

Mr: But, okay that's, I guess that's as valid as (inaudible)

I: Uh huh. We take your best:: information.

(NHIS, U family)

This sequence is most immediately striking for the preference accorded Mrs. U's responses over her son's, in spite of Mrs. U's own disclaimers that her knowledge of what he does during the day at school is limited. We cite the sequence here not for the trouble this creates between family members, but for the extent to which the interviewer manages to engage in the appearance of an interaction over the meaning of the question without ever really offering an alternative, clarifying version or an elaboration. She thereby adheres to the injunction against deviating in any way from the interview schedule. What is reportable here is defined according to an agenda that restricts codable illnesses to those that force one to "cut down on activities for more than half a day." We take this to be a screening question that, we assume, is intended to differentiate between more serious and less serious illness episodes. The intent of the question is delimited by an obviously deliberate construction, but according to criteria and for purposes opaque to the parties engaged in administering and answering it. So the interviewer's care to read the question precisely as written is undermined by the vagueness of what "cutting down on activities" could mean, and just what constitutes half a day (is that half of a twenty-four-hour day? Half of an eight-hour workday?). Each of these determinations is left to the respondent's imagination. Moreover, whereas "half a day" is a unit of measurement that may seem a more objectively measurable quantity than "serious," it is not a natural unit for many activities. So one may be limited in doing some everyday activities such as writing, eating, shopping, exercising, and the like that don't extend throughout the day, or even half a day, but are important activities nonetheless. Similarly, just how is the respondent to interpret "cutting down"? It may be that a respondent does, in some way, all of his or her normal activities but that he or she is dragging through the day, doing none of them quite up to par. Our concern is that rather than preserving the question's intended meaning, the injunction that it be read as written, without elaboration, in this case leaves interpretation up to the respondent, but in an entirely uncontrolled way.

Detection and Repair of Misunderstanding

Through the careful use of language, questionnaire designers attempt to craft survey questions that will be subject to a single intended hearing.[6] Ordinary talk, however, is replete with alternate interpretations of meaning, which, to the extent that they can be seen to affect the adequacy of the communication in consequential ways, must be identified and remedied by the participants. The occurrence of these alternate interpretations, moreover, is not a product of sloppiness in the use of the language, but inheres in the language in ways that only situated interaction can resolve. Successful communication is not so much a product of the avoidance of misunderstandings as of their successful detection and repair.[7]

6. In fact, some innovative research on the design of survey questions has emerged over the past few years. For example, the movement to study cognitive aspects of survey methodology has led to a change in the conception of pilot testing of surveys in several agencies of the federal government. The National Center for Health Statistics, the Bureau of Labor Statistics, and the Bureau of the Census have established laboratories in which techniques of cognitive psychology are routinely applied to the design of survey questionnaires. Using analyses of "think-aloud" and retrospective protocols and other cognitive interviewing techniques, investigators iteratively refine questions so that their meaning to respondents matches those intended by the survey designer and required by the underlying concept for which the data are being gathered. Such laboratory pretesting does not obviate by any means the need for field testing to be sure that a questionnaire "works" under production conditions, but it does permit much more careful and flexible crafting of questions than does a system that follows minimal pretesting directly with full-scale field testing.

7. For the importance of repair to conversation see, for example, Jordan and Fuller (1975) and Schegloff, Jefferson, and Sacks (1977).

Whereas the survey interviewer is trained to read questions without variation, he or she seems less prepared to listen for misunderstanding and effect its repair. The consequence of undetected misunderstanding is a hidden source of invalid data. A particularly striking example of failure in this regard occurs in the supplementary interview with Mrs. U about her drinking practices. Mrs. U reports that during the two-week reference period prior to the interview she has had one to two glasses of wine every night with dinner, and that this amount of drinking is typical of her drinking not only for the past twelve months but also for the past six years. The interviewer then asks:

I: During the past year, in how many *months* did you have at least one drink of any alcoholic beverage. In other words, out of the twelve months of the year, in how many months did you have at least one drink.

Mrs: One drink. Uhm, and alcohol. I'd guess, uh, I would say four months? Five months? Five months.

(NHIS, U Family)

Hearing this question in light of the previous response, one is struck by the apparent inconsistency in Mrs. U's answers. If she had a drink every day during the two-week reference period, and she reports this as typical of her drinking during the past six years, the implication that there were seven of those months in which she had no drink at all is surprising. One infers a possible miscalculation or a misunderstanding. Further evidence of the latter comes in the next series:

I: Was there ever a period in your life when you considered yourself to be a light drinker.

Mrs: (smiles) I guess yes.

I: For how many years were you a light drinker.

Mrs: You know, do you define, how would you define light drinker?

I: Well this is ho— we would have you define it,

Mrs: Right.

I: Uh huh.

Mrs: You know, well, if having one or two glasses of wine every night with dinner is (laugh) a light drinker, then I guess I would be characterized a light drinker.

I: Uh huh. Uh, see we want to know for ho, uh, if there was a period in your life when you *considered yourself* to be a light drinker, and I believe you said yes.

Mrs: I did, yes.

I: Now, for how many years were you a light drinker.

Mrs: (pause) A light drinker. If a light drinker is defined as having one or two glasses of wine a day, I'd say:: for about five years. Under that definition of light drinker (laugh).

I: Uh huh, see this is, the, the next question, see we had you say that you considered yourself to be a light drinker, and you said for about five years. Now, when you were a *light* drinker, how many drinks of alcoholic beverages did you have in a week.

→ Mrs: Oh, of alcoholic beverages in a week?

I: Uh huh.

→ Mrs: Very ra— you know,

I: That would be the total.

→ Mrs: Out of five months, five months out of the year:: I said that I may have alcoholic beverages. But to say in a week?

I: Uh huh.

→ Mrs: That's—during those five months? Maybe I'd have two::

I: Now uh, mm hm, now uh,

Mrs: See I::

I: Now there, uh, if it, there's also the possibility that you might not consider yourself to be a light drinker, in which case you might say that you were never a light drinker as such, uh. Was there ever a period in your life when you considered yourself to be a very light, occasional, or infrequent drinker.

I: Well, you know, once again, you know, that category sounds right, if you, however you want to define::

I: You think that would be more accurate than, than the light drinker then.

→ Mrs: Especially since it *seems* that drinker refers to alcoholic beverages::

I: That's right.

Mrs: Then in that case I would be an infrequent (pause) drinker.

I: Alright, let's, let's change that then, and uh, move down here to this one.

Mrs: Someone might consider me a wino, but I (laughs) . . .

(NHIS, U Family)

In her response Mrs. U reminds us that she drinks one or two glasses of wine with dinner, and by that definition she does in fact characterize herself as a light drinker. What follows is confounded by several problems, however. First and most serious, it becomes apparent that Mrs. U is making a distinction, which the question writer did not intend, between alcohol or hard liquor and wine. (In retrospect this explains the apparent contradiction between her report that she drank alcohol during only five of the previous twelve months, and her earlier report that her daily drinking during the two-week reference period was typical of her drinking during those same twelve months.) The confusion is compounded when the interviewer repeats the question, "When you were a light drinker, how many drinks of alcoholic beverages did you have in a week." Taking the "alcoholic beverages" to refer to hard liquor, Mrs. U has trouble answering. In response to this trouble, the interviewer offers her the next question that provides the option of characterizing herself as a *very* light drinker, to which Mrs. U concedes (again with the understanding that "drinker" now refers to hard liquor). The interviewer does not seem to hear this misunderstanding and, in fact, unwittingly confirms the misinterpretation by answering, "That's right" in response to Mrs. U's clarification that "it seems that drinker refers to *alcoholic* beverages." Finally, the confusion is exacerbated by the past tense of the questions, which presupposes that she no longer considers herself to be a light or very light drinker.

The completed questionnaire shows Mrs. U to consider herself an occasional rather than light drinker, a response based on the misunderstanding of type of drink involved. This discrepancy, obvious from the interaction, is not visible in the interview schedule. What is visible is an apparent inconsistency in her answers; namely, that she now reports two drinks in a typical week, where earlier she reported twenty-five in two weeks. The credibility of both responses is thereby cast into doubt, yet the questionnaire provides no means for their reconciliation.

Validity
and the Collaborative Construction
of Meaning in Survey Interviews

As anthropologists interested in talk-in-activity, we see the face-to-face survey interview as a deeply consequential form of interaction for both social science and the public that makes up its object of inquiry. Our intent in this discussion, however, is not to present a critique of the survey enterprise. We have not, as several of our commentators have pointed out, attempted to consider the competing goals (e.g., large sample size) and requirements (e.g., budgetary constraints) of that enterprise.[8] Neither did we set out to propose detailed solutions to the troubles we have unearthed. Rather, we have tried to say something about what we see in the materials available to us that might be structural rather than thoroughly idiosyncratic aspects of the face-to-face

---

8. See Suchman and Jordan (1990) and the associated commentaries.

survey as a form of talk-in-interaction. We are convinced that whatever lessons might be drawn from our work, they will need to be drawn not by us but by practitioners in the field.

We have framed the contrast between the survey interview and ordinary conversation as a matter of distant, externally imposed versus local, internally produced determinations of what gets talked about in what way and by whom. Even more than the lecture or debate (where speakership and topic are also determined ahead of time but by at least one of the participants) the survey interview presents two parties with an agenda conceived by a third, the question writer, who is not present in the event. Validity in survey research therefore involves the extent to which a question is heard in the way that this third party intends.

Put simply, our view is that valid data are those that measure what the researcher intends to measure. In contrast to a thermometer or other instrument of measurement, an interview, no matter how standardized, remains fundamentally an interactional event. Invalid data are those that suffer from what Fienberg (1990, p. 243) calls "errors of the third kind," that is, errors that arise from the discrepancy between the concept of interest to the researcher and the quantity actually measured in the survey. One obvious way to reduce such errors is to make sure not only that questions are worded to maximize the likelihood of an intended reading, but also that the interviewer is in a position to clarify the meaning of a question whenever that necessity arises. It is true that allowing more local control of the survey interview between interviewer and respondent would lead to greater heterogeneity in the questions asked and answered. But in our view this does not present a problem, since what we are looking for is not standardization of the interaction but stability of meaning across situations and respondents. As Fienberg puts it, "in surveys, if the use of ordinary conversation produces stability of meaning across interviews, then this should lead to valid estimates of the quantities of interest" (p. 243).

At the same time, we are not proposing that survey researchers abandon the structured interview in favor of something called "having a conversation." The question we raise is not whether the quantity of structure involved in the survey interview should be somehow less (analyses of conversation show there to be no such thing as an unstructured conversation, in any case), but rather from where the structure should come. The structure of conversation is not missing; it comes from inside the interaction. That is to say, it is generated by the participants in and through the course of their talk together, rather than being imposed from outside. Nor does saying that the structure of the interaction must be endogenously produced preclude an agenda given by the researcher. It simply acknowledges that the realization of the researcher's agenda is an irremediably local achievement of the participants in a specific interview interaction.

The problem of assessing the meaning of questions and responses extends beyond the interview situation. Even if questions and answers are interpreted in the way that their authors intend, it is by no means assured that other users of the data will share this understanding. Every researcher who employs survey data for descriptive or inferential statistics needs to know the sense in which the question was heard and answered in order to use the data legitimately. It follows that validity requires a mechanism to assure that all parties involved in the enterprise (including the author of the question, the interviewer, the respondent, the coder, and the analyst of the data) have a common understanding of what the question means and how the answer is to be taken. The only hope for such stable interpretations, and therefore for validity, is active collaboration between all of these parties.

To take this view seriously would mean rethinking the relations between participants in survey work to focus on the achievement of a joint sense of the meaning of questions. The questionnaire itself is the record of the question writer's agenda. Whereas the business of filling it out is, in some sense, the joint accomplishment of interviewer and respondent, it is the interviewer who directly controls the work. The interview schedule determines the course of the interaction, and is physically as well as cognitively the focus of the interviewer's attention. At the same time, the form is unavailable to the respondent, who at best is able to watch the interviewer read and write. The respondent thus is required to focus his or her attention on something to which he or she has no direct access and to hold the floor for the interviewer across major gaps in the interaction. The consequence is an awkward, if not untenable, position for the respondent; namely, to be participating in an event that is organized by the task of filling out the form and, at the same time, not to have a role in its management.

A material aspect of a more collaborative interview, therefore, might be a questionnaire that is at least visually available to both parties. One could imagine a technological improvement in the form of an interactive computer screen, where the interviewer acts as a kind of navigation guide for the respondent. But the same principle can be incorporated in interviews that use manual recording techniques. As well as increasing the respondent's participation and engagement, access to the record might also afford a check on its accuracy as well as a greater commitment to producing a codable answer. For example, rather than concealing the option of "don't know," the interviewer might enlist the respondent in the project of producing a response with something like, "What we want to do if we can is to avoid 'don't know' answers, because they are not counted, and your voice won't be heard."

Most importantly we would recommend, as an alternative to the present injunction against interviewer-respondent interaction, allowing the interviewer to talk about the questions, to offer clarifications and elaborations, and to engage in a limited form of recipient design and common-sense inference. This change emphasizes the interviewer's role as the principal mediator between the intended meaning of the question and the interpretations of the respondent. By bringing the resources of everyday conversation to bear and engaging in interaction with the respondent, the interviewer might be better able to see how it is that the respondent is hearing a given question. Insofar as the interviewer is briefed on the intent of a question, she or he can then act as a kind of stand-in or representative of the question writer, thereby contributing to effective standardization. To the extent that in the survey interview negotiation of meaning is suppressed, resources are lost through which the intent of the question writer could be communicated or the interpretations of the respondents assessed. And insofar as the meanings of questions and answers remain uncertain, so also does the validity of the measures produced.

Some practitioners of survey research in the field assert that interviewer practice is, in fact, more open to interaction between interviewer and respondent than our limited view of it in simulated interview situations made evident. We find this not implausible, given that life "outdoors," to use Lave's (1988) phrase, is always more contingent, more subtly fitted to its circumstances than any form of simulated activity would suggest. If survey researchers know that the troubles we identify do not occur in the field, then all is well. But though we acknowledge the limits of our access to interviewer practice, we wonder to what extent anyone really does know what happens when interviewer meets respondent not in simulated or laboratory settings, but in her or his natural habitat. More seriously we are concerned with a response to the troubles that we identify that locates the problem with the interviewer. In that regard we find a certain double bind for the interviewer in critiques like that offered by Kovar and Royston (1990). They seem to propose that the interviewers we studied failed to follow the instructions in the NHIS interviewer handbook. At the same time they fault the interviewers for having worked too much "to the rules" when videotaped. We believe that this points not to a failing on the part of these interviewers, but rather to a contradiction in the system of rules with which they are asked to comply.

The point that we hope to make is precisely that the rigid form of interviewer behavior that we have seen in these materials is what interviewers do when they act in the way that they believe they are supposed to act. If the reality of their everyday practice is otherwise, this could be taken to mean either that their real practice is a flawed version of the ideal, or (and this is the implication we would hope our readers draw) that the ideal model of interviewing practice fails to acknowledge the reality of what actual practice necessarily requires. Accordingly, our call is for some investigation into possible revisions to the current ideal—revisions that would make the model of good practice for interviewers more conforming to actual practice and thereby more genuinely useful to those who are trying to upgrade the craft.

It might be reasonable to expect that when participants are given the opportunity to discuss the meaning of questions and answers, interviews will be longer or fewer questions will be manageable within a single interview. But this is by no means a forgone conclusion. It could well be the case that more natural interaction might actually make the interview more efficient. It is clear that to recognize the interviewer's role as the representative of the researcher to the respondent and as the adjudicator of meaning does assign to him or her greater responsibility. However, that assignment may be less a change than an acknowledgment of what is already the case. To acknowledge the interviewer's role and to equip him or her with the means to fill that role more effectively might have a sufficient value with respect to the validity of the data to offset the costs of additional compensation and training. In the final analysis, if data are invalid, it matters little how cheaply we can obtain them.

This analysis raises questions that are themselves open to empirical investigation. Rather than speculate further on the answers, we would propose that research be conducted on such issues as:

- What are the effects of joint access to the survey instrument?
- How can interviewer bias be avoided while admitting the negotiation of question meanings?
- How difficult is it to train interviewers to discriminate between the two?
- How might data quality be more rigorously assessed?
- How much improvement in data quality might be obtained for what additional cost?

Among the questions we have tried to raise is just what might be the difference between *bias* (bringing to the interaction, in consequential ways, some evidence of one's own point of view) and *clarification* (attempting to arrive at a specific understanding of the point of view of the question's designer.) Our analysis should be understood as a very preliminary move in the direction that Schegloff (1990) calls a general inquiry into the survey interview as a form of talk-in-interaction. As we begin to understand such phenomena as the preference for agreement in conversation (see Pomerantz, 1984; Sacks, 1987), we can begin to investigate such issues as how interviewers might be trained not to ask questions in ways that imply agreement. Our analysis is a call for such investigations, not a proposal for unreflective abandonment of the structure of the interview.

Through this analysis we have attempted to "raise major methodological questions whose answers potentially might change the practice of the traditional survey interview" (Fienberg, 1990, p. 241). Our summary recommendation is that survey researchers acknowledge the fact that the survey interview is fundamentally an interactional event. At present the standardized interview question has become such a fragile, technical object that it is no longer viable in the real world of interaction. We believe that it can be made more robust through a finer discrimination between clarification and bias. The validity of data obtained through survey questionnaires hinges on the extent to which researchers who write the questions communicate their intended meaning to interviewers who, in turn, convey the questions' meaning to respondents. Taking this fact seriously recasts participants' interactional expertise as a resource for survey research rather than a problem. In particular the interviewers, rather than administering a set of questions designed by a third party whose intentions they do not know and for which they are not prepared to take responsibility, might then see the work of data collection as an enterprise for which they have some appreciation and about which they have something to say.

An earlier version of this chapter appeared in *Journal of the American Statistical Association* (1990) under the title, "Interactional Troubles in Face-to-Face Survey Interviews." Those parts that are repeated are reprinted with permission.

We thank the Committee on Cognition and Survey Research for lively and productive discussions of the problems considered in this paper, while absolving them of responsibility for its shortcomings. Particular thanks go to Judith Tanur for her stewardship of the project from its inception to its conclusion. Careful commentary on earlier drafts was provided by JoAnne Goldberg, Robert Hahn, Emanuel Schegloff, and Ron Simons. Our analysis benefited greatly from insights offered by members of the Interaction Analysis Laboratories at Michigan State University and Xerox Palo Alto Research Center.

References

Briggs, C. (1986) *Learning How to Ask*. Cambridge, England: Cambridge University Press.

Converse, J., and Schuman, H. (1974) *Conversations at Random: Survey Research as Interviewers See It*. New York: Wiley.

Fienberg, S. (1990) Comment on Suchman and Jordan. *Journal of the American Statistical Association* 85 (409) 241–244.

Goodwin, C., and Heritage, J. (1990) Conversation analysis. *Annual Review of Anthropology* 19, 283–307.

HUNT, L. M., BROWNER, C. H., and JORDAN, B. (1990) Hypoglycemia: Portrait of an illness construct in everyday use. *Medical Anthropology Quarterly* 4, 199–210.

HUNT, L. M., JORDAN, B., IRWIN, S., and BROWNER, C. H. (1989) Compliance and the patient's perspective: Controlling symptoms in everyday life. *Culture, Medicine, and Psychiatry* 13, 315–334.

JABINE, T., STRAF, M., TANUR, J. M., and TOURANGEAU, R., eds. (1984) *Cognitive Aspects of Survey Methodology: Building a Bridge Between Disciplines.* Report of the Advanced Research Seminar on Cognitive Aspects of Survey Methodology. Washington, DC: National Academy Press.

JORDAN, B., and FULLER, N. (1975) On the non-fatal nature of trouble: Sense-making and trouble-managing in *lingua franca* talk. *Semiotica* 13, 1–31.

KOVAR, M. G., and ROYSTON, P. (1990) Comment on Suchman and Jordan. *Journal of the American Statistical Association* 85 (409) 246–247.

LAVE, J. (1988) *Cognition in Practice.* Cambridge, England: Cambridge University Press.

LEVINSON, S. (1983) *Pragmatics.* Cambridge, England: Cambridge University Press.

MISHLER, E. (1986) *Research Interviewing.* Cambridge, MA: Harvard University Press.

POMERANTZ, A. (1984) Agreeing and disagreeing with assessments: Some features of preferred/dispreferred turn shapes. In ATKINSON, J. M., and HERITAGE, J. (eds). *Structures of Social Action: Studies in Conversation Analysis.* Cambridge, England: Cambridge University Press, pp. 57–101.

SACKS, H. (1987) On the preference for agreement and contiguity in sequences in conversation. In BUTTON, G., and LEE, J. R. E. *Talk and Social Organization.* Clevedon, England: Multilingual Matters, pp. 54–69.

SACKS, H., SCHEGLOFF, E., and JEFFERSON, G. (1974) A simplest systematics for the organization of turn-taking for conversation. *Language* 50, 696–735.

SCHEGLOFF, E. (1990) Comment on Suchman and Jordan. *Journal of the American Statistical Association* 85 (409) 248–250.

SCHEGLOFF, E., JEFFERSON, G., and SACKS, H. (1977) The preference for self-correction in the organization of repair in conversation. *Language* 53, 361–382.

SUCHMAN, L., and JORDAN, B. (1990) Interactional troubles in face-to-face survey interviews. *Journal of the American Statistical Association* 85 (409), 232–253.

PART
VI
GOVERNMENT
APPLICATIONS

13

A Review of Research at the Bureau of Labor Statistics

CATHRYN S. DIPPO
and JANET L. NORWOOD

Federal statistical agencies have a long history of research on data quality and collection methods. Much of the early work was on improved methods of sampling and error calculation, but in recent years research has focused increasingly on methods for reducing nonsampling error. In fact, early research on the influence of the interviewer on the accuracy of survey data was done at the Bureau of the Census (Hanson and Marks, 1958), and Neter and Waksberg's (1964) study of response errors in expenditure data collected in the Survey of Residential Alterations and Repairs was the first comprehensive investigation of the effects of alternative data-collection procedures on respondent recall of consumer expenditures.

In most of the investigations of survey error carried out by the federal government until about ten years ago, however, the primary investigating method was through field studies. Field tests were used extensively, for example, in research related to improvement of the questionnaire wording in the Current Population Survey (CPS), which profiles the labor market and provides an estimate of the monthly unemployment rate. Fieldwork was also involved in the extensive program of return visits to re-collect data from sample households in order to examine the variation in interviewer application of questionnaires. A special field test panel was used from 1963 to 1967 to investigate the feasibility and possible effects of questionnaire changes recommended by the President's Committee to Appraise Employment and Unemployment Statistics (Gordon Committee). The effects of detailed probing for hours worked, dependent interviewing using prior month's data, self-enumeration by mail, alternative respondent rules (restrictions on the use of proxy respondents), and one-month recall were also investigated (Deighton, 1967; Waksberg and Pearl, 1965; Williams, 1969). In addition, the Monthly Labor Survey was used to test new questions about the employed, the unemployed, and persons outside the labor force (Stein, 1967; Stein and Levine, 1965). In the 1970s the effects of telephone interviewing and other data collection issues related to the CPS were tested in a special Methods Development Survey (Roman, 1981). And again in the 1980s, when computer-assisted telephone interviewing was proposed as a method to improve the quality of CPS data, a field test was used to examine the feasibility and effects on the survey data (Shoemaker, Bushery, and Cahoon, 1989).

Most of these field studies were designed to determine the effect of alternative questions or procedures, where the alternatives were based on common sense. The studies were not designed to test hypotheses about *why* respondents provide different answers when questions are asked in different ways or when different collection procedures are used; nor were the alternatives guided by cognitive principles. Most of these field tests were not preceded by laboratory studies of even a few respondents.

Thus, the 1980 "Workshop on Applying Cognitive Psychology to Recall Problems of the National Crime Survey" (Biderman, 1980) represented a radical departure from the status quo for the federal statistical system at that time. This workshop brought about some tests of cognitive applications to a government survey, but did not result in any lasting recognition of the need to apply interdisciplinary techniques to survey research in the federal government. Nevertheless, the fact that the workshop occurred was in itself important, because it set the stage for further cooperation between government and academe on these issues in the future.

It was possible for this cooperation to take place because federal survey statisticians often employed techniques that paralleled those used in the cognitive sciences in questionnaire development, even though they did not use cognitive theories or laboratory methods (Office of Management and Budget, 1983). Some of this government research can be seen in the studies undertaken for the 1980 Census of Population and Housing (Rothwell, 1985). This program was developed to provide "useful general principles for the design of self-administered questionnaires and mechanisms for applying these principles systematically in Census Bureau data collection programs" (Rothwell, 1983). The program included laboratory experiments on alternative form layouts and one-on-one observations of subjects filling out a form. These were the first small-scale experiments and observational studies of questionnaires conducted by the Bureau of the Census in conjunction with questionnaire research.

Previously, questionnaires had been tested on only a few respondents, in large part because the Federal Reports Act of 1942 provides that a federal form cannot be tested on more than nine members of the public without prior approval of the Office of Management and Budget. Such testing was usually limited to an examination of skip patterns and internal consistency of the proposed questionnaire. The system permitted detection of obvious problems with question wording, but did not permit an investigation of respondents' thought processes to determine if their understanding of the question matched that of the survey sponsor.

The step needed to formalize the integration of the methods and concepts of the cognitive sciences with survey research came in 1983, when the National Science Foundation (NSF) funded a Committee on National Statistics-sponsored Seminar on the Cognitive Aspects of Survey Methodology (CASM). At this seminar representatives of both government and academe, a partnership that had its roots in the 1980 workshop on the National Crime Survey, tackled the generic and more basic issues involved in bringing together the cognitive sciences and survey methodology. Surveys were examined as a vehicle for cognitive research, and possibilities for the use of cognitive methods to improve surveys were considered.

The CASM conference used the National Health Interview Survey, sponsored by the National Center for Health Statistics (NCHS), as a case study in the application of the techniques of the cognitive sciences to the development of a survey questionnaire. And, as a result of this conference, NCHS obtained NSF funding to sponsor collaborative cognitive research (Brewer, Dull, and Jobe, 1989; Lessler, Salter, and Tourangeau, 1989; Means, Swan, Jobe, Esposito, and Loftus, 1989). A second NSF grant was used to establish a laboratory for research on cognition and survey measurement at NCHS. The Bureau of Labor Statistics (BLS) and the Bureau of the Census have since established their own laboratories for pretesting questionnaires, investigating redesign options, and carrying out basic research.

The formal integration of cognitive theories and techniques in survey design research is thus a relatively recent phenomenon in the federal government. Nevertheless, a number of different types of applications have already been developed. The remainder of this chapter reviews the work at BLS over the last few years, first by describing some of the applications attempted, and then by reporting on various accomplishments with an emphasis on laboratory-based research related to questionnaire design. We recognize, of course, that laboratory-based questionnaire research is only one of the many areas where interdisciplinary research is taking place or being planned, but since so little is known about laboratory-based research, it seems wise to focus on it in the sections that follow. Although laboratory-based questionnaire research is taking place at all three federal laboratories,[1] the emphasis here is on research conducted or sponsored by BLS because the authors are more familiar with this work.

Application

Federal government efforts to integrate the cognitive sciences and survey research have thus far centered on the use of cognitive laboratory techniques to develop and improve survey questionnaires. At BLS, much of the Collection Procedures Research Laboratory's (CPRL) resources have been concentrated on improving the questionnaires used in the Current Population Survey and Consumer Expenditure Surveys (Dippo, 1989). The self-administered forms used in several of BLS's establishment surveys have also been the subject of laboratory research.

In many ways, however, cognitive research in government laboratories should go beyond the specific application to questionnaire design envisaged in this volume. For example, laboratory techniques, such as focus groups, protocol analysis, and paraphrasing, can usefully be applied to all aspects of data collection, including developing manuals and training interviewers, as well as the interface between people and machines associated with computer-assisted interviewing. The interdisciplinary approach can also be applied to data processing, where the techniques from the cognitive sciences can be especially helpful in developing the knowledge bases needed for expert systems and evaluating software usability.

Some nonquestionnaire laboratory projects at BLS include an examination of the interface between interviewers and laptop and notebook-style personal computers for computer-assisted personal interviewing (Couper, Groves, and Jacobs, 1990), and interviewer knowledge and behavior studies for improving training. These studies indicate that the theories and techniques of the cognitive sciences have a much broader field of application than just the questionnaire.

Survey research in government laboratories needs to be wide-ranging with many aspects, in part because federal surveys are not limited to face-to-face communication with individuals responding about themselves. In order to restrain cost and to save time, many government household

1. Willis, Royston, and Bercini (1989) summarize the types of problems found in NCHS survey questions through the use of cognitive-based interviewing techniques. Rothwell (1985) reviews the types of laboratory and laboratory-like methods used in studying the population and housing census questionnaire.

surveys ask respondents to provide information first about themselves, and then to serve as a proxy and provide information about others in the household. Until we know more about communication within households as understood by developmental psychologists, psycholinguists, and sociolinguists—what knowledge is transmitted among household members and how that knowledge is transmitted—it will be difficult to develop adequate models of proxy response. BLS is taking an initial step in this area by funding laboratory research on communication patterns within households using artificial intelligence techniques. The focus is on the types of autobiographical information collected in BLS surveys, for instance, job and job-search activities and personal expenditures.

Because a significant proportion of interviews in many surveys is conducted over the telephone or through the use of mailed questionnaires, the interdisciplinary aspect of the work has in some cases been extended beyond the cognitive sciences and survey research by including experts in other areas, for instance, specialists in human factors. It seems clear that research issues associated with computer-assisted interviewing can benefit from the work of human-factors experts, and that specialists in information exchange processes can help us to understand better the entire survey interviewing process.

At BLS we have found the team approach to research to be especially successful. Teams include economists, statisticians, and cognitive social scientists, such as psychologists, sociologists, or anthropologists. The inclusion of an expert to clarify the concept to be measured and to explain the analytical use for which the data are collected can help to ensure that the survey process yields data of high quality for the intended uses.

Although simple cognitive tasks may be generalizable across most segments of the population, many of the cognitive tasks involved in responding to national surveys may not be. Thus, it is important to consider what social and economic factors might affect the response process and reach out to include the appropriate demographic, socioeconomic, or geographic subpopulations in the laboratory research. For example, a primary goal of current CPS questionnaire research is an evaluation of the effectiveness of alternative questions in determining the labor force status of survey respondents—whether they are employed, unemployed, or out of the labor force. This can only be done with a pool of subjects sufficient to cover the margins between unemployment, employment, or not in the labor force for the many different kinds of socioeconomic groups in the country. In order to reach selected segments of the labor market—for example, migrant workers—we have found it necessary to take the laboratory on the road to visit employment offices in areas of the country where the labor market distribution is different from that in the Washington area.

Research has also been conducted outside of the CPRL in another area in which BLS is especially interested—the application of cognitive techniques to establishment surveys. Most of the cognitive laboratory procedures were developed for application to persons reporting about themselves; the procedures require modification for use in business surveys. Questionnaires used in business surveys are designed to retrieve information stored in the records of a company rather than in the memories of respondents. In this retrieval process, a questionnaire designed and structured so that a business respondent understands what is requested as well as alternative approaches to interviewing respondents are important. Company officials cannot be expected to visit a laboratory in Washington. Instead, our researchers need to visit company sites equipped with relevant procedures and protocols for use by business professionals on a tight time schedule.

BLS first applied cognitive techniques to the development of an establishment survey questionnaire for the Survey of Employer Assistance Programs (Palmisano, 1988). With assistance from state and regional offices, think-aloud interviews were used to test survey questions and concepts with nine companies. The interviews were taped for further study. Since then, in-the-field laboratory-type interviews have been used regularly as a tool for evaluating new establishment survey instruments. Telephone interviews with establishment survey respondents using retrospective think-aloud procedures have also been used in testing question and concept comprehension.

Laboratory Experience at BLS

This section highlights the diversity of knowledge gained from laboratory-based research for BLS-sponsored surveys. These results are, however, just a beginning. We are still a long way from having a synthesis of results built into a theoretical model of response that can be tested and modified for applicability across the many dimensions of survey data collection. Yet, one of the most important benefits of the laboratory approach to survey research is that it permits methodical investigation of various aspects of survey design in which the focus of problem solving can be shifted from reaction to anticipation and from haphazard to systematic.

Even though laboratory-based research related to survey questionnaires is relatively new, a significant body of literature has appeared documenting the results of its use. The review that follows is organized within the framework of an information-processing model (Cannell, Miller, and Oksenberg, 1981; Tourangeau, 1984), which has four distinct stages: comprehension, retrieval, judgment, and communication. As applied to respondents, these stages refer to comprehension of the question, retrieval of pertinent information, judgment about the accuracy of the information retrieved, and communication about this information within social and other restrictions imposed by the interview situation. As applied to interviewers, these stages refer to comprehension of the question, retrieval of appropriate ways to say the question aloud, judgment about whether the respondent has understood the question, and communication to ensure the question has been understood (such as by rereading it) or, if the question has apparently been understood, to indicate that another question is about to be presented.

Comprehension

Question comprehension clearly requires that the terms making up a question be correctly understood. The accuracy of term comprehension has been shown by numerous psycholinguistic investigations to differ as a result of a number of factors, including whether the term has multiple meanings or diverse meanings (see Clark and Schober, chapter 2 in this volume). In self-administered questionnaires, the format of the questionnaire can also affect comprehension. Research at BLS has focused particularly on the cognition of meaning and format.

MULTIPLE MEANINGS OF TERMS.   A term may lead some respondents to answer inappropriately because it conveys a meaning different from that intended by the survey designer. Many seemingly simple words possess multiple meanings. For example, *bank* may mean a "financial institution" or an "embankment alongside a river or stream." Even when the context of a sentence may make clear the intended meaning of a term, a respondent may be tired or tense and interpret the meaning in the wrong way. Usually the multiple meanings that are confused are close; for example, *bank* may mean a "full-service bank" or a "savings and loan." Often such close distinctions are crucial to the goals of a survey. Consequently, much of our research in this area has attempted to determine the extent to which response accuracy may be biased by misunderstandings due to terms having multiple meanings.

When the topics being asked about are sensitive, misinterpretation of term meaning increases. Anxiety distracts people and impairs their ability to concentrate. As a result, when a research initiative at BLS is begun, an attempt is made to identify terms with alternative meanings that are not made explicit by the phrasing of questions and that might be misinterpreted.

Research into comprehension of multiple-meaning terms has begun for the Consumer Expenditure (CE) Interview Survey with the sections on medical and health expenditures, owned living quarters, and trips and vacation expenditures. Specifically, it was hypothesized that the term *payments* in the section on medical and health expenditures may be misinterpreted by respondents because it lends itself to alternative meanings.

Research indicates that *payments* indeed does involve multiple meanings, such as "anything paid for medical services" and "money issued in the form of a check" (Miller and Downes-Le Guin, 1989). Since our results indicate that people interpret *payments* in different ways, the section on medical and health expenditures has since been modified to minimize misinterpretations of this term by including a definition for *payments*.

Sometimes, alternative meanings of terms are related to very different response task difficulties. For example, *monthly payment on your mortgage* might be interpreted to mean the "full amount paid to a mortgage holder each month" or the "sum of principal and interest." Homeowners who pay the lender fees for mortgage life insurance, prorated property taxes, or other fees have to recall several components and perform subtractions if the phrase is interpreted as principal and interest only. In these cases respondents may choose to simplify their task by providing rough estimates rather than more accurate information that they could recall if they made the effort (Krosnick and Alwin, 1987). We found that more explicit cues or separate questions clarify what is being asked for and counteract this tendency by respondents to select the interpretation that makes their response task easier.

BREADTH OF TERM MEANING.   Issues of comprehension are especially critical to the accuracy of the data used to produce statistics on employment and unemployment from the Current Population Survey, one of the oldest and most carefully produced labor force surveys in the world. Since employment status is of considerable personal significance to most people (Bailar and Rothwell, 1984; Edwards, Levine, and Cohany, 1989), questions about employment status are likely to induce at least some anxiety (especially in the unemployed or those with insecure employment). The misinterpretation of employment status terms may easily occur in a survey such as the CPS (Martin, 1987).

Previous research has demonstrated that the terms that are used in the classification of respondents as employed, unemployed, or out of the labor force are not always understood by the persons responding to the survey in the manner intended by the survey designers (Rothgeb, 1982). Thus, much of the research on respondent comprehension in the CPS has been predicated on the hypothesis that respondents have a broader interpretation of two key terms concerning unemployment status, *on layoff* and *looking for work*, than BLS. The BLS definition of unemployment in the CPS refers to persons who were not employed during the survey week, were available for work, and had made specific efforts to find employment sometime during the prior four weeks. Persons who are waiting to be recalled to a job from which they have been laid off need not be looking for work to be classified as unemployed. As expected, research demonstrates that these terms are sometimes misinterpreted by laboratory respondents to the CPS. Specifically, *on layoff* is interpreted too broadly to include persons who have been fired or lost their jobs due to plant closings (Palmisano, 1989). Similarly, *looking for work* is found to embrace, for some respondents, some activities that are not included in the BLS definition, for instance, merely studying the want ads (Campanelli, Martin, and Creighton, 1989; Palmisano, 1989).

Given that the data confirm expectations of misinterpretation of the terms *on layoff* and *looking for work*, modifications to the language of the CPS are being tested in an attempt to avoid misinterpretation of these terms. For example, in the case of *on layoff*, we are investigating the addition of probing questions to determine whether a person identified as being on layoff has been given a date to return to work and, if not, whether the person has been given any indication of recall within the next six months. The *looking for work* test question employs more encompassing wording and the response categories include more alternatives.

DIVERSE MEANINGS OF TERMS.   Diversity of term meaning may also impair comprehension. People often acquire an imprecise meaning for a term. For some people this meaning is too narrow and for others too broad. Terms with diverse meanings dispose respondents to produce too limited or too general answers. Infrequently used terms, such as technical terms, often have diverse meanings. Since establishment surveys often use technical terms that are familiar to survey designers and researchers but not to all respondents, it has been hypothesized that technical terms may possess variable meanings across respondents, and their use may lead to misinterpretations.

For example, in a recent pilot survey of business establishments, respondents were asked to report all *nonwage cash payments* to employees during the calendar year. BLS defines the payments to include bonuses and awards, lump sum, cash-profit sharing, and severance payments, as well as nonregular commissions; but since this technical term probably is not too familiar to respondents, the meanings of *nonwage cash payments* can be expected to vary across respondents. When the interpretations of this term by respondents were investigated, we found that respondents interpreted *nonwage cash payments* in a diverse fashion. Some interpreted it too broadly to include payments in kind, such as a new car (Boehm, 1988), and some, too narrowly to include only cash and not cashable checks (Phipps, 1990). Another group of respondents who indeed had made such payments simply checked they had made no payments because of a lack of understanding of what the term included. Respondent exclusion and nonreporting of payments that contributed to underreporting were more serious comprehension errors than inclusion of inappropriate payments.

QUESTIONNAIRE FORMAT PROPERTIES.   When respondents answer a written survey or form directly, the format of the instrument may play a crucial role in the respondents' comprehension. If the format does not make it clear what parts of instructions are essential, respondents may overlook these parts and respond inappropriately (DeMaio and Bates, 1989). Also, even if a respondent is successful in finding the necessary instructions in an otherwise confusing format, the respondent may become anxious—and more prone to error—in the process.

In establishment mail surveys, detailed instructions and definitions are often printed in an entirely different location than the question-and-answer space. Thus, with this type of layout, respondents are forced to discover their own way to proceed through the questionnaire. Telephone interviews with respondents have indicated that reference to the separate instructions and definitions is inconsistent (Phipps, 1990). Reporters state that they overlook or do not understand that they are to provide data items explained in instructions and definitions.

For example, in the Nonwage Cash Payments Pilot Survey (Phipps, 1990), instructions, definitions, and examples were on the back of a one-page questionnaire for which two different layouts were used. One layout required respondents first to provide an annual nonwage cash payment total and an annual payroll total, then answer a set of yes/no questions asking if they made specific types of nonwage cash payments. The second layout placed the set of yes/no questions first, with the payments and payroll totals requested at the bottom of the page. Reporters receiving the second layout were much less likely to provide the annual payroll total, stating in retrospective interviews that they overlooked it or did not understand they were to provide it. Many of these respondents had indicated in the yes/no questions that they did not have nonwage cash payments. Without any instructions, they simply stopped at that point rather than going on to the annual payroll section. Thus, the survey form played an important role in the respondents' comprehension of survey items. The layout of the second form, combined with a lack of instruction, caused an entire section of the form to be overlooked.

Retrieval

Because cost and burden constraints frequently make it impossible to conduct surveys on a weekly or monthly basis, many of the large household surveys sponsored by the federal government have reference periods that require respondents to retrieve information from memory about events that may have occurred some time ago. For example, interviewers in the Consumer Expenditure Interview Survey visit sample households five times at three-month intervals. During each visit the interviewers collect households' expenditures since the first of the month, three months ago. Respondents to the Current Population Survey are asked to recall if they were working or if they had a job from which they were temporarily absent last week. If they did not have a job last week, they are asked if they have looked for work in the last four weeks. If they have, they are asked about when they began looking and when they last worked at a full-time job or business for two consecutive weeks or more, which could require recall over very long periods of time. (For further discussion of memory retrieval errors in CE and CPS, see Dippo, 1989.)

Memory researchers have recognized for nearly two decades that people sometimes appear to forget but can later be shown not to have forgotten after all. One way to elicit a memory is to present cues that remind a person of this memory. Another way is to induce a person to employ a specific information-processing strategy. Finally, people retrieve best that which they know best. Interpretation of a respondent's memory performance, therefore, may be sounder if it takes account of the respondent's expertise for what is being asked about.

CUES.   Often a situation is inadequate in the cues it presents for retrieval. When enough appropriate cues are presented, a person is able to retrieve the previously forgotten memory. Whereas some information is probably lost from memory due to diseases and environmental influences (such as alcohol), cues clearly play an important role in retrieval. Accordingly, a number of investigations have attempted to increase response accuracy in surveys by providing additional cues for retrieval (Lessler, Salter, and Tourangeau, 1989; Martin, Groves, Matlin, and Miller, 1986; Means et al., 1989). A variety of cuing methods have been used in these investigations to good effect. However, it is important to recognize that some cues can be misleading and ensure that a respondent does *not* retrieve the appropriate information. Cues facilitate only when they correctly direct retrieval.

In telephone follow-up interviews with respondents to the Nonwage Cash Payments Pilot Survey, a list of specific types of bonus and award payments was read to company representatives. Approximately 11% of the respondents who had not reported such payment types during the regular survey recalled them when given the specific cues. At least 15% of those who had unreported payments attributed their failure to report them to memory (Phipps, 1990).

Certain cues may be more effective than others. Depending upon the generality of the cues, they may enhance recall for the mentioned items while interfering with the recall of unmentioned items. In the Consumer Expenditure Diary Survey, cues with varying levels of generality have been tested in a field study of three alternative diary formats (Tucker and Bennett, 1988; Tucker, Miller, Vitrano, and Doddy, 1989). In the study, expenditures were reported more often for specific cuts of beef when they were listed on the diary as *Ground beef, chuck roast, round roast, other roast, round steak, sirloin steak, other steak, other beef* and *veal* than when a general category heading *Beef (ground, roasts, steaks, briskets, etc.)* was used. Underreporting was greater with general cues for certain items, as the memory literature suggests, particularly in the case of nonfood items. On the other hand, the level of reporting for many food items was not affected by the type of cues (Tucker and Bennett, 1988).

STRATEGIES.   Memory for activities in everyday life may be localized in time. Typically, people reconstruct their past from schemas of how routine events recur. For example, people have a general understanding of what is involved when they go to a restaurant: They choose items from a menu, order these items, eat, pay the bill, and leave. To recall accurately past events, people need to retrieve schematic information that pertains to the event, along with the mental records about the event, for example, details about the particular restaurant and meal. People typically recall events strategically by using schematic knowledge to reconstruct their memory for the actual particulars of an event. Since strategies are known to guide recall in general, our research has attempted to determine how strategy use may facilitate the data-collection process.

Several strategies to get respondents to access their memories of actual experience (Lessler, Salter, and Tourangeau, 1989) have proved useful in our investigations of the "hours worked last week" question on the CPS. Laboratory research on this question indicates that most respondents' errors in reporting their own hours worked can be classified as motivation errors rather than memory retrieval errors (Edwards, Levine, and Cohany, 1989); that is, the respondent does not attempt to access episodic memory to retrieve the details of specific hours worked each day last week in order to answer the question, but instead relies on a schema of usual hours worked.

Alternative questionnaires have been developed and tested that attempt to impose a specific recall strategy on the respondent. One strategy first asks the respondent for the number of hours usually worked per week to anchor the response, then adjusts for extra hours worked and time off from work last week. A second strategy has a respondent consult a calendar while the interviewer suggests the respondent decompose events recalled into smaller events (that is, write down the hours worked each day). Research at BLS has replicated the effectiveness of these strategies as found at NCHS and has extended this research in certain ways. For example, we have found that respondents vary in the extent to which they employ the strategy that they were instructed to use. Only one-third of the laboratory subjects instructed to use a particular strategy when responding to questions on their hours worked actually used the strategy (Edwards and Levine, 1990).

EXPERTISE.   Research has shown that people encode and remember attributes of personal events differently than attributes of events concerning others. The efficiency and accuracy of encoding and the durability of retention has been shown to depend very clearly on the amount of experience people have had with the kind of information at issue. The more expert people are with a particular topic, the more quickly and more precisely they will register an experience, the longer they will retain the information, and the faster and more accurately they will recall the information. Consequently, research at BLS has been concerned with how expertise affects survey data.

As noted earlier, most government surveys allow one adult member of a household to report for all members. In a laboratory study of household respondent pairs using the Current Population Survey questionnaire, proxy responses were different from those of the self-respondent approximately one-third of the time (Boehm, 1989). In another laboratory study investigating the accuracy of reports on the number of hours worked last week (Edwards, Levine, and Cohany, 1989), respondents were found to overreport and proxy respondents to underreport the hours worked. Proxy respondents were more likely than self-respondents to make errors, and their errors tended to be larger. The study indicated the underreporting by proxy respondents increases for subjects who work on weekends and for those who generally work more hours. Moreover, proxy respondents' errors were greater if the respondents were unrelated to or of a different generation than the person for whom data were being collected.

Judgment

People may recall information correctly to themselves but not produce it overtly because they do not realize the information is correct. They may recall incorrectly but judge what they recall as accurate. Or they may decide accurate information cannot be recalled (or it is too much work) and use a response strategy based on judgment. In the first two cases the correct response is not produced because people are unable to judge the accuracy of the knowledge or information process. In the third case people judge the knowledge retrieval process to be inaccurate or unworkable and substitute an alternative information process. For example, instead of trying to recall specific hours worked last week, many people respond with an estimate of their usual hours worked; or, instead of looking at the records of their utility payments for the last three months, many people respond with an estimate.

Research shows that sometimes flawed judgment may be detected by people, enabling them to make a correct response after all. Accordingly, BLS has been investigating ways to facilitate the judgment process and increase response accuracy.

It was noted earlier that field research on the Consumer Expenditure Diary Survey indicated specific cues were often more effective, that is, they led to less underreporting than general cues (Tucker and Bennett, 1988). In this survey, respondents are instructed to record all purchases on the diary form. When specific cues, such as *White bread (nonrefrigerated), round roast,* and *other fresh milk and cream,* are used, they are preprinted on individual lines of the diary and respondents are instructed to "Mark (X) if item purchased." When general heading cues, such as *Bakery products (fresh or frozen bread, cakes, cookies, pies,* etc.*)* and *beef (ground, roasts, steaks, briskets,* etc.*)*, are used, respondents are asked to "Describe item purchased" on the blank lines of the diary.

Whereas the specific cues may increase reporting, further laboratory investigation indicates respondents have difficulty making judgments about where to categorize items not individually listed on the diary form containing specific cues (Tucker et al., 1989), thus affecting the accuracy of reports. Moreover, the specific cues may also make the reporting task more onerous to the respondent by forcing him or her to make many detailed judgments.

For several situations in which respondents are likely to judge an estimation strategy to be superior to or easier than an episodic memory recall strategy, BLS has investigated the use of imposed recall strategies. For an example, see the above section on retrieval strategies.

Interviewers' judgments are crucial when responses to open-ended questions are not recorded verbatim, but are instead classified by the interviewers into one of several categories listed on the questionnaire. The effects of alternative categories and category wording on the reliability of interviewers' judgment have been studied with respect to the open-ended questions in the Current Population Survey (Fracasso, 1989). The laboratory study shows that modifications to the terms used in response categories, as well as additions to and deletions from the list of response categories, can affect interviewers' judgments. For example, modifying the response categories *Own illness* and *On vacation* to the CPS question, "What is the reason . . . worked less than thirty-five hours LAST WEEK?" to be more specific—such as *Illness, injury, medical appointments,* and *Vacation, personal day*—results in responses that belong in these categories being more accurately coded by interviewers. With the first set of categories, responses such as "Doctor appointment" are frequently coded as *Other* rather than as *Own illness*.

Communication

A considerable amount of survey research has shown that a number of factors can influence a respondent's decision at the communication stage, including the sensitivity of the question, the social desirability of the answer, and the expectations of the interviewer. Respondents may be reluctant to answer sensitive questions honestly. They may feel a need to give favorable impressions of themselves, or they may want to adapt their response to what they perceive to be the expectations of the interviewer. They may recall correct information, know it is correct, but express it inappropriately because they misconceive how responses are to be expressed. Because communication is crucial to correct responding, the CPRL has been directing some of its research attention to investigating how communication should be considered in evaluating survey data.

Although BLS has yet to complete an investigation of communication, it has recently begun several such investigations. First, research is being conducted on the psycholinguistic factors that persuade a respondent to provide confidential information in a survey. This research will ascertain the degree of trust elicited by the use of different protection terms (confidential, private, secret, concealed). Subsequent work will examine how the trust induced by these terms is moderated by the topic of information to be protected and by the nature of the agency responsible for maintaining the protection.

Second, we are examining the influence of interviewer errors on the errors of respondents, using techniques developed by Cannell (Cannell et al., 1981; Cannell et al., 1989). The paraphrasing, verification, and skip-pattern errors of CE interviewers are being coded from audiotapes of over ninety field interviews and linked with the various answers provided by respondents. We hypothesize that the quality of answers produced by respondents will vary with the quality of the interviewers' presentation of a question.

Similar types of behavior investigations are being conducted for the CPS, Consumer Price Index-Housing, and Current Point of Purchase surveys to determine if people respond in the same manner in a computer-assisted telephone interview (CATI) as they do in a personal interview. It has been suggested that the personal interview insures better attention from the respondent, whereas it has also been suggested that CATI elicits information that otherwise might not be disclosed because the respondent feels less personally involved when interacting with an interviewer on the telephone. In various ways our research is addressing these alternative expectations about CATI.

Third, in the Current Employment Statistics Survey, BLS is experimenting with touch-tone data entry (TDE) as a form of data collection. With TDE, respondents with touch-tone telephones can call a toll-free number at their convenience and enter data using their telephone in response to computer-synthesized voice requests for numbers of employees, average hours, and earnings data. To investigate respondents' behaviors when trying to communicate using this system, data on the number of times a respondent reenters items, how often the respondent waits until the second request to enter an item, and if and when a respondent hangs up during a call are being collected. These data should indicate when respondents are having difficulties with the questions, the pace of the interview, and the machine interface.

Conclusion

Most federal surveys attempt to collect factual information from respondents about themselves, their households, or their places of work. The existence of survey measurement problems has been known and well documented over the years. However, the methods for investigating the effects of alternative question wording and ordering, variations in questionnaire form design and structure, and mode of data collection, to name just a few survey design variables, have been largely limited to experimental designs carried out by data-collection staff. While these methods have advanced the field of survey methods research significantly by showing the effects of alternative procedures, they have added little to our basic understanding of *why* different procedures elicit different data from respondents. The theories and methods of the cognitive sciences provide a framework and tools for conducting the research needed to address this issue.

Much remains to be done to develop a true interdisciplinary science for investigating survey research methods. At the Bureau of Labor Statistics, we have taken our first tentative steps toward the integration of statistical and psychological sciences: the construction of a Collection Procedures Research Laboratory; the hiring of a staff of enthusiastic psychologists, sociologists, and anthropologists to work with the mathematical statisticians and economists at the bureau; and the establishment of research contracts with private and academic research institutions. The applied laboratory research conducted over the last few years has yielded practical results, which we have used to improve the quality of data collected by BLS. Furthermore, the results have indicated areas in which basic research is needed. Plans for conducting such research are underway, and as the laboratory becomes more established, the variety and scope of research will expand (Dippo and Herrmann, 1991).

As the agency responsible for producing many important statistics for governing the nation and setting public policy, the mission of the bureau is to provide the most accurate data possible. We view the laboratory as another tool in our program of total quality management. As such, we expect laboratory research to expand to other aspects of survey design and to other noncognitive aspects of survey research.

This review of research at the Bureau of Labor Statistics is based on the work of the BLS Collection Procedures Research Laboratory staff, many of whom have contributed portions of the discussion. The authors are especially indebted to Douglas Herrmann, whose insights have significantly improved the focus of the discussion.

References

BAILAR, B., and ROTHWELL, N. (1984) Measuring employment and unemployment. In TURNER, C., and MARTIN, E. (eds.). *Surveying Subjective Phenomena*. New York: Russell Sage Foundation, pp. 129–142.

BIDERMAN, A. (1980) *Report of a Workshop on Applying Cognitive Psychology to Recall Problems of the National Crime Survey*. Washington, DC: Bureau of Social Science Research.

BOEHM, L. (1988) CES nonwage cash payment prepilot interviews. Washington, DC: U.S. Bureau of Labor Statistics' internal memorandum to Alan Tupek dated December 16.

_____ (1989) The relationship between confidence, knowledge, and performance in the Current Population Survey. In *Proceedings of the Section on Survey Research Methods*. Washington, DC: American Statistical Association, pp. 486–489.

BREWER, M., DULL, V., and JOBE, J. (1989) Social cognition approach to reporting chronic conditions in health surveys. *Vital and Health Statistics*, series 6, no. 3 (DHHS Publication No. PHS 89–1078). Washington, DC: U.S. Government Printing Office, pp. 3–36.

CAMPANELLI, P., MARTIN, E., and CREIGHTON, K. (1989) Respondents' understanding of labor force concepts: Insights from debriefing studies. In *Proceedings of the Fifth Annual Research Conference*. Washington, DC: U.S. Department of Commerce, Bureau of the Census, pp. 361–374.

CANNELL, C., FOWLER, F., KALTON, G., OKSENBERG, L., and BISCHOPING, K. (1989) New quantitative techniques for pretesting survey questions. In *Bulletin of the International Statistical Institute*, pp. 481–495.

CANNELL, C. F., MILLER, P. V., and OKSENBERG, L. (1981) Research on interviewing techniques. In LEINHARDT, S. (ed.). *Sociological Methodology*. San Francisco: Jossey-Bass, pp. 389–437.

COUPER, M., GROVES, R., and JACOBS, C. (1990) Building predictive models of CAPI acceptance in a field interviewing staff. In *Proceedings of the 1990 Annual Research Conference*. Washington, DC: U.S. Department of Commerce, Bureau of the Census, pp. 685–702.

DEIGHTON, R. (1967) Some results of experimentation with self-respondent interviewing procedures, February 1965–June 1966. Internal memorandum dated February 28. Washington, DC: U.S. Department of Commerce, Bureau of the Census.

DeMaio, T., and Bates, N. (1989) Using cognitive research methods to improve the design of the Decennial Census form. In *Proceedings of the Fifth Annual Research Conference*. Washington, DC: U.S. Department of Commerce, Bureau of the Census, pp. 267–285.

Dippo, C. S. (1989) The use of cognitive laboratory techniques for investigating memory retrieval errors in retrospective surveys. *Bulletin of the International Statistical Institute*, vol. 53, book 2, pp. 363–382.

Dippo, C. S., and Herrmann, D. (1991) The Bureau of Labor Statistics' collection procedures research laboratory: Accomplishments and future directions. In *Statistical Policy Working Paper 20*. Washington, DC: U.S. Office of Management and Budget, pp. 253–267.

Edwards, S., and Levine, R. (1990) Further research on hours of work questions in the Current Population Survey. Final report prepared for the Bureau of Labor Statistics. Rockville, MD: Westat.

Edwards, S., Levine, R., and Cohany, S. (1989) Procedures for validating reports of hours worked and for classifying discrepancies between questionnaire reports and validation totals. In *Proceedings of the Section on Survey Research Methods*. Washington, DC: American Statistical Association, pp. 496–501.

Fracasso, M. (1989) Categorization of responses to the open-ended labor force questions in the Current Population Survey (CPS). In *Proceedings of the Section on Survey Research Methods*. Washington, DC: American Statistical Association, pp. 481–485.

Hanson, R. H., and Marks, E. S. (1958) Influence of the interviewer on the accuracy of survey results. *Journal of the American Statistical Association* 53, 635–655.

Krosnick, J. A., and Alwin, D. F. (1987) Satisficing: A strategy for dealing with the demands of survey questions. Paper presented at the annual meeting of the American Association for Public Opinion Research.

Lessler, J., Salter, W., and Tourangeau, R. (1989) Questionnaire design in the cognitive research laboratory: Results of an experimental prototype. *Vital and Health Statistics*, series 6, no. 1 (DHHS Publication No. PHS 89–1076). Washington, DC: U.S. Government Printing Office.

Martin, E. (1987) Some conceptual problems in the Current Population Survey. In *Proceedings of the Section on Survey Research Methods*. Washington, DC: American Statistical Association, pp. 420–424.

Martin, E., Groves, R., Matlin, J., and Miller, C. (1986) Report on the development of alternative screening procedures for the National Crime Survey. Washington, DC: Bureau of Social Science Research.

Means, B., Swan, G., Jobe, J. B., Esposito, J., and Loftus, E. F. (1989) Recall strategies for estimation of smoking levels in health surveys. In *Proceedings of the Section on Survey Research Methods*. Washington, DC: American Statistical Association, pp. 421–424.

Miller, L., and Downes-Le Guin, T. (1989) Improving comprehension and recall in the Consumer Expenditure Interview Survey: Discrepancies in comprehension and recall as a source of nonsampling error. In *Proceedings of the Section on Survey*

Research Methods. Washington, DC: American Statistical Association, pp. 502–507.

NETER, J., and WAKSBERG, J. (1964) A study of response errors in expenditures data from household interviews. *Journal of the American Statistical Association* 59, 18–55.

OFFICE OF MANAGEMENT AND BUDGET (1983) Approaches to developing questionnaires. Statistical Policy Working Paper 10, Washington, DC.

PALMISANO, M. (1988) The application of cognitive survey methodology to an establishment survey field test. In *Proceedings of the Section on Survey Research Methods.* Washington, DC: American Statistical Association, pp. 179–190.

——— (1989) Respondent understanding of key labor force concepts used in the CPS. Paper presented at the annual meeting of the American Statistical Association.

PHIPPS, P. (1990) Applying cognitive techniques to an establishment mail survey. In *Proceedings of the Section on Survey Research Methods.* Washington, DC: American Statistical Association, pp. 608–612.

ROMAN, A. M. (1981) Results from the methods development survey (phase I). In *Proceedings of the Section on Survey Research Methods.* Washington, DC: American Statistical Association, pp. 232–237.

ROTHGEB, J. (1982) Summary report of July followup of the unemployed. Internal memorandum to K. A. Riccini dated December 30. Washington, DC: U.S. Department of Commerce, Bureau of the Census.

ROTHWELL, N. (1983) New ways of learning how to improve self-enumerative questionnaires: A demonstration project. Paper for the Bureau of the Census, Washington, DC.

——— (1985) Laboratory and field response research studies for the 1980 Census of Population in the United States. *Journal of Official Statistics* 1(2), 137–157.

SHOEMAKER, H., BUSHERY, J., and CAHOON, L. (1989) Evaluation of the use of CATI in the Current Population Survey. In *Proceedings of the Section on Survey Research Methods.* Washington, DC: American Statistical Association, pp. 361–366.

STEIN, R. L. (1967) New definitions for employment and unemployment. In *Employment and Earnings and Monthly Report on the Labor Force.* Washington, DC: U.S. Department of Labor, Bureau of Labor Statistics, pp. 3–13.

STEIN, R. L., and LEVINE, D. B. (1965) Research in labor force concepts. In *Proceedings of the Social Statistics Section.* Washington, DC: American Statistical Association, pp. 218–226.

TOURANGEAU, R. (1984) Cognitive science and survey methods. In JABINE, T., STRAF, M., TANUR, J., and TOURANGEAU, R. (eds.). *Cognitive Aspects of Survey Methodology: Building a Bridge Between Disciplines.* Washington, DC: National Academy Press, pp. 73–100.

TUCKER, C., and BENNETT, C. (1988) Procedural effects in the collection of consumer expenditure information: The diary operation test. In *Proceedings of the Section on Survey Research Methods.* Washington, DC: American Statistical Association, pp. 256–261.

TUCKER, C., MILLER, L., VITRANO, F., and DODDY, J. (1989) Cognitive issues and research on the Consumer Expenditure Diary Survey. Paper presented at the annual Conference of the American Association for Public Opinion Research.

WAKSBERG, J., and PEARL, R. (1965) New methodological research on labor force measurements. In *Proceedings of the Social Statistics Section*. Washington, DC: American Statistical Association, pp. 227–237.

WILLIAMS, L. E. (1969) Methods test phase III: First report on the accuracy of retrospective interviewing and effects of nonself response on labor force status. Internal memorandum to Walter M. Perkins dated June 24. Washington, DC: U.S. Department of Commerce, Bureau of the Census.

WILLIS, G., ROYSTON, P., and BERCINI, D. (1989) Problems with survey questions revealed by cognitively-based interviewing techniques. In *Proceedings of the Fifth Annual Research Conference*. Washington, DC: Bureau of the Census, pp. 345–360.

Name Index

Abelson, R. P., xi, xvi, xvii, xxi, 7–9, 68, 89, 97, 99, 209, 232
Aborn, M., xv, 5, 9
Abramson, P. R., 138, 139, 151
Adam, E., 103
Aderman, D., 87
Ajzen, I., 189, 209
Alba, J. W., 86, 87
Aldrich, J. H., 189, 190
Allen, H. M., Jr., 218
Allen, J. L., 222
Allgeier, A. R., 85
Allison, D. E., 187
Allport, F. H., 181
Alwin, D. F., 278
Amador, M., 163, 164
Anderson, B. A., 138, 139, 151
Anderson, D., xix
Anderson, R. C., 67, 155, 163
Aneshensel, C. S., 76
Arnold, W. E., 181
Asch, S. E., 180n
Atkins, J. L., 192

Baddeley, A., 120
Bailar, B., 278
Bailey, S., 181
Baker, S. M., 222
Baldridge, B., 189
Barclay, C. R., 70
Bargh, J. A., 175, 222, 224
Barnes, A. B., 103
Baron, R. S., 192
Bartlett, F. C., 67
Bates, N., 280

Batts, V., 210
Bean, J. A., 103
Belson, W. A., 27, 50
Bem, D. J., 71
Bennett, C., 281, 282, 284
Bercini, D., x, 274
Berent, M. K., 182, 190, 191
Berger, P. L., 74
Bergstralh, E., 103
Biderman, A., ix, 5, 272
Biemer, P. P., xx
Bienias, J., x
Birren, J. E., 87
Bishop, G. F., 36, 38, 192, 193
Black, J. B., 70
Blankenship, A. B., 191
Block, G., 97
Block, J., 87
Bobo, L., 210, 218
Bobrow, D. G., 134
Bodnar, J., 68n
Boehm, L., 279, 283
Boninger, D. S., 182
Booth, A. L., 154
Borgida, E., 181, 185, 190, 191
Bower, G. H., 100
Bradburn, N., 180, 183, 192–193
Bradburn, N. M., 9, 10, 26, 35, 67, 88, 113, 181
Bradley, L., xix
Brehm, S. S., 87
Brennan, S. E., 24, 36
Brent, E., 181
Brewer, M. B., xvii, 225, 273
Briggs, C. L., 51, 242
Broedling, L. A., 5

Edwards, C., 192
Edwards, S., 278, 282, 283
Eich, E., xx, 75, 79
Ely, R. J., 184
Epstein, S., 68
Ergas, Y., 68n
Ericsson, K. A., 73
Erikson, E. H., 68
Erikson, R. S., 191
Esposito, J., 273
Ester, P., 179, 187
Estrada, A. L., 76
Evans, M., 68
Evans, N., 222
Ewing, T. N., 179, 180, 183

Fagot, B., 79
Fathi, D., 9, 103, 107, 134
Fazio, R. H., xxi, 8, 10, 73n, 174, 175, 181, 182, 186
Fee, J., 28
Feldman, J. J., 116
Ferber, R., 35, 50
Festinger, L., 189, 190
Fetterman, J. G., 122
Fiedler, J., 7, 9, 97, 123
Fienberg, S. E., 3, 8n, 9, 10, 135, 262, 265
Fillmore, C. J., xvii
Fine, B. J., 184
Fishbein, M., 189, 209
Fisher, R. P., 7, 97–99, 152
Fiske, S. T., 115
Fitzgerald, J. M., 70
Fletcher, G. J. O., 71n, 74
Fowler, F., xx
Fracasso, M., 284
Freund, T., 208
Fricke, T., xxi
Fricker, R. S., 154
Fulero, S., 68
Fuller, N., 258n
Fultz, N., xi, xx, 6–7

Gaertner, S. L., 175, 210, 211, 216, 217, 219, 221–222, 224, 226
Gallup, G., 191
Garofalo, J., 35, 113

Geiselman, R. E., 154, 155, 163, 164
Gerhard, D., 88
Gibbs, G., 78
Gibbs, R., xx
Gilbreath, F. B., 115
Glaser, R., xviii
Glover, R. L., 122
Glucksberg, S., xx
Goethals, G. R., 71, 86
Goldstein, H., ix
Gomberg, E. S. L., 82n–83n
Goodwin, C., 243n
Gorenflo, D. W., 187, 191
Gorn, G. J., 184
Graff-Radford, S. B., 75, 79
Graham, J. W., 76, 86
Granberg, D., 181, 189
Greene, R. L., 122
Greenwald, A. G., xi, 7, 74, 89, 97, 209, 218
Grice, H. P., 16, 22
Griffin, M., 87
Griffitt, W., 189, 190
Groves, R. M., xi, xvi, xvii, xviii, xx, xxi, 6–7, 36, 274, 281
Gurtman, M. B., 225
Guttman, L., 180, 181

Haberman, S. J., 148
Hahn, H., 184
Halvorsen, P. K., xvii
Hamilton, D. L., 67
Hamilton, S., 79–81
Hansell, M. J., 76
Hansen, W. B., 76, 86
Hanson, R. H., 271
Hardee, B. B., 210
Hardy, D., 192
Hartley, E., 28
Hartman, D. A., 181
Hasher, L., 86, 87, 114
Hastie, R., 67
Hastorf, A. H., 206
Haviland, S. E., 18
Hedges, L. V., 10
Heider, F., 189
Heritage, J., 243n
Herman, C. P., 78, 181, 185
Hermann, D., 286, 287

Subject Index

abilities, implicit theories of change in, 69

abortion attitudes, 186

academic skills-improvement programs, 66, 77–79

accumulation, principle of, 19, 24

accuracy: and comprehension, 278; and degree of bias, 86; of health memories, 104, 111–112, 113, 114; of health memories, and two-time-frame procedure, 123, 127–128; and judgment, 283–284; of recollection, 4, 70, 72, 111–112; of self-reports of voting, 138–152

adjacency pairs, 34

Advanced Research Seminar on Cognitive Aspects of Survey Methodology (CASM Seminar), 5, 9, 273

affect responses, 53, 54

age and recall, 113, 114, 120

ageism, 225

"aided" recall methods, 88, 154–169

AIDS-testing attitudes, 186

alcoholics, personality of, 81–82, 82n–83n

Alcoholics Anonymous (AA), 81, 85

anchors: and attitude strength, 187; and recall, 67, 88, 89, 282

"Applying Cognitive Theory in Public Health Investigations" (Fisher and Quigley), 154–169

"Attempts to Improve the Accuracy of Self-Reports of Voting" (Abelson, Loftus, and Greenwald), 138–153

attitude(s), 171–237; accessibility, 178, 230; affective-cognitive consistency, 178; affective salience, 178; ambivalence or certainty, 178, 179, 180, 180n, 181, 182, 183, 184, 186, 192–193; and behavior, 7–8, 10, 73–74, 73n, 204–205, 208–216; -behavior relation, 204–205, 207–208, 209–216, 230; centrality, 180n; -change hypothesis, 184–185; -change manipulation studies, 87; cognitive complexity, 178; cognitive elaboration, 183; conflict, 180n; crystallization, 183–185; ego preoccupation, 183; embeddedness, 178; emotional commitment, 183; expression, mode concept of, 174; flexibility, 178; and implicit theories of stability, 69, 72, 84; importance, 179, 180, 180n, 181, 182, 184, 185, 186, 188, 189, 190, 191, 192–193; intensity, 178, 179–180, 181, 183; laboratory-induced change in, and recall, 71–74, 71n; magnitude or extremity, 178, 179, 181, 182–185, 182n–183n, 186, 186n; measurement of, and processing mode, 208–216; naturally occurring change in behavior and, 74–75; new technologies for direct and indirect assessment of, 204–232; no strong prior, 174; overtness, 178; and perceptions of others' attitudes, 187–188; -relevant information, memory for, 190–191; -relevant knowledge, 178, 179, 181, 183, 184, 186, 189; salience, 178; and social-desirability, 216–218; strength concept, 7–8, 174, 175, 177–194;

299